"The Path of Energy provides an elegar῀
understanding of the many faces and fε
clearly a very accomplished expert in th
and the practical application of its move.
whole-heartedly endorse this fine book, ν ..ιust read for all
of us in the healing field and for anyone interested in the flows of life
force energy that fill us, surround us, and align us with Spirit in this
most amazing Universe. Well done!"

—Meredith Young-Sowers, D. Div., founder and director of the
Stillpoint School of Integrative Life Healing
author of *Spirit Heals* and the *Angelic Messenger Cards*

"Meditation is the key to body, soul, and spirit health. *The Path of
Energy* is both an inner and outer guide to understand why and how
the proper flow of life connects us with an ongoing plan of Love.
These guidelines are important to improve our lives as conscious
beings in experiencing the thrill of keeping healthy and open minds
for the greater dimensions of Reality."

—Drs. J.J. Hurtak and Desiree Hurtak,
Academy For Future Science, The Keys of Enoch

"My long research career into a multiplex of scientific subjects has
included consciousness and the human brain's ability to effect its
surroundings. Through my wife Synthia I experienced firsthand a
physical reaction within my body, changing my health for the good,
that was accomplished through a process she knowingly directed.
I believe that Synthia Andrews holds an important piece of future
scientific study."

—Colin Andrews, author/researcher/investigative journalist coauthor of
*Circular Evidence, Signs of Change,
The Complete Idiots Guide to 2012,*
and *The Complete Idiots Guide to the Akashic Record*
author of *Government Circles*

"If you've always known that there's more to you than you learned in Biology 101, but find yourself intimidated by the technical language of science, this is the beautiful book you've been waiting for! In 21 concise chapters, Synthia Andrews, ND, draws upon 30 years of direct experience to describe our quantum relationship with ourselves, and the world. In a responsible, well-researched, and practical manual that you'll want to keep at your fingertips during your personal practice, the easy-to-use step-by-step techniques give everyone the opportunity to experiment with their own quantum field to discover for themselves what works best."

—Gregg Braden, *New York Times* best-selling author of *The Divine Matrix* and *Fractal Time*

The
Path of Energy

Awaken Your Personal Power
and
Expand Your Consciousness

By Dr. Synthia Andrews, ND

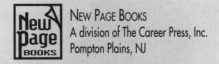
New Page Books
A division of The Career Press, Inc.
Pompton Plains, NJ

THE PATH OF ENERGY
EDITED BY JODI BRANDON
TYPESET BY EILEEN MUNSON
Cover design by Lucia Rossman/Digi Dog Design
Images on pages 17, 32, 41, 54, 61, 117, and 261 by Mark Johnson
Image on page 80 by Wayne Mason
Cover art contributions from Wayne Mason and Dmitri D'Alessandro
Printed in Canada

To order this title, please call toll-free 1-800-CAREER-1 (NJ and Canada: 201-848-0310) to order using VISA or MasterCard, or for further information on books from Career Press.

The Career Press, Inc.
220 West Parkway, Unit 12
Pompton Plains, NJ 07444
www.careerpress.com
www.newpagebooks.com

Library of Congress Cataloging-in-Publication Data

Andrews, Synthia.
  The path of energy : awaken your personal power and expand your consciousness / by Synthia Andrews.
    p. cm.
  Includes bibliographical references and index.
  ISBN 978-1-60163-172-5 -- ISBN 978-1-60163-654-6 (ebook) 1. Consciousness.
2. Vitality. 3. Chakras. I. Title.
  BF311.A5914 2011
  131--dc22

                                                                2011010736

*This book is dedicated to
Johanna Sayre,
whose friendship is a touchstone in my life and
whose insight, wisdom, and fullness of spirit
grace every page of this manuscript.*

Acknowledgments

First and foremost, I must thank the artists who put themselves full-heartedly into this project, dedicating time and talent for little in return: Mark Johnson, who created the artwork throughout the book; Johanna Sayre, who created the directional illustrations on the Website *www.the-pathofenergy.com*; Wayne Mason, who contributed cover art and Website art; and Dmitri D'Alessandro, who contributed to the cover art. Each of these people brought more than talent; they brought excitement and enthusiasm, engaging the concepts with curiosity and encouragement. Each bolstered me, and this project, at essential moments on the path.

I owe a tremendous debt of gratitude to Barbara Marciniak for writing the wonderful Foreword to this book and for her support and encouragement. A thank you as well for the teachings she courageously brought forward over the past 30 years. The first time I sat in a channeling, I felt I had come home. She talked of energy before it was popular and opened those who listened to new vistas.

A thank you to the many teachers and mentors on my path, especially Louisa Poole, Iona Marsaa Teegarden, founder of Jin Shin Do Bodymind Acupressure, Debbie Valentine Smith, and my two favorite psychics, Deb Hastings and Pam Hogan.

As always, tremendous thanks to my husband, Colin Andrews, who helped with all the loose ends and my children, Erin and Adriel, who are constant sources of inspiration.

And a second thank you is due to Johanna for the tireless editing of query letters, proposals, rewrites of proposals, rewrites of rewrites, and, finally, the manuscript.

Thank you to my agent, John White, and the staff at Career Press, who believed in the project on first sight.

Heartfelt thanks and gratitude to Meredith Young-Sowers, Dannion and Kathryn Brinkley, Dr. Edgar Mitchell, Gregg Braden, Drs. J.J. and Desiree Hurtack, and my husband Colin Andrews, for taking the time to read my material and for providing encouragement and endorsement for this book.

Last but not least, thank you to my clients, who leave me speechless with their greatness of spirit.

Contents

Part I: Transformation and the Art of Moving Energy
17

Part II: The Sea of Life Force
67

Part III: Empowering Your Life
117

Appendicies
261

"The circumstances of your life do not describe and cannot constrain the greatness of your soul."

—Synthia Andrews

FOREWORD

You create your reality. When I first encountered that phrase in the late 1970s in *The Seth Material* by Jane Roberts, I knew it was true. Some part of me intuitively recognized the power, freedom, and responsibility the statement conveyed as an essential key to experiencing life in a higher state of consciousness. To test the depths of my own power to create my reality, I have spent more than three decades enthusiastically exploring the many fascinating avenues and intriguing paths to higher consciousness. Essentially, every path appears to lead to a vista common to us all: the recognition of our inner power and how we use it to create our experience of life.

A crisis in consciousness appears to be fully underway on Earth. As formerly reliable systems fall away and uncertainty grows, the vast complexities of navigating modern society are challenging us to awaken to our inner power and use it to be more responsible for ourselves and our own well-being. A paradigm shift, a momentous transformation of consciousness, is upon us. Even though the growing prevalence of chaos and confusion is scrambling our senses and desensitizing us to the speed at which things are changing, the global turmoil is actually compelling us to enter into a new territory of perceptual experience where new ideas stretch our minds into new panoramas of awareness.

Expanding our consciousness involves becoming much more aware of how our thoughts, feelings, and words create frequencies of energy that we broadcast into existence. Our personal inner songs are telepathic expressions of energy that send out signals about our beliefs and expectations of reality. Accepting responsibility for all we create is not always easy; yet as we expand our consciousness to look for the larger purpose and significance of our encounters, a grander multidimensional vista inevitably unfolds.

Multidimensional experiences definitely change the way we see reality; yet having such experiences is one thing, and really understanding them is quite another. Multidimensional ventures move our focus beyond the boundaries of linear time to a place where we experience the interconnectedness of existence. We become much more aware of our own telepathic abilities as we begin to detect the great commerce of energies and ideas that are exchanged between various eras of time and other dimensional realities. When time slips away to reveal the rich facets of existence, the conscious mind is sometimes left scrambling to understand what is occurring. When we are grounded and secure in this reality, our nervous system eventually adapts to the explorations into other realms of consciousness. Exercising the mind takes practice, playful determination, and very clear intentions for a safe and meaningful expansion of consciousness.

Love, trust, and respect for the body are important keys to higher consciousness. I have learned to trust that my body will reliably respond to what I am energizing. Our bodies are brilliant biological computers, and we must value and feel more at home in them in order to access the vast treasure of inner knowledge that waits our attention. A belief that the body can function in a healthier and more life-fulfilling capacity is a very noble and generous thought. We must personally examine the relationship we have with our physical form. Do our beliefs and actions really promote our well-being? The higher mind and physical body are always seeking balance, and when inner balance is maintained, the outer world manifests in balance as well.

Our beliefs and perceptions about the nature of reality are quickly expanding. We are experiencing a most profound process of awakening to new realizations about the nature of existence. We are fully aware that all of existence is imbued in some manner with subtle vibrating frequencies of energy; from ancient to modern times we called this energy chi, qi, prana, ether, life force, electrons, protons, particles, and waves. Frequencies of energy are instilled with forms of consciousness that interact with and respond to our growing awareness. Our cells read and vibrate with the energy of our thoughts and everything around us. As we become more aware of how we use our energy and what we project into the outside world, our nervous system becomes more finely attuned. We naturally become more psychic, telepathic, and sensitive to our surroundings as we realize that all of existence is filled with energy that is responsive, alive, and intelligent. Everything is alive with energy!

Awareness is a subtle partner of expanding consciousness. Our awareness expands when we take time to reflect on things, see each day as an extension of our energy in the physical world, and take responsibility for all our creations. Learning to manage energy leads to the creation of health and inner peace, a stronger energy field, a more productive, happy, and creative life, protection from unseen forces, greater psychic awareness, enhanced intuition and insight, and healing the body, mind, and soul/spirit. When we raise our awareness of how we use energy, we can move blocked energy in the body by looking for and recognizing the reasons for and significance of the imbalance. We change our ideas and beliefs when we see things from other perspectives. Exploring the body's myriad avenues of energy offers us the opportunity to venture into exciting new frontiers. Our bodies are filled with wisdom and great intelligence, and our creativity and vitality soar when we learn how to manage our energy to create inner balance.

With the speed of life accelerating, we must discipline ourselves to slow down and become more aware of the energies we are broadcasting. Expanding our perceptions includes being aware of energy and learning how to direct and focus our most valuable attention into these subtle realms. This takes time, discipline, and practice. The power of the imagination activates the inner subtle energy patterns, and being in Nature extends our senses into the natural environment, where we feel more vital and alive when we entrain with Earth's energy grid and the cosmic influences of the planets and stars. Deep rhythmic breathing calms the body and opens the mind to the realms of energy. Devoting 10 minutes every day for mind relaxation through energy meditations will reward you with brand-new wonders of the mind.

Consciously interacting with subtle energies is a most powerful and productive use of our minds. In a very grand sense, as we traverse the terrain of new possibilities of the mind, we have a spiritual duty to take charge of our lives, to search for the valuable ancient inner wisdom, and to use it to improve the quality of our lives. When we learn how to create from within, we broadcast frequencies of energy that inspire others to tap into and use their own inherent energy to create new possibilities. We can demonstrate a sacred way of exploring multidimensional realities through subtle energies with reverence for the presence of a grand intelligence of which we are all part.

Vibrant health, a wealth of happiness, and a safe harmonious experience of reality all display a productive use of creativity that serves as a major contribution to our purpose for being here: to pioneer and make practical use of our inner abilities. My Pleiadian friends have said: "Energy is like money; it doesn't care who owns it, it never sleeps, and it is freely available to be directed by you. Subtle energies can offer you so much when you learn how to communicate with them. There is no shortage of energy, creative and otherwise."

Synthia Andrews has created something very special in *The Path of Energy*, a most generous and thoughtful map for navigating and exploring the wonderful realms of subtle energy. When I first met Synthia almost 20 years ago and she performed her magic on me, I quickly realized that she was a very talented body therapist who understood the realms of subtle energy patterns and their effects on the body. Her longtime work in the arena of energy has imbued her with a deep understanding of how these forces of life and intelligence can indeed alter our perceptions and experiences of physical and nonphysical reality. In *The Path of Energy*, Synthia provides a most valuable and grounded understanding of the forces at play as she guides the reader into higher states of consciousness through clear and practical applications and explanations of how to move confidently into the exciting new and ancient territory of mind and energy. During the transformation of consciousness, her book helps us to get in touch with the energies we all use to create our realities. Whatever spiritual path we pursue, the signs of the times are urging us to delve much deeper into the potentials of human energy systems to support, sustain, and enhance our lives. By applying what we learn, we contribute to the flowering of consciousness that is expanding our understanding of human affairs and our place in the cosmos.

Barbara Marciniak
Author of *Path of Empowerment*,
Earth, Family of Light, and
Bringers of the Dawn
December 2010

Introduction

You already know that behind the circumstances, events, and conditions in your life is energy. If you didn't, you wouldn't be looking at this book. To change your life, you need to first shift the energy patterns that hold conditions in place. You may have a sense that you know how to do this, yet somehow you just can't remember. This book is a resource to help you remember.

The world in which we live contains more than what we see, feel, and hear with our current senses; it contains a sea of energy from which the circumstances and events of life unfold. There is a paradigm shift underway—an awakening to the knowledge that subtle energy is the substance of reality and the vehicle of consciousness. Your body is wired to navigate this sea of life force, and you are equipped with everything needed to engage it and change your life.

Right now, inner senses are stirring as people awaken to the energy matrix of life. Many are experiencing levels of awareness that were previously available only to the initiate. Perhaps you are having experiences you haven't had before and don't completely understand. Do you feel energy moving in your body? Do you know who is on the phone when it rings? Do you think of people only to have them appear around the next corner? Do you see lights in the sky and auras around people?

The purpose of this book is to support you in understanding, developing, and using your energy awareness to find new solutions to personal and global problems. Ultimately this shift is an awakening to a deeper connection with your spiritual essence. However, there is no attempt to define this; it is for each person to decide his or her spiritual source and connection. This book can be adapted to different belief systems, and every suggestion and practice has been tried firsthand and proven effective. With awareness, you can navigate the world of subtle energy, expand your consciousness, and creatively generate the circumstances of your life.

How This Book Works

Part I (Chapters 1–4) consists of 13 meditations to activate and move energy. They are the heart of the book and include instructions with simple descriptions, benefits, and uses. Instructions are very basic, are easy to follow and understand, and allow the freedom of individual discovery. Part I also explores principles of subtle energy, explains the resources and tools you will use to activate the energy patterns, provides simple guidelines, and offers a troubleshooting guide to pinpoint difficulty.

Part II (Chapters 5–9) of this book is an exploration of consciousness that puts personal experience into a larger context. If you're having difficulty understanding some of the meditations, reading this section first may be helpful. For many, this will be old hat and skipping it is the right thing to do. This section provides a discussion of what consciousness is, contains a description of energetic anatomy, explores the relationship between energy and emotions, assists in translating energy information, helps develop intuition, and examines the role of attitudes and beliefs in creating our human experience.

Part III (Chapters 10–20 and Conclusion) provides hands-on exercises for everyday use. The more you experience and practice moving energy, the more useful this section will be. It covers basics such as how to ground and center, create protection, clear space, manifest your dreams, vision your life, and build intimate relationships. It also helps develop higher awareness through expanded perception, remote sensing, channeling your higher self, and more. This section provides a path for you if the forest of possibility seems overwhelming. The recipes for creating change are suggestions only—examples of what is possible. They can be used as is, be modified, or provide validation for your personal practice.

Appendix A provides a brief description of the inception of the meditations, how they came into being, and how they were originally used. Most of them are original or taught to me by mentors. Some are modifications of traditional patterns, such as the meditations involving the chakras and the Great Central Channel of the Traditional Chinese Medicine meridian system.

Appendix B is a resource guide with a list of books, Websites, and resources for further study into energy reality.

Appendix C contains a comprehensive glossary of the words and terms used throughout the book.

Part 1

Transformation and the Art of Moving Energy

Circle of Life

If you're like most people, you want to transform some aspect of your life. You may be seeking more joy or a more fulfilling career, looking for greater spiritual connection, or desiring deeper, more committed relationships. Perhaps you're searching for better health, yearning to understand your purpose and path, looking for better life solutions, or simply craving a more authentic life. We all want to set aside the self-imposed limitations that keep us from experiencing inner freedom and self-realization. This book provides the missing link: tools to activate your energy body and power your dreams.

This book of 13 energy meditations is a resource for change. As you activate your energy field, you will clear old patterns, find new solutions to life problems, and awaken unknown inner resources and abilities. Transformation often requires letting go of the old to allow the new to grow. It's not always easy. Practicing the activating meditations will assist a smoother transition.

Most importantly, the meditations can deepen your inner journey and strengthen your connection to your authentic self. They seek to bring you into alignment with Spirit, allowing you to live fully in the present moment. Everything you need you already have; energy meditations help you access it.

Chapter 1

The Terrain

Energy, Matter, and Awareness

Einstein's groundbreaking equation $E=MC^2$ (energy equals matter times the speed of light squared) explains that energy and matter are the same substance separated only by their rate of vibration. Energy and matter live in a perpetual dance of transformation: energy entrained in matter, matter released back to energy. This multifaceted interface creates the spectrum of the world you know—all you can see, feel, hear, taste, touch, and sense. Your bodymind is the instrument through which you experience and explore this world.

You are equipped with all the senses and extensions of the senses you need to fully engage the universe. Every experience you have you are biologically wired for. You cannot experience anything you are not designed to experience. You cannot physically see in the frequencies outside the scope of your eyes; you cannot physically hear frequencies outside the design parameter of your ears. On the other hand, every experience you do have, you have *because* you are designed for it.

No matter how strange it seems, spiritual and psychic events, such as visions, astral projection, telepathy, and energy projection, happen because every person has extensions of the senses necessary to engage this level of reality. Most of the time we all ignore the information coming to us from this realm. However, we are all capable of so much more than we allow ourselves to experience. We have been civilized right out of our senses!

The Adventure

New science says that the energy phase of the dance is the creative phase—that matter is held together by energy, and to organize matter there must first be an energy template. Energy templates can be accessed through your awareness, making the science of the mind the new frontier. Thoughts, emotions, and beliefs are energy. As the mystics of the past have said, the energy of your mind and heart co-create the reality you experience. In order to change your world, you must first change your mind. In order to change your mind, you must change the attitudes and beliefs that direct your thoughts. Are you ready for an adventure?

You have all the tools necessary. Your bodymind is equipped with everything you need. The energy that holds your body in form is accessible. You know how to do it; you have just forgotten. The energy activations in this book can awaken your memory. No more theory is necessary—no philosophy, historical perspective, warnings on what might go wrong, or directions on the "right experience" are needed. You were not born with an owner's manual on how to use your living energy body, and no one can give you one. You can only remember/learn this through experiencing it. It's your experience. No matter what anyone else has to say, including me, only you know what's true for you. These meditations are maps. Feel free to change them as you chart your own territory.

Energy Keys: Quick Access Summary

If the world of energy is new territory for you, you may want to read Part II of this book to get familiar with energy anatomy, terms, and so forth. The following concepts form the foundation of these meditations. You may agree with these concepts or not; it won't affect the power of the work. Ultimately what you believe determines your experience; however, your beliefs don't have to match mine for the meditations to be effective. People generally read information to validate their inner truth. If your inner truth is validated, it will make your commitment to the practice stronger. If your belief is challenged, it can make your desire to explore and discover stronger. If your reaction is incredulity and ridicule, you probably won't try the meditations.

$E=MC^2$

This equation means that energy and matter are the same stuff; the only difference between the two is the rate at which they vibrate. Light is the first order of *measurable* matter stepped down from pure energy. Light is both a particle (matter) and a wave (energy).

Energy and matter express along an electromagnetic continuum.
The lower end of the spectrum vibrates slower than the higher end.
Slower vibrations translate as a more physical expression.

Energy and matter are in perpetual exchange.
Influencing one impacts the other. You can interact at either end of
the spectrum, physical or energetic.

*Everything that exists in the material world has an energy template,
including your body.*
The human template is created before birth and holds a record of
your karma and the original design of perfect health and wholeness. It
also holds instructions for your purpose, path, and life plan. This template is accessible through awareness.

The energy template is called an aura.
The template manifests as radiance around the body and is called the
aura. It organizes and enlivens physical form. Everything has an aura:
humans, animals, plants, rocks, the planet. You can access information in
your aura to manifest health, growth, awareness, and expansion, allowing
you to live a more authentic life.

A dialogue is happening between your mind, body, spirit, and aura.
Your aura holds the record of your past and the direction of your
future. What you think, feel, and experience lives in the aura and impacts
the expression of your original design. The interaction between your
original design and your experience is your growth edge.

The energy involved is called vital energy or life force.
All cultures have a concept of this energy and a name for it. Some of
the names are prana, chi, ki, pneuma, mana, ruan, and orgone.

Key descriptions, qualities, and functions of vital energy are:
- It is the organizing principle behind matter.
- It is cohesive, binding matter in form.
- It is unifying, the interconnecting web of life.
- It nourishes and sustains.
- It is encoded with, carries, and transmits information.
- It is a vehicle for consciousness.

Energy flows through matter in organized channels.
Vital energy flows through the Earth in channels called ley lines. It flows through the body in channels called meridians. Information is coded on the energy flowing through these channels. Ley lines and meridians can be interacted with to improve balance, harmony, and health.

Energy centers occur when energy paths intersect.
Energy centers are areas of higher vibration, or frequency. In the Earth, these centers are called vortexes or sacred sites. In the body, they're called chakras. Chakras and sacred sites gather and amplify energy. They also transform energy from one frequency to another.

The nature of energy is to move.
Moving energy nourishes and sustains life. When energy stagnates it can cause illness, emotional disturbance, pain, lack of motivation, disillusionment, fear, and any number of ailments. Stagnating Earth energy creates a noxious environment.

There is no such thing as negative energy.
Energy may be held in patterns that produce "negative" effects; be directed by someone with harmful intent, flow backward, or become stagnant and produce limitation. However, when the pattern is broken, the ill-intending sender enlightened, the life-force realigned, and the flow reestablished, the energy released is simply energy.

Each of us is responsible for our own space.
No one else created it; no one else can change it.

How energy flows depends on what a person thinks, feels, and imagines.
Energy is directed with your mind through your attention, thoughts, feelings, and emotions.

In Oriental medicine: Blood follows chi; Chi follows mind; Mind follows Shen; Shen follows the Tao.
In other words, your physiology (blood) responds to vital energy (chi) which is directed by your mind. When your mind follows your inner spirit (Shen), you are living authentically and in harmony with your path (Tao).

In a perfect world, your mind is in harmony with your spirit.
In this perfect world you make choices that support your highest and best good. There is no such thing as a perfect world. On the other hand, all of your choices support growth, no matter how difficult growth appears.

We are each the sum total of our choices.
Although born to specific circumstances, how we respond and what we do are choices.

To change your life you must first change your mind.
This requires two things: awareness and discipline.

We are spiritual beings having a human experience.
You have access with your soul and spirit to spiritual realms. You are biologically wired for the experience, and your bodymind is the instrument you have to traverse these realms.

You have access to guidance, which you can receive in myriad forms.
Everyone receives guidance differently. Every way is right.

Only love is real.
Unconditional love is the most powerful and transformative force in the universe.

You are never alone.
We live in a spiritual universe and are connected to all other sentient beings. Support is always present.

Chapter 2

THE TOOLS

Meditation, Visualization, Attention, and Discipline: The Master Keys of Awareness

The meditations in this book activate patterns of energy flow in the body that stimulate specific states of awareness. Energy is dynamic and interactive. It flows through you along precise pathways (meridians), is gathered and transformed in identifiable centers (chakras), and radiates through your energy field (aura). Energy, as vibration, streams through these structures creating an ever-changing mosaic of geometric patterns. Each pattern is a particular response to an individual event and is directed by your thoughts, feelings, attitudes, and beliefs. How you manage your energy flow reflects the quality of your being, and the quality of your being attracts your life. Activating these energy flows can change your life.

Activating Energy

Your bodymind is the vehicle you have to explore the sea of vital life force we live within and is fully equipped for the journey. The configuration of your internal energy flow determines your level of awareness, whereas your thoughts, attitudes, emotions, and attention direct the configuration of your energy. Using energy activations impacts two key capabilities: They enhance your energy sensitivity, and they increase your ability to consciously interact in this realm.

Imagine the energy pathways as highways with exit ramps and subsidiary roads. There are several routes you can take to get to any particular place. Your energy takes different roads in response to different stimuli. For example, consider how your energy might flow at the moment something awful happens. Perhaps your energy will mobilize along the kidney and bladder meridians to give you a boost of physical strength. At the same time, imagine a surge into your Root chakra, activating survival instincts, and a flood to your Third Eye chakra, activating higher perception. Your aura may radiate a protective shield. As much vital life force as possible will be directed into these structures, creating a configuration of energy flow that ensures your survival. If you could freeze-frame your energy at this moment, you would see a very precise pattern of activation.

Look at how your energy might respond to a different event. Consider participating in an important ceremony such as getting married. In this case, your energy might mobilize along the heart meridian as you access your spirit. Your Second chakra of creative sexual energy and passion might be filled, along with your Heart chakra and your Crown chakra. Your aura might be glowing in the outer layers with high frequency love energy. Freeze-framing this pattern reveals an entirely different level of activation from the previous example and invites an entirely different level of awareness.

If you're like most people, you're unaware of the movement and patterning of energy at any given moment. However, energy is moving all the time and, because it responds to your emotional and mental focus, it tends to travel in the same pattern over and over, just as your thoughts do. Just as your thinking and expectations get stuck in patterns, so does your energy flow. The more a pathway is used, the more likely it is to be used in the future.

Since energy creates reality, using the same pattern creates the same outcome. For example, many people are stuck in survival patterns even when there is no threat. By seeing every situation as threatening, the same configuration develops and the same life conditions are attracted. Being stuck in one pattern causes you to miss opportunities. The meditations in this book help you shift out of firmly lodged, reactive patterns and into higher realms.

Meditation

Meditation is the practice of quieting the mind. In the quiet you can hear the deeper thoughts underlying the background clutter of your mind. The incessant chatter of surface thoughts that most people experience maintains a continuous cycle of reviewing the past and anticipating the future. In this state, it's easy to lose awareness of the present. The point of power is always in the present moment. Being fully present in the moment intensifies focus and allows for expansion of awareness. Quieting the mind involves giving less attention to habitual thoughts and freeing your attention for a deeper experience of the present moment.

The key to meditation is the breath. Paying attention to the flow of your breath brings your awareness more deeply into your body and promotes inner stillness. Slowing your breath changes your brain-wave states, allowing you better access to your subconscious mind. In this state of awareness you can connect with your energy structures and assess the flow and vitality of your life force. The free attention gained in meditation can connect you to what is and to what you truly feel and believe. This knowledge guides your choices to fit who you really are and what you truly want.

Different states of awareness occur with different brain waves. Very simply speaking, beta waves govern everyday awareness, and as the mind quiets you move into alpha, theta, and delta brain-wave states. Alpha states enhance creativity and imaging, theta states enhance deep meditation and intuition, and though delta states are mostly related to sleep, in meditation they can produce detached awareness. Delta brain waves are accessed by Tibetan monks and provide the greatest gateway to the divine intelligence.

Solid meditation skills are the foundation of the art of moving energy. If your meditation is not as deep as you would like, there are many tools you can use to move into different states. Specially designed meditation music or hemi-sync tapes can be useful. Hemi-sync tapes synchronize the right and left hemispheres of the brain and change brain-wave states. They were developed by the Monroe Institute in Virginia and can be obtained on its Website (*www.Monroeinstitute.org*).

Visualization

Visualization is the practice of constructing images in the mind's eye. It utilizes the meditative state of mind to increase focus and the ability to create clear intentions. Some might consider visualization mere imagination; however, your body responds to every thought you think. If you think of something scary, your energy enters a survival pattern, your muscles tighten, and chemicals flood your body to prepare you to flee or fight. This is a very real response. On the other hand, if you think of someone you love your energy centers open, your face opens, your body softens, and energy flows in patterns of upliftment. Where your mind goes, your energy follows and your physiology responds. This is why visualization is used by successful people in all fields, including athletes, business CEOs, and scientists, to increase creativity and performance.

Moving energy in your mind's eye moves energy in your body and aura, and interacts with energy in the universe. Visualization initiates a flow of energy from the point of power in the present moment to the future we are choosing. How compelling is the future you are envisioning? How grounded is the present moment from which your future is sprouting?

The 13 meditations you are about to learn rely on visualization to activate energy flows. Meditation quiets the mind, and visualization activates the energy flow. Your body provides you with the feedback to know whether or not you are successfully moving energy. What you feel, sense, and experience becomes your guideposts on the journey.

Experiencing Energy

The first step in developing energy awareness is paying attention to your body. Your body is continually translating the energy flows in and around you into body events such as muscle tension, breathing patterns, emotions, gut feelings, sensations, thoughts, memory associations, and a multitude of other communications (see Chapter 9).

As you become aware of energy movement in your body you will feel distinct sensations. Feeling energy is different for everyone. You may have only one of these sensations, all of them, or none of them. As you engage this practice you will learn the energy language of your own bodymind. There is no wrong experience.

Some people feel a "quickening" as if their body is vibrating. Others describe a feeling of softening as muscle tension dissolves. Many have a sense of opening that may be accompanied by the sensation of warm water, warm honey, or lava flowing through the body. For some, their body seems to expand and take in more and more sensation. People's experience can include feeling "rushes," electric tingling, warmth, pressure, magnetism, electric shocks, and an assortment of other sensations. Some see flashes of light or undergo changes in awareness.

Whatever your experience is, it's important to take note of your sensations (perhaps by cataloging them in a journal), so that you can begin to recognize when shifts in energy are happening around you and what they mean.

Attention and Discipline

Experiencing the world from an energy perspective can be elusive. You are probing for something very subtle when all of your past training was probably focused on paying attention to the obvious. Many people don't even inhabit their bodies enough to be able to feel whether or not they have tense muscles or are breathing fully into their diaphragm. How many times have you been told to relax when you thought you were?

Disciplining yourself to pay attention to and interact with the information from your bodymind opens the door to energy awareness. Discipline requires that you maintain a fraction of your awareness on your body at all times. This is part of what is meant by "being present"—in other words, being in your body for the events that are taking place. Get in the practice of taking inventory. Right now, at this moment, where are you tense? Where are you relaxed? What do you feel, other than simply "better," when you release a muscle tension? How deeply are you breathing? Becoming fully present is embracing the now.

Authenticity

Using the combined tools of meditation and visualization you can develop your energy awareness. Through observing how your energy responds to both the outer world of events and relationships and your inner world of thoughts, beliefs, attitudes, and emotions, you can begin to make conscious the choices that shape your life. With meditation you can become aware of your deeper beliefs, where they came from, and whether they serve your authentic self. By paying attention to your energy flow you can observe how your beliefs direct your choices and create the circumstances of your life. Using visualization, you create connection between your authenticity and what you think, choose, and do. In this way, your world begins to reflect the core of who you are.

Chapter 3

Patterns of Light

The 13 energy meditations in this chapter activate particular energy flows that open different levels of awareness. Using them opens lines of force between you and the objectives of the pattern. They are divided into three types: Foundations, Explorations in Light, and Master Activations.

Together, the first group, the *Foundations* (meditations one through four), open your energy body and provide the foundation for the rest of the meditations. They introduce you to the basic human energy structures of the aura, chakras, Hara line, and meridians, and how they relate to the larger universe. Understanding and working with these structures is the first step in expanding awareness.

The second group, *Explorations in Light* (meditations five through 10), open new patterns of energy flow to shift your perceptions. Working with them welcomes conscious co-creation of your life circumstances and experiences.

The last group, *Master Activations* (meditations 11 through 13), accelerate individual and planetary growth. They function in a larger capacity than personal development, opening doorways into universal consciousness.

The final meditation, *Dancing with the Elements*, is not an activation; it's a moving exercise to integrate your energy senses. It is in honor of Louisa Poole, my first energy teacher.

If you are experienced with meditation, visualization, and moving energy, you probably want to jump right in and explore the patterns. However, if this is new to you, here are some guidelines for getting started. If you have a hard time visualizing the meditations because you don't know what the energy structures being referred to are, then go to Part II to obtain a basic construct.

Prepare a quite comfortable space.
It's helpful to practice in a quiet, comfortable location, free from interruption. When you're proficient, you'll be able to shift your energy patterns anywhere, anytime. In fact, to use the meditations as a tool of awareness requires that you be able to access them as needed, any time, in any situation.

Open sessions with the first meditation, the **Spiral Pillar of Light,** *and keep it active during the session.*
This creates a sacred space and establishes an intention aligned with unconditional love. It also keeps your own energy contained so that your attention remains focused.

Use your breath to help move energy along the intended pathways.
Conscious breathing uses the diaphragm to breathe deeply into the lower abdomen. Use your inhalation to build energy and your exhalation to disperse energy. Vision the pathway you wish to activate being filled with your breath when you inhale. Vision your breath as light. You might find the light changes colors to activate different aspects of a meditation.

You do not need to practice the patterns in order.
The first four meditations are arranged to complement each other and become the foundation of the rest. If you're just starting out, you may find it useful to practice them first, as they help open perceptions you will use throughout the practice. However, the meditations can be used in any order. The order in this book is *not* the order in which they were developed, so don't limit your exploration.

Trust yourself. If the flow seems wrong for you, change it.
Use your body to feel or sense the rightness of any particular pattern. If it doesn't feel right, explore it and find out how it wants to be different with you. The practice is interactive. Energy has consciousness and, as you work with it, you will co-create your own patterns that match specific needs in your life.

Activation of these energy patterns can be done in a split second.
At first, you will need to use the directions to activate the patterns. Through time, you will be able to activate the pattern by simply visualizing the pathway. Later, you will only need to think of the name of the pattern, or feel the need for one and it will activate automatically.

Keep a journal of your experiences.
It's a good idea to keep a journal and, at the end of a meditation session, record what you felt, saw, sensed, and experienced. You're making a library of energy experiences to guide your energy awareness. This book is a guide, not an authority; each of us has access to our own inspiration and internal authority. This is your record of your journey that you will use to chart and navigate your own path; it's your library of energy information.

Pay attention to communications from guidance.
Communications may take the form of dreams, synchronicity, strong intuitions, a sense of knowing, abrupt new thoughts, unusual feelings, and body sensations, and also by more direct means such as telepathy, clairaudience, clairvoyance, or visitations. Do not discard any one form over another. Spirit speaks to each of us uniquely and personally.

Enjoy yourself! Joy is the point.

The Foundations

Earth and Sky

SPIRAL PILLAR OF LIGHT

(Adapted from a meditation of author/channel Barbara Marciniak.)

Keyword: Centering

Description: This meditation activates the boundaries of the aura, creating a powerful circle of safety and healing. The pattern pulls energy in spirals from the heavens to the center of the Earth, creating a pillar of living light. This is the center of the storm: The winds are howling all around; within this space is calm and peace. It is sacred space, a place to go for connection, protection, renewal, and resolve. It is unconditional love.

Benefits:

- Strengthens boundaries and promotes centering.
- Harmonizes the aura and supports spiritual alignment.
- Enhances inner strength and resolve.
- Promotes calmness, inner peace, balance, clarity, and focus.
- Provides protection from unwanted influences.

Use to:

- Create sacred space.
- Cleanse rooms, buildings, gardens, and so on.
- Enhance focus and clarity in times of mental exertion.
- Establish balance when feeling off center, overwhelmed, or in shock.
- Establish safety.
- Maintain your boundaries during chaos, conflict, or draining situations.
- Contain and transform your own destructive projections.

Flow Pattern:

1. Sit, stand, or recline.
2. Visualize yourself standing on the Earth.
3. Breathe in deeply and, with each inhalation, imagine cascading spirals of light descending into, through, and around you.

4. Visualize this energy filling and enveloping you as it descends into the Earth. See the light becoming a pillar of safety and healing.

5. Imagine this spiral pillar coming from a specific source in the sky, a star that represents your spiritual Source and connection.

6. While suspended within this spiraling energy, invite spiritual guidance to be present with you for the highest and best good. Let the source in the star be your spiritual Source—your star.

7. Breathe into this image; notice your feelings, sensations, emotions, and thoughts.

8. Expand your inner strength and calmness with peace, focus, and clarity.

9. Radiate your energy outward to meet the circumference of light.

10. Merge with the spiral pillar of light, coming into alignment with higher frequency.

Variations:

➤ Eliminate the spiral; see the energy as a pillar of light; or eliminate the pillar and imagine a cone of spiraling energy. Does one feel more comfortable? Does one have more energy, strength, or flow? What is activated in you with each?

➤ The descending energy can be any color you tune in to. Is there a color your body is craving, a specific emotion you want to radiate? Choose the color that magnifies this emotion and create the spiraling pillar of light in that color.

➤ When feeling internal negativity, activate the spiral pillar to avoid projecting your emotions onto others in a harmful way, or hooking into their energy field and draining them.

➤ Let your projections of fear, pain, or anger extend outward to the edge of the pillar. Here they can be absorbed, transformed, and returned as loving self-acceptance and understanding.

EARTH AND SKY

Keyword: Grounding

Description: The *Earth and Sky* meditation opens the Hara line, the channel of energy that runs up the vertical core of your body. This meditation establishes your place as the bridge between Heaven and Earth; the point of exchange between energy and matter. When you become the fulcrum between polarities, you are in a position of power and able to move in any direction. It's the difference between reacting and responding; here you are free to respond with balance and confidence.

Benefits:
- Promotes grounding and centering.
- Strengthens the Hara line.
- Integrates material and spiritual polarities.
- Balances masculine and feminine principles.
- Facilitates inner balance between polar or conflicting concepts/ideas.
- Promotes wholeness.

Use to:
- Bring ideas and concepts into physical form.
- Create inner strength on all levels: physical, spiritual, mental, emotional.
- Promote balance between conflicting life demands.
- Maintain a grounded, practical approach to life circumstances.
- Integrate conflicting desires and beliefs in decision-making.
- Find and follow your path.
- Reduce stress and manage anxiety.

Flow Pattern:
1. Sit or stand. Take a few deep breaths, and calm your mind and body. Bring your awareness to the core of your body.
2. Connect with the channel running between your perineum and the top of your head through the center of your body. This is often called

the Hara line, and it connects your star in the sky to the center of the Earth and vice versa.

3. Focus on your Crown chakra while inhaling. Imagine your breath is drawing light from the sky into your Hara line, filling your body with freedom, space, light, and air. Be free.

4. Exhale and send energy downward through your body, out of your sacrum into the ground, sending roots deep into the Earth. Feel the solidity, stability, and safety of the Earth. See yourself safe.

5. Inhale and imagine pulling Earthlight up into your body through your sacrum, bringing the stability and safety of the Earth into your Hara line. Feel yourself strong, safe, and flexible.

6. Exhale, sending Earth energy out through the top of your head, sending branches into the sky, and sending the strength of the Earth to the heavens.

7. Repeat this alternating flow of energy in your natural breathing rhythm: Send Earth energy into sky; bring sky energy into Earth.

8. Take your natural place as a bridge between Earth and sky. Integrate the energies within your body, becoming strong, safe, balanced, and free.

Variations:

➤ Use color in your breathing. Often, people use green for the Earth and blue for the sky.

➤ Notice which polarity, Earth or sky, is more difficult for you to integrate. Breathe in from that polarity exclusively until it is easy to do and feels balanced, then resume breathing from both Earth and sky to promote integration.

CIRCLE OF LIFE

Keyword: Energizing

Description: This meditation activates your meridians by circulating energy along the Great Central Channel of Chinese medicine. This channel feeds and interacts with your entire meridian system, while nourishing and defending your bodymind. The meditation has two distinct flows. In one, energy travels down the center line of the front of your body, under and then up your back. Sometimes this pattern is called the Microcosmic Orbit. In the second flow, a circle is created by energy traveling up the internal central core of your body, the Hara line, becoming a fountain when it crests the top of your head. Like a fountain, the energy flows down around the boundary of your aura, pooling under your Base chakra, where it is gathered together and re-circulated up your core. The *Circle of Life* nourishes and revitalizes all aspects of your physical, mental, and emotional being. It helps prepare your nervous system to handle larger quantities of high frequency energy.

Benefits:
- Promotes balance between nourishment and defense.
- Supports your physical, mental, emotional, and spiritual constitution.
- Revitalizes, renews, and rejuvenates.
- Balances excess/deficient energy.
- Creates even distribution and smooth flow of energy.
- Clears your thinking and focuses your actions.
- Opens psychic perception.
- Prepares the body for higher spiritual frequencies.

Use to:
- Improve health and strengthen the immune system.
- Regain physical strength after trauma, depletion, or exhaustion.
- Clear old, stagnant ideas and beliefs; create positive action.
- Prepare for spiritual and/or healing work.

Flow Pattern:
1. Sit comfortably with your back straight and well supported.
2. Breathe in, center, and ground yourself, letting go of unnecessary tension.
3. Relax your jaw and place your tongue lightly on the roof of your mouth. Contract your perineum as though holding your bladder.
4. Inhale, drawing the breath in below your belly button to an area called the Hara or Sea of Energy, where vital life force is stored. Breathe light into this area until your belly feels full and vibrant.
5. While breathing, on your inhale imagine light flowing from your belly down under your torso into your sacrum, up your spine, and over the top of your head.
6. On your exhalations, imagine energy flowing down your face and through your tongue, down the front of your body, curling under your torso, and up your spine.
7. In tandem with your breathing, keep the energy flowing along this pathway until your bodymind feels awake and alive.
8. At the completion of the meditation, draw all the energy into your Hara for storage.

Variations:
➤ Instead of focusing on your Hara when building energy, focus on your coccyx, the very base of the spine. This is useful if you have restless legs or vibration in your coccyx, symptoms of Kundalini getting ready to rise. (See Chapter 7 for more information.)
➤ As energy circulates, send beams of light from the Central Channel into each chakra to clear and energize each center. (See the *Chakra Fibers* meditation.)
➤ Imagine the energy flowing in different colors.
➤ Change the circuit by drawing energy up your Hara line and letting it spill out the top of your head like a fountain. Keep it flowing, allowing the energy to form a Torus of energy that looks like a donut.

Caution: It's easy to become over-stimulated with this exercise. To avoid this, begin your practice with shorter sessions. If you do become over-stimulated, send the excess energy out of your hands and feet. With practice you will be able to handle both larger quantities and higher frequencies of energy.

CHAKRA CLARITY

Keyword: Growth

Description: This meditation activates all seven of the major chakras. Chakras are vortices, often called "wheels of light" that emerge from the Hara line and project outward into the aura. Chakras are centers of higher frequency that accumulate and transmit vital life energy. Your chakras are involved in all aspects of your health, growth, development, and spiritual awareness. Each chakra governs a specific aspect of evolving consciousness and is associated with a specific color, sound, spiritual challenge, gift, and set of emotions. Working with the chakra system is an intricate, lifelong process. Although this is a basic meditation, it can take you into a very deep practice.

Benefits:
- Improves emotional clarity.
- Enhances spiritual awareness, expansion, and personal development.
- Promotes the specific benefits of each chakra. (See Chapter 7.)
- Deepens awareness of self-limiting attitudes, beliefs, and behaviors.
- Helps to discover inner resources.

Use to:
- Expand your awareness as part of daily spiritual practice.
- Promote balance in all aspects of bodymind.
- Change yourself when confronted by self-sabotaging behavior.
- Balance extremes of emotion during times of stress.
- Remove obstacles on your path.

Flow Pattern:
1. Sit or lie down. Keep your spine as straight as possible or imagine sitting with a straight spine.
2. Relax. Calm the mind and open the *Spiral Pillar of Light* and/or *Earth and Sky* meditations for grounding and to charge your system.

3. Imagine the seven vortices of energy that are rooted in the Hara line and blossom in the aura. Try to feel all of them as vibration affecting the body area with which they connect.

4. Begin with the Base chakra and inhale energy into one after another, using your attention to notice how each feels. Here are the locations: First or Base chakra is in the pelvic bowl facing down to the Earth; second or Sacral chakra is above the pubic bone and below the belly button, facing front and back; third or Solar Plexus chakra is below the ribcage above the belly button, facing front and back; fourth or Heart chakra is on your breastbone in the center of your chest, facing front and back; fifth or Throat chakra is in your throat, facing front and back; sixth or Third Eye chakra is between your eyebrows, facing front and back; seventh or Crown chakra is at the top of the head facing up.

5. Experience the content of each chakra individually: What color is it? What are the quality and shade of color? Is it clear, cloudy, vibrant, dull? How much energy does it emit? Is it full or empty? Is it perfectly or ill-shaped? Round or oval? Is the chakra spinning? If so, clockwise or counterclockwise? What is the emotion of the chakra? How does it feel? Is it tight, expansive, energized, depleted? Is it hot, cold, or neutral? Do you enjoy the sensation here? There is no need to change anything, simply be in the moment with what you feel.

6. As you sit with each chakra, you may or may not notice that the chakra is asking for something, perhaps a color, light, more vibrancy, or space.

7. Inhale and imagine your breath providing the chakra with whatever it needs. Notice what thoughts, emotions, feelings get in the way of receiving and also notice what assists you in being able to receive.

8. Does this area have an image, perhaps an animal or light being? Is there a message for you?

9. After exploring each individual chakra, step back and visualize the entire path. Does one chakra draw your attention more than another? Is there flow between each? Is any chakra energetically isolated? What do you feel, sense, experience, and imagine as you look at your chakra system? Do you identify with the emotion or spiritual challenge of any particular chakra?

10. Breathe through the entire chakra system, letting go of anything you no longer need while strengthening that which you want to keep.

11. Just sit and enjoy the sensation of your chakras vibrating with each other.

12. Take the time to write down your experience.

Explorations in Light

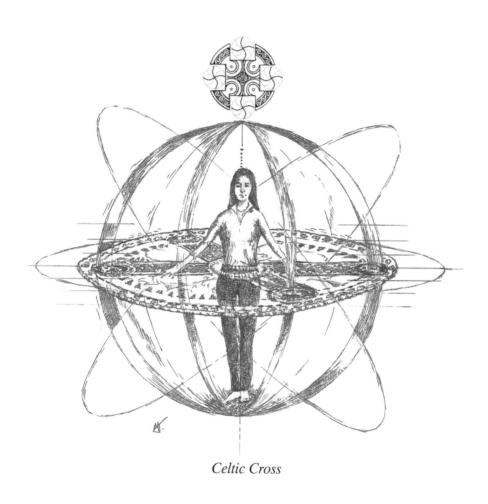

Celtic Cross

Chakra Fibers (Light Filaments)

Keyword: Connection

Description: The *Chakra Fibers* meditation expands your imagination and increases inspiration while helping you stay grounded. A chakra can be experienced as a rotating vortex in the aura, as in the previous meditation, or as a nexus of energy fibers used to explore and connect with your environment. Where you place your attention is where your fibers explore. When your fibers anchor in one place, you become grounded in that reality and way of seeing the world. When they are unattached, you have free attention open to explore new ways of thinking and new realities. A balance between anchored and unattached fibers allows for stability, integrity, grounding, and commitment while fostering flexibility of thought, openness to new ideas, freedom from limiting beliefs, creativity, and acceptance of others.

Benefits:
- Anchors your reality.
- Deepens connection to other people, animals, and light beings.
- Maintains connection to locations, the environment, and experiences.
- Maintains grounding and direction on your path.
- Provides creative inspiration.
- Increases intuition.
- Provides an avenue for psychic awareness.
- Draws insight, ideas, beliefs, and attitudes from your experiences.

Use to:
- Deepen connection in relationships, human and non-human.
- Release outgrown attachments and old relationships.
- See different perspectives and approaches to life.
- Strengthen connection and ability to work with Earth energies.

⟐ Experience oneness and interconnection with all life and the god force.

Flow Pattern:

1. Sit or lie with straight spine. Relax, center, ground, and create sacred space.

2. Bring your attention to each chakra, one at a time, and then focus on the one that draws your attention.

3. Imagine energy fibers flowing out from the center of each chakra into the space around you: reaching, feeling, attaching, releasing, and exploring.

4. Observe the fibers. Notice their color, thickness, flexibility, length, amount of light, and so on. Do the fibers move freely and easily, or are they tangled and enmeshed in each other? Are they lively and awake, or dull and listless?

5. Breathe vitality into your fibers and allow them to be full of life, freedom, and joy.

6. Notice what percentage of your fibers are attached to your surroundings. Can you see what they are attached to and how firmly? How many are free to explore?

Variations:

≻ Think of a specific person. How many of your fibers are attached to this person? Notice the quality of the attachment; does it take more energy than you receive? Does it bring you joy? Does it bring joy to the other person? Does the attachment help or hinder you? Is one person growing at the expense of the other? Know that at any time you can recall your fibers from someone, as well as release any fibers that are attached to you. (See Chapter 16.)

≻ Think of something you enjoy in nature such as a garden and send your awareness into this garden. Watch your unattached fibers explore, and allow thoughts and inspiration to flow to you.

≻ Think of a project you are working on. Notice how your fibers are behaving. Are they anchored in one place? Are you inspired with new ideas? Is this the way you want it to be?

≻ Imagine having a spiritual guide and notice the light connections between you. Be open to receiving insight.

WEAVING THE NADIS

Keyword: Serenity

Description: This meditation impacts the quality of energy flowing through your body and energy field. The Nadis are pathways of energy interacting with the meridians and weaving between the chakras. There are thousands of Nadis in the body, with a main set linking the seven major chakras and maintaining communication among them. The Nadis also sustain a smooth energy flow. When they are too tight or too loose, flow is uneven: constrained and restricted in some areas while too loose in others, creating wild rapids and stagnating pools. Clear flowing Nadis help prepare the nervous system for managing higher frequency and amplitude of energy. They also prepare you for the rising of Kundalini, a powerful spiritual experience. Kundalini is a spiritual energy residing in the sacrum that rises naturally as your awareness expands. You don't need to invite Kundalini to rise; it will do it organically as the pathways are cleared. This weaving meditation is the sweetest of all the meditations, providing a truly sublime serenity.

Benefits:

- Regulates the flow of energy among chakras.
- Promotes peace and harmony.
- Allows communication and integration among chakras.
- Nourishes and cleanses chakra energy.
- Prepares the Hara line for receiving Kundalini, which opens psychic perception.
- Maintains balance between left and right; up and down.
- Increases integration of insight from your experiences.
- Expands awareness, promoting new attitudes and beliefs.
- Improves the quantity and quality of energy used for daily living.

Use to:

- Calm the mind and soothe the spirit.
- Reduce fatigue by stimulating stagnating pools of energy.

◈ Improve focus by reducing the frenetic quality of undirected energy.

◈ Improve quality of sleep and reduce insomnia.

◈ Reduce the impact of trauma on the physical and emotional body.

◈ Integrate emotional trauma and restore balance.

◈ Increase unconditional love and acceptance.

◈ Invite spiritual uplifting.

Flow Pattern:
1. Sit or lie comfortably; do an opening meditation to create sacred space.
2. Focus your awareness on your Base chakra and breathe into it, energizing it.
3. Visualize the Nadis in your mind's eye and imagine weaving energy from the first chakra all the way up to the seventh.
4. Begin by bringing energy up your left leg into the left side of the Base chakra. Imagine the flow leaving the right side of the first chakra and flowing on a loop of the Nadis into the right side of the second chakra. See it flowing out the left side of the second chakra up to left side of the third chakra. Continue weaving the energy up through the chakra system.
5. At the sixth chakra, the energy exits from that chakra's left side into the Nadis and curls over the top of the head, moving through the upper levels of the seventh/Crown chakra, then exits the Crown chakra into the right side of the sixth chakra and flows down through the chakras in reverse order, forming an alternating pattern.
6. If you are someone who learns through feeling, it might be helpful to trace this pathway on your body with your hands before starting the meditation.
7. When the descending pathway reaches the Base chakra, send the energy out the chakra's right side and down your right leg into the Earth.
8. Maintain a continuous cycling of energy using your breath as a pump.

Variation:
➤ Expand and contract the width of the Nadis to slow down or speed up the flow of energy.

FIVE-HEARTS OPEN

Keyword: Sensitivity

Description: The *Five-Hearts Open* meditation is used to enhance your awareness of the subtle energy within matter. The five "hearts" of Chinese medicine consist of four small chakras, one in the palm of each hand and in the soles of the feet, plus the large Heart chakra in the middle of the chest. The chakra in the palms of your hands feel the world around you; the chakras from the soles of your feet connect to the ley lines of the Earth. *Five-Hearts Open* is a moving meditation that opens awareness to the energy within physical form, increasing your energy sensitivity. It plugs you into the Earth's energy circuit and enhances the direct experience of how interconnected all life is.

Benefits:
- Increases energy sensitivity and awareness of energy connections.
- Increases contact with the people around you.
- Increases connection to nature and the natural environment.

Use to:
- Increase energy sensitivity.
- Better feel auras in people, animals, crystals, and so on.
- Feel the energy flows in the Earth.
- Understand the energetic quality of a situation, group, place, event.
- Plug into Earth energy and charge your energy system.
- Explore and discover deeper connection and meaning in life.
- Increase inspiration and guidance.

Flow Pattern:
Ideally, this meditation is done outdoors, although indoors works as well.
1. Sit quietly and do an opening meditation creating sacred space.
2. Using awareness and breath, direct your attention to your Heart chakra.

3. With each inhalation, draw conscious, living light into your head and down your Hara line to your heart, expanding it with light and joy.

4. Let light shine from your heart into the space around you. Become an extension of light as your fibers explore nearby objects, plants, animals, and, with permission, people.

5. Bring your awareness and energy back to your heart. Using your breath, recharge your Heart chakra, then focus on your palms, sending streams of living light down your arms and into your hands. You may notice your palms tingling and/or becoming hot.

6. Open a pathway from your heart to the soles of your feet, allowing them to come alive with awareness.

7. When all five hearts are open, stand up and visualize the energy in your feet descending deep into the Earth. Walk slowly and deliberately, engaging your entire foot as your weight shifts. When your foot lifts, keep your focus on the connection it still has to the Earth. No matter how far off the ground your foot rises, feel energy streaming out of the sole, plugging into the Earth's energy circuit.

8. Breathe Earth energy up into your body through your feet, charging your system.

9. Approach a tree or plant and ask permission to connect with its spiritual essence. Stream energy out of your heart and hands toward this Being. With light-filled hands, explore the space around the plant, feeling for the radiance emanating from its core. Pulse your hand toward and away from it, building energy. You may notice a magnetic repulsion/attraction between your hand and the plant.

10. Notice changes inside yourself as you connect energetically with life.

Variation:

➤ Do the same as above, only blind-folded. Be sure to have a friend present for safety.

Queen Nefertiti's Headdress

Keyword: Perception

Description: This meditation brings freedom from old, emotional patterns by re-creating the ancient Egyptian headdress worn by Queens and Pharaohs. The headdress is a unique energy amplifier. Shaped like a cone and worn with the narrow end around the head and the wide end opened to Spirit, it channels spiritual energy downward into the Crown chakra. The layered striations of the headdress align with the seven layers of the aura. Each striation connects to its associated layer. As higher frequencies are drawn into the headdress, the aura begins to vibrate. Each layer of the headdress, and thus each layer of the aura, vibrates at a different rate. Thought forms, limiting beliefs, and old emotional patterns cannot maintain their structure and, like bubbles, burst and disperse, allowing new inspirations to emerge. This meditation brings upliftment, expanded consciousness, and freedom from limitation. It allows you to perceive reality without your standard lens and bias.

Benefits:
- Cleanses and purifies the aura.
- Expands consciousness and shifts to higher planes of awareness.
- Raises frequency for higher connections and guidance.
- Removes bias and outmoded perceptions.

Use to:
- Remove negative thought forms and old emotional patterns.
- Remove energy attachments.
- Eliminate energy projections from other people or situations.
- See situations, people, and self clearly.

Flow Pattern:
1. Sit comfortably; do opening meditation to create sacred space.

2. In your imagination, put on the cone-shaped Egyptian headdress so that the narrow end rests on your head and the wider end is open to the heavens.

3. Gently drop your chin and stretch the back of your neck, aligning the cone directly heavenward and activating the Hara line.

4. Using breath and intention, invite energy to fill the headdress. As the headdress fills, the energy within vibrates at faster speed and intensity.

5. Imagine the energy flowing into your aura along the energy pathways defined by the striations of the headdress. Use your breath to assist this process and mentally invite energy to flow down the striations and into the layers of your aura.

6. Notice that as your aura fills with light, its different layers begin to vibrate intensely and at slightly different rates.

7. Mental and emotional disturbances, negative thought forms, projections from other people, and psychic hooks reveal themselves as areas that vibrate more slowly. They may feel sluggish, blocked, or dense, and have a dark color. You may notice emotional content such as fear, guilt, greed, shame, anger, or victimization.

8. Focus your awareness and, with your breath, increase the light coming into the headdress. As your aura increases in vibration, the unwanted energy will vibrate beyond ability to maintain form and burst, releasing all the trapped energy.

9. Let yourself feel light and free.

Variations:

➤ After dispersing unwanted energy forms, imagine the energy reversing direction and passing out of the headdress through the opening at the top, vacuuming your aura and pulling psychic residue and debris out of your field to be released.

➤ Finish by brushing your aura. Use your fingers as a comb to separate the light filaments and untangle snarled areas, fluffing the aura by brushing light, space, and color into your field.

THE WINGED DISK

Keyword: Healing

Description: The *Winged Disk* meditation activates healing patterns by linking the physical body with its perfect energy template. The winged disk of ancient Egypt, like the Zuni Eye of God, recognizes the God force at the heart of all creation. The winged disk was said to fly across the sky, keeping watch over creation and bringing energy from the God-side of reality onto Earth when the Earth plane was out of balance. This meditation focuses on health as an outcome of balanced and abundant life force. It channels healing energy in the form of higher frequencies that promote transformation. The *Winged Disk* meditation acts as a star-bridge for people in the healing arts, channeling templates for physical reality from the God-side of creation.

Benefits:
- Increases vitality and free flow of energy.
- Brings spiritual information into the physical and emotional system.
- Opens powerful flows of energy from the creative life force.

Use to:
- Promote healing—physically, emotionally, spiritually.
- Enhance immune function.
- Assist during healing work of all kinds:
  - To energetically assess life force, flow, and obstruction.
  - To align and balance energy flow within the body.
  - To transmute frequencies holding patterns of dis-ease.
  - To transmit higher frequencies of unconditional love, the source of all healing.
- Manifest your dreams that are aligned with higher ideal.

Flow Pattern:
Prior to starting this meditation, be sure to have permission from anyone to whom you are intending to send energy. This is basic respect for another's personal path.

1. Open sacred, protected space and invite higher assistance.
2. Align your intention to the highest and best good. Increase energy along the Hara line using the *Earth and Sky* meditation.
3. Imagine tiny, golden, dancing stars entering your Crown chakra and descending along the Hara line to your Heart chakra.
4. Allow the stars to increase and dance faster and faster within your heart as your Heart chakra vibrates and expands in harmony with them.
5. Allow starlight to flow down your arms into your hands. What color is it?
6. Maintaining awareness of the dancing stars, place your attention on an imbalance of yours, or in a person, situation, or place where you want to offer support.
7. Place your hands directly on or over the imbalanced area, or over a picture of the person on whom you are working, or the map of an area you want to energize, or intention you want to manifest. You can also simply hold the image of the person or event in your mind's eye.
8. Breathing through your Crown chakra, invite the dancing stars into the imbalanced area, stating that the person has the right to accept or reject your offering.
9. Imagine molecules vibrating into alignment with ideal reality, reflecting the perfect template that already exists in the energy matrix.
10. Release all judgment of what the ideal is "supposed" to look like and allow it to be whatever it is.
11. Hold this sacred space, allowing your hands to move as it seems they must until the flow of light from your hands to the receiver decreases, indicating the conclusion of the healing.
12. Sit in silence, holding sacred space and allowing thoughts, impressions, and feelings to emerge.
13. Close the channels to your hands and continue to let your heart fill with light.
14. Close the meditation with your own heart full of light, energizing all the pathways in your body.

CELTIC CROSS

Keyword: Protection

Description: This pattern provides a protective shield when in physical, psychological, or psychic danger. The Celtic Cross consists of five energy balls: one large, central ball surrounded by four satellites. When you stand in the center and energetically connect the satellites in the Celtic Cross pattern, an impenetrable wall of safety is created. Any ill-intentioned energy sent toward a person or place protected by the Celtic Cross is blessed and reflected back to the sender as love. This formation magnifies your energy field, expanding your personal space and creating power and strength. It helps to activate your survival instincts while calling on higher powers to assist your safety. Although not an aggressive pattern, it is fully protective. It can also act as a filter, allowing higher energy to come in while shielding you from thought forms, projections, and hooks. (See Chapter 12.)

Benefits:

   ❂ Creates an energetic shield around yourself, people, objects, and places.

   ❂ Helps to focus and solidify your attention.

   ❂ Gathers all your resources necessary for strength and action.

   ❂ Facilitates the highest and best outcome for all involved parties.

   ❂ Allows you to rest when under extended external pressure.

   ❂ Filters harmful energy from the matrix of energy you receive.

Use to:

   ❂ Protect from psychic attack or extreme situations.

   ❂ Maintain boundaries and facilitate peaceful resolution during conflict.

   ❂ Assist a safe outcome when in physical danger.

   ❂ Help protect and shield loved ones.

   ❂ Protect property.

- Activate filtered protection when in group situations.
- Filter energy during telepathic or psychic explorations.
- Act as vehicle for out of body exploration.

Flow Pattern:
1. Activate the *Spiral Pillar of Light*.
2. Align the outer edge of the pillar with the outer edge of your aura.
3. Imagine four spheres/balls of light circling several feet beyond your aura: one in front of you, one behind, and one to either side of you. They are connected around you through a horizontal tube of light circling your torso.
4. Visualize a tube of energy flowing from the sphere in front, over your head and through the one behind you, then flowing under your feet and returning to the ball in front. Keep energy flowing along this circular tube.
5. Connect the balls on either side in the same way. Imagine a tube of energy flowing from the sphere on your left, over the top of your head through the one on your right, under your feet, and back to the ball on the left. Keep energy flowing along this route.
6. Maintain a continuous energy flow in the two circuits.
7. Spin the circuits, creating a gyroscopic field that repels and/or filters approaching energy.

Variations:
- Use color to magnify the effect; metallic silver is one of the strongest.
- Construct this pattern around your house, family, individuals, animals, personal property, or objects that need extra protection.

Master Activations

Pyramid Purification

MYSTIC TRIANGLE

Keyword: Intention

Description: The *Mystic Triangle* is a master communication tool. It aligns with and opens the third eye, promoting higher level communication. It magnifies both the ability to see higher truth and to manifest it in the physical world. It can open a portal between dimensions, different levels of reality, or different places in time and space. This is a Master Activation and requires a developed nervous system to sustain. It invokes the archetype of the Earth Mother, the Spiritual Mother who gives birth to higher truth and nurtures it in this reality. This is a protective and sustaining activation.

Benefits:

- Establishes mental, emotional, and spiritual clarity.
- Creates a portal to higher planes.
- Connects with guides, guardians, the angelic realm, and Nature Spirits.
- Manifests spiritual principles and aligns to higher path and purpose.
- Provides connection between people in different locations or times.
- Enhances telepathic ability.
- Provides protection during spiritual development.
- Activates the Pineal Gland and the Third Eye.

Use to:

- Provide inspiration during creative projects (art, writing, problem-solving).
- Communicate telepathically with others.
- Remote view distant events or places and explore psychic realms.
- Enhance therapy sessions, healing work, prayer, meditation, manifestation.
- Channel or develop extra-sensory perception.

Flow Pattern:
1. Center, ground, and open sacred space. Invite your guides to participate.
2. Sit or stand with arms at your side, about 45 degrees away from your body, palms facing forward. Use the four activations that follow for different purposes.

> **Intuitive Opening:** Visualize a triangle at your Third Eye. Imagine it as electric, cobalt blue with energy pulsing along the edges, creating an energetic beacon into the ethers. Invite spiritual energy to flow into this triangle. Be open to inspiration, communication, upliftment, heightened perception, and so on. Keep this triangle activated while performing your spiritual practice.

> **Transmitting Energy:** Create a triangle with the apex the triangle in your Third Eye and the corners of the base in the palms of your hands. Allow the Third Eye to energize this larger triangle. As the Third Eye and palms of your hands vibrate, use the vibration to transmit your highest intentions for healing, manifestation, and transformation into the world. This vibration overrides lower energy impulses and only transmits pure intentions and manifestations for the highest spiritual good.

> **Opening a Communication Portal:** Move the triangle into a horizontal plane by keeping the base stable in your hands and imagining the apex falling forward, away from your Third Eye, until it is on the same plane as the base. Invite any person, spiritual being, or group with whom you wish to communicate to sit in the apex of the triangle. This activation protects you from lower-level influences or attachments.

> **Charging your System:** Visualize a triangle, its apex in your Third Eye, base in your palms. Create two smaller triangles inside this larger one; one with apex at the Heart chakra, the other with apex at the Solar Plexus. All three triangles share the same base. Note your Hara line bisects the midpoint of the bases at the level of your coccyx bone (tail bone), seat of Kundalini, in the Base chakra. Allow energy to lift up the Hara line to energize and amplify the Third Eye, activating the Solar Plexus and Heart chakras as it rises. The Third Eye is now fully activated and charged. Use to incorporate higher frequencies, remote view, transmute lower level energies, and so forth.

PYRAMID PURIFICATION

Keyword: Cleansing

Description: This is a cleansing meditation. True spiritual growth requires that we own both our light and the shadow it casts. Our thoughts and emotions generate energy forms that fill the aura and atmosphere of the Earth, move along the surface of the planet via rivers and oceans, and travel beneath the surface of the planet on ley lines. Heart-centered thoughts and emotions create connection and advancement. They stabilize the planet and promote harmonics of spiritual growth. Destructive thoughts and emotions create energetic pollution, poisoning the planet energetically just as our industrial pollution poisons the air, water, and soil we depend on to live. This activation cleanses and purifies destructive emotional manifestations which are transformed and broadcast as unconditional love. It is our opportunity to call home our shadow and embrace it, merging the shadow with light, becoming whole.

Benefits:
- Establishes inner congruence.
- Promotes self-acceptance, self-love, inner peace, and forgiveness.
- Promotes healing by removing obstacles to health.
- Transmutes karma.
- Cleanses your soul of old pain, trauma, anger, and destructive patterns.
- Creates spiritual uplifting and freedom.
- Cleanses and clears the Earth.
- Harmonizes the Earth's aura and stabilizes Earth energy.

Use to:
- Generate love, peace, light, forgiveness, and grace.
- Cleanse personal space, houses, offices and so on, especially after conflict.
- Clear battle grounds, murder sites, sites of traumatic events.
- Take responsibility for your choices and actions.

◈ Make an intention of peace on the planet.

◈ Clear energetic pollution.

Flow Pattern:

1. Sit with straight back in cross-legged position or on chair, feet flat on the ground. Activate the *Spiral Pillar of Light* to establish sacred space.

2. Breathe and establish your intention to cleanse the bodymind and reclaim the shadow self.

3. Extend your awareness above your head and see that you have higher level energy centers in your aura. These are chakras that are aligned with your higher dimensional self and linked to multidimensional planes. Their function is to tune into spiritual reality.

4. Imagine a four-sided pyramid with the apex above your head at the level of one of the higher energy centers.

5. The base of the pyramid sits on the Earth and the pyramid may be all one color or multicolored. What color(s) is it for you?

6. Activate the pyramid by focusing on the apex while holding the intention to take responsibility for all of your emotions, thoughts, and actions.

7. Allow the outline of the pyramid to light up with energy. See a vortex forming along your Hara line, drawing energy up through your chakras and forming a spiral within the pyramid. The spiral may look like a violet flame.

8. The base of the pyramid is connected to lines of energy coming into it from the matrix of the planet. As the pyramid activates, past, destructive energies are drawn in along these lines for the clearing. You may see dark vapors being pulled into the base and fed into the violet flame. As your thoughts and emotions are transmuted into light, embrace your shadow, that small hurt part of self, and welcome yourself home.

9. Accept yourself. Allow all the cells of your body to be bathed in love and joy.

10. Feel the rips and tears in your light body mend as you expand.

Variation:

➤ This pattern can be used for Earth healing, singly or in groups. The directions are in Chapter 14.

THE LIVING MATRIX

Keyword: Transcendence

Description: *The Living Matrix* is the Master Activation for higher consciousness. According to the ancient Maya, three-dimensional consciousness is woven on a loom of 20 vertical warp lines and 13 horizontal weft lines, creating the matrix of life. Everything we see and experience resonates to the ratio of 13:20. It is the golden ratio of nature; it governs the cycles of time and harmonizes the music of the celestial spheres. The human body is woven into the matrix through the 20 fingers and toes. Thirteen major joints (ankles, knees, hips, wrists, elbows, shoulders, and neck) create connecting points to the galaxy. When your toes anchor your meridians into the ley lines of the Earth and your fingers weave your meridians into the energy pathways of the heavens, the 13 joints become portals to dimensional reality. This is the awakening of true paradigm shift.

Benefits:
- Initiates shifts into higher consciousness.
- Harmonizes you to higher frequency.
- Opens dimensional perception.
- Activates the light filaments in your DNA.
- Brings singularity consciousness into expression.
- Increases planetary love.

Use to:
- Activate your intuition.
- Merge with your higher self.
- Manifest your dreams and goals.
- Envision, create, and anchor higher reality.
- Align with new frequency.
- Bring humanitarian ideals for all life into consciousness.

Flow Pattern:
1. Lie or stand with your arms and legs spread in the manner of da Vinci's drawing of Man. If you can't do this physically, visualize.

2. Breathe in through your Crown chakra and send energy into your heart chakra, filling it with light.

3. When your heart is full, split the energy in four streams of light flowing into your arms and legs and out your fingers and toes.

4. Imagine the energy flowing from your toes and joining the ley lines of the Earth. Feel yourself an anchor for higher frequency coming into the Earth.

5. Imagine energy flowing from your fingers into the energy pathways of the sky. Feel yourself part of expanding awareness.

6. Maintain this flow into your crown and out your fingers and toes.

7. Allow your vibration to become finer and finer as you experience yourself as a link in a network grid of light. All of your mentors are before you, you are a mentor to those behind, and all are part of the One.

8. Know that we are all part of the shift under way and none of us makes it unless all of us do. Send energy and light to humanity.

9. Repeat the Mayan phase "In lak'ech—I am another yourself." Let go of judgment and condemnation.

10. Become pure light, pure love.

Variation:
Send this energy to the highest dream you can envision for manifestation.

Integration Exercise

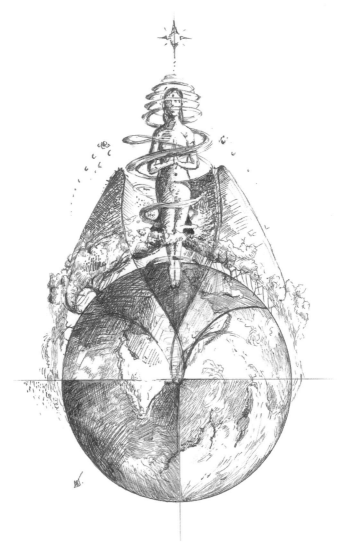

Dancing With Elements

Dancing with the Elements
(A Gift From Louisa Poole)

Keyword: Exploration

Description: All life is interconnected and interdependent: energy flowing into, through, and around matter, forming and unforming, in perpetual exchange. Quantum physics is based on the realization that light can be either a particle or a wave. It can be either the matrix or the form within the matrix. Each particle is a specific window into reality, a perspective, a unique small experience of the whole. We choose whether we are the whole or the part, but either way, each contains all. *Dancing with the Elements* is not an activation; it is the celebration of all that is awake within.

Benefits:
- Increases energy awareness.
- Deepens or awakens connection to nature, self, and the universe.
- Awakens gratitude and appreciation.

Use to:
- Celebrate being alive.
- Overcome depression.
- Wake up the senses.
- Play and have fun.
- Experience and express joy.
- Honor and experience the sacred in nature.
- Get over one's self importance.

Flow Pattern:
Wear loose, comfortable clothing; barefoot is best if your feet can do it.

1. Stand outside at dusk, dawn, or early night. (Well, okay—any time is fine!)

2. Open the *Spiral Pillar of Light* and create sacred space.

3. Open the Hara line and feel yourself suspended between Earth and Sky.

4. Become a puppet whose strings are controlled by the elements. Focus on your senses and let yourself be moved by what you feel, see, and hear.

5. Follow the wind. Let it push you, pull you, send you down the road, across the beach, into the field.

6. Conduct the orchestra of the birds, the cars, the waves.

7. Follow the smell, low down, up high, swirling into, out of. How does it smell? How does it move? Where does it go? Does it have shape? Can you dance to it?

8. Move with the insects, move with the flowers, move with the clouds, move with the sunlight, moonbeams, starlight.

9. Send your energy out of your arms, out of your legs, out of all parts of your body. Send your energy into the wind, into the Earth, into the sky. Can you say if the wind moves you or you move the wind? Can you say if the birds call you or if you call the birds? Who is the leader? Who is the follower? Is there a difference?

Variation:

➤ Dance with the elements blindfolded. Be sure to have a guide who keeps you safe and stays out of the way.

Chapter 4

Troubleshooting

If you're having trouble establishing any of these meditations you may be falling prey to one of these common mishaps:

> You may need a better foundation in meditation practice. If you have never meditated before and are having difficulty, start with a practice of standard meditation or join a meditation class, and then return after you've developed basic focusing skills.

> If you're having difficulty with the more advanced meditations, it's possible you haven't established enough energy in your field to maintain the complexity of the patterns. Stay with the foundational patterns until you are able to establish and maintain the flows comfortably before moving to more complex patterns.

> You may have too much investment in the outcome. These are processes and the object is to experience them; outcome orientation limits possibility and creates self-doubt. Release any expectations and simply do the meditations for fun. Whatever happens, happens. If nothing happens, that's something, too. Accept the experience and continue to practice just for the sake of discipline.

> The directions are described in very visual terms. You may not be a visually oriented person and may be having difficulty accessing the experience. Try translating the instructions into terms you can relate to:

   - Engage your auditory sense. Instead of using light as a metaphor, use sound or tones. Instead of creating visual structures, create sound architecture.

   - Engage the kinesthetic senses:

> ≻ Try drawing the patterns, letting yourself feel them in your body.

> ≻ Draw the patterns very large in your backyard or driveway. Walk them until you feel them in your body.

≻ You may have difficulty with the subtleness of the energy experience. Maybe you're separated from the feelings and sensations in your body, or maybe this is so different that you're unsure of what you're experiencing. Working with an experienced, trained energy practitioner can boost your confidence and awareness. A few good energy sessions should help you in discerning your inner energy flows.

≻ If you find yourself falling asleep during your practice don't discount your experience. You may be accessing higher realms in your sleep state. Ultimately you want to be able to access deeper brainwave states while maintaining conscious awareness. You might want to practice your meditations while sitting up, or start with the moving meditations until you can maintain wakefulness while in a deep meditative state.

≻ If you have trouble staying focused or taking the work seriously, practicing alone may not provide enough initial support. Practicing with other people can magnify energy and also provide validation for your experience.

≻ Some people need an intellectual construct to align to. If your mind needs further engagement, read Part II of this book before continuing with the meditations.

Part II

The Sea of Life Force

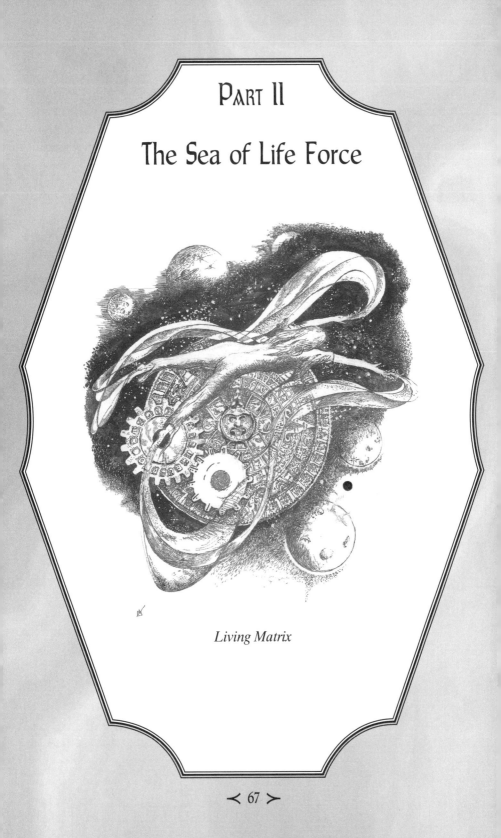

Living Matrix

Did you find it challenging to interact with the internal flows of energy introduced in Part I? It can be helpful to have a framework to organize your experience. Part II provides key constructs in the understanding of subtle energy. It's important for some people to understand the meditations and what they do. For others, too much intellectualizing gets in the way. If this section seems too complicated, skip it. Activating the energy patterns is enough; it's your experience that's important.

Constructs are models for organizing information. They're not written in stone; they evolve as new information is added. The structures that organize energy in our body, the aura, chakras, and meridians, are themselves simply constructs. As humans evolve and as the planet's energy changes frequency, there's no reason to think our energy structures won't change as well. Read the information in Part II as a guide to how things might be for you, not as a directive of how they have to be. Your body will confirm what's true for you and what isn't.

Information in this section is metaphysical. Although science is beginning to bridge the gap between energy and matter, there is little, if any, scientific verification of what is being described. When scientific principles are used to portray subtle energy mechanisms, they are used as metaphor, not mechanisms. It will be up to the scientists of the future, exploring mind, matter, and inner space, to describe this reality in terms of pure science.

Chapter 5

Expanding Consciousness

The flow of your internal energy—its amplitude, its clarity, and the connection between one structure in your energy anatomy and another—is a reflection of your consciousness. Interacting with the movement of your energy and the pattern of its flow opens your mind to new levels of awareness, promoting expansion. What the structures are and how energy flows between them is covered in Chapter 7, and how to interact with the flows to makes changes in your life is the focus of Part III.

Understanding the connection between subtle energy and consciousness helps to clarify how the meditation practices in this book can expand your life.

Consciousness Defined

You may have heard the phrase *consciousness is the new frontier*, but what exactly is consciousness? The dictionary defines it as self-awareness, implying that the more aware you are of the processes that direct you, the more conscious you will be. Other definitions include:

- The whole of a person's experience.
- The energy or force behind awareness and intelligence.
- God, the Source, or the Totality of all that is.
- The animating and directing principle of the universe.

In short, consciousness is the part of you that connects to everything else and harmonizes with the rhythms of the universe. It's the force that directs human evolution, guiding your development from a vessel of infinite potential to one of spiritual self-realization.

The definitions of consciousness are very similar to the descriptions of subtle energy. Although they are not the same, the two are inseparable.

Subtle energy transmits the information of consciousness that organizes matter. It nourishes and sustains life, flowing into and through everything, creating an interconnected and interdependent universe.

As with subtle energy, definitions of consciousness are more related to how it functions than to what it is. The best description of consciousness includes three components:

First, it is a vehicle. If, as author Bob Frissell claims, people are spiritual beings having a human experience, then consciousness, as expressed through the creation of our bodymind, is the vehicle for this experience. It's the part of you that has the ability to process and respond to the physical and spiritual universe. Every idea, every thought, every belief you embrace contributes to your vehicle.

Second, consciousness is a perceptive tool. If the purpose of being human is to expand awareness and perceive with greater parts of self, then consciousness is the perceptive tool each person is developing to achieve this purpose. As you expand your consciousness, you are developing your ability to perceive deeper levels of reality.

Third, if we're learning to co-create the universe, then consciousness is the force we're learning to use. In becoming conscious of yourself as a spiritual being, you're acknowledging that you have creative capacity. Spiritual evolution is learning how to responsibly use that capacity to its fullest potential.

Your mind, emotions, physical sensations, perceptive tools, and awareness—the "self" you inhabit—are extensions of who you are, but they are not the whole of you. Your spiritual essence is much more than the instrument you are developing. When human identity became linked to the physical vehicle of the body, we lost our freedom.

The problem, however, is not the vehicle; it's the misidentification. Elevating your consciousness is the act of moving beyond this trap. It's returning to the knowing that you are the source *and* the instrument. The ultimate goal of raising consciousness is freedom.

> "You are not bodies, you are not minds, and you are not identities; you are the source of these things, and you can create better."
>
> —Harry Palmer, author of *Living Deliberately*

In short, the aspects of consciousness that can be defined are twofold. First, consciousness is the vehicle for an extraordinary journey, and is complete with both the sensing tools and power necessary for exploration and creation. Expanding consciousness is the act of developing these tools and generating greater power to invest in creative living. Secondly, consciousness is that which is traveling in this vehicle, something immensely more than our individual expression.

Holographic Consciousness

A helpful construct for thinking about consciousness is the hologram. When holograms were discovered, they changed how scientists viewed both the universe and the capacity of our brain to process information. Through the study of holograms, consciousness can be seen as an all pervasive and indivisible whole, where each part has access to the information contained in the whole.

Holograms have become quite common in our everyday world. We see holographic ID cards, advertisements, and knickknacks in every store. They have become so commonplace that we rarely think of what they really are and limit them to simply a three-dimensional photograph. However, that is the smallest part of what they have to offer.

To make a holographic photograph, an object is illuminated with a laser beam. A laser beam differs from regular light in that it has a high level of coherence among the light photons. Photon coherence is the reason for a laser's brilliance. A second laser beam is bounced off the reflected light of the first laser beam, creating an interference pattern where the two beams intersect. The interference pattern is captured on film. The developed film looks to be a meaningless swirl of lines. When these meaningless swirls are illuminated with a third laser beam, a three-dimensional image of the original object appears. Have you ever looked at a Magic Eye picture? This is utilizing the principles of holography, with your brain creating the coherence of a three-dimensional picture.

Its three-dimensional quality is not the most important aspect of the hologram. What is most remarkable is how information is contained in the picture. If a holographic picture of an image is cut in half, you don't have two halves of the picture as you would if you tore an ordinary photograph in half. Instead, each half contains the entire image. If the halves are divided again, each piece still contains a smaller, but intact version of the original image. In fact, every part of a hologram contains all the information possessed by the whole. This concept has changed scientist's view of nature, consciousness, the universe, and the functioning of our brains.

In holographic consciousness, the universe is not made up of separate, individual "I's." Rather, each person is part of the same whole, experiencing his or her own individual awareness at different places within the whole. Every part of this awareness is important. Every type of experience is integral and holds valuable insight. There are no mistakes. From wherever you are right now in this moment, the job is to become fully awake, aware, and alive. This is how to maximize your contribution to the whole of consciousness.

Dimensions of Consciousness

The term *dimension* has different meanings in different contexts. In mathematics and physics, a dimension is defined by the minimum number of coordinates needed to specify each point within it. Each point on a line requires only one coordinate, making it one-dimensional. A plane requires two coordinates, and three-dimensional forms require three coordinates: width, depth, and height.

Einstein introduced the idea that time is a dimension, suggesting we live in a four-dimensional world of space-time. The String Theory of physics predicts that physical space has 10 to 11 dimensions (some say 26) that can't be seen or measured due to the folding of space. In quantum physics, different dimensions often refer to alternate universes, as each possible choice creates its own alternate universe.

Metaphysically, a dimension is a state of consciousness and different states are reflected in specific planes of existence. Each plane or dimension inhabits the same physical space, vibrating at different rates. Different spiritual traditions describe different numbers of dimensions. The Hindu model describes seven dimensions of reality and consciousness. The Maya described nine dimensions of Heaven and seven dimensions of the underworld.

Many ancient texts, including those of the Mayans, Egyptians, and Hindus, have predicted a change in paradigm related to an expansion of consciousness that seems to relate to this time in history. This higher level of consciousness is that of multidimensional awareness. In a holographic model, expanding consciousness doesn't mean moving your awareness from one projection, or dimension, within the hologram to another. The view might be prettier, and your life might even be more fun; however, you will still be a singular perspective. The shift to multidimensional consciousness means becoming aware of yourself as one with the entirety of the hologram and able to experience all dimensions, a concept mystics have talked about for eons.

How the Meditations Work

The energy pathways in your aura form structured geometries of light and are your energetic expression in the world. The geometries connect different elements within your energy anatomy at the same time that they network with the world around you, linking you to the larger picture. In this manner, you're interconnected with the rest of life through a flow of energy to specific people, places, guides, the planet, and so forth.

Pathways in your energy structures are similar to neural pathways in the brain. Stanford neurophysiologist Karl Pribram has illuminated the study of the brain with holographic models. Author Michael Talbot reports:

> Pribram believes memories are encoded not in neurons, or small groupings of neurons, but in patterns of nerve impulses that crisscross the entire brain in the same way that patterns of laser light interference crisscross the entire area of a piece of film containing a holographic image. In other words, Pribram believes the brain is itself a hologram.[1]

In this analogy, the storage of information in the brain exists as patterns of neural activity in the same way patterns of perception exists as crisscrossing flows of energy in your aura. Your beliefs and perceptions are charges in your energy field that influence the direction and configuration of your energy flow. When you act in habitual ways, your energy flows in predetermined patterns. The meditations in this book activate new pathways of energy, creating new connections into the world and opening new arenas of perception and awareness.

Chapter 6

Understanding Subtle Energy

Subtle Energy = life force (chi, prana, vital energy)

Consciousness = life force + information + Love + the unknowable

We live in a sea of energy coursing through and around us. It organizes matter, creating form, structure, and life. This doesn't happen randomly. Humans have energy structures in and around the body that filter incoming energy and radiate outgoing energy in an organized manner. They consist of the aura, a field of energy that surrounds the body in seven distinct layers; the chakras, energy centers originating in the layers of the aura and permeating the physical body; and the meridians, channels within the body that feed each cell with vital life force. (If you're not familiar with these structures, what they are and how they function are covered in Chapter 7.)

The Frequency of Life

Subtle energy, chi, or life force is not some mysterious force that only exists in the realm of the supernatural. According to Einstein's famous equation, the speed of light is the reference point for the exchange of matter and energy, and $E=MC^2$ (energy equals matter moving at the speed of light squared), matter and energy are the same substance just moving at different speeds. Matter doesn't necessarily move faster and faster in a straight line until it reaches the speed of light squared, when it suddenly transforms into energy. Movement is also vibration, or back-and-forth motion. Matter vibrating at a high enough frequency becomes energy.[1]

The physical world—everything we see, feel, hear, and experience—is an expression of vibration. Based on Einstein's equation, light is often described as the building block of matter. The basic unit of light is a photon, or bundle of energy, which is entrained in the vibratory nature of subatomic particles. Quantum Physicist David Bohm has gone so far as to describe matter as frozen light.

Vibration can be measured along an electromagnetic spectrum from low frequency to high, where frequency refers to both the speed or rate of the propagation of energy waves and the speed or rate of vibration. As the photon is the basic unit of light, it is also the basic unit of electromagnetic energy. A photon can be described as a bundle of energy that carries electromagnetic radiation. Although light is commonly considered energy, in reality it is both energy and matter, a wave and a particle.

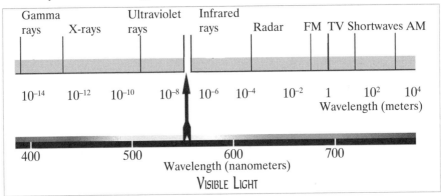

Electromagnetic Spectrum. The physical world is comprised of vibration expressed along an electromagnetic spectrum from low frequency to high.

Subtle energy exists outside of the measurable electromagnetic range. That doesn't mean it's supernatural. It means science hasn't discovered the technology to measure its rate of vibration. Radio waves, microwaves, and all the other measurable expressions of the electromagnetic spectrum were once outside of the range of technology, and many believe it is only a matter of time before subtle energy is measurable through accepted scientific means.

Metaphysically, subtle energy provides the matrix from which matter is formed. Vibration within the matrix creates the organizational focal point, as is discussed in the next section. Ancient traditions assert that this realm is influenced by our thoughts and intentions, which is why mental discipline and positive thinking are powerful tools of change. Additionally, since light is the reference point, it is the carrier of information from the higher vibration of energy to the lower vibration of matter. In all traditions, spirit, inspiration, healing, and spiritual connection are associated with being engulfed by or filled with light.

Organizing Principle

"The field is the sole governing agency of the particle."
—Albert Einstein

The definition of physical energy is the ability to do work, or affect matter. The forces that generate energy and effect the movement of matter include:

> Gravity, which allows us to swing big balls from cranes and knock down buildings.

> Chemical forces, which drive the making and breaking of bonds and all metabolic functions.

> Electromagnetic forces, which we have harnessed for our technology.

> Solar energy, which is entrained in matter and drives the processes of life.

One of the effects energy has on matter is organizational; energy is an organizing principle. Some of the forces of gravity organize the orientation of life; trees, people, and animals grow up, not down. Life orients to the field of gravity. The forces that guide chemical bonds direct the geometries inherent in nature. Ice crystals look the way they do based on the amount of energy in the bonds between water molecules. Electromagnetic energy flows in fields that organize magnetized particles. Solar energy becomes entrained in matter and organizes the complexity of life. The more solar energy a life form entrains, the more complex it can be.

Dr. Hans Jenny, a Swiss medical doctor and naturalist, investigated the impact of vibration in organizing matter in a science he named "Cymatics." Using audible sound frequency, he demonstrated that vibration creates patterns in material substances such as sand and oil. Different frequencies vibrate particles of sand suspended in oil into unique, complicated and sustained designs. Alternating frequencies create undulating, or moving, patterns.[2]

Although Jenny used audible sound frequency, the action of higher, inaudible frequency is the same; the higher the frequency, the more complex the pattern. Jenny's work demonstrates that vibration creates energy templates that can organize matter. Changing the frequency of the vibration changes the pattern of the template and therefore the physical structure.

Another demonstration of this principle comes from a Japanese author, Masaru Emoto, who demonstrated that the crystalline structure of frozen water is impacted when exposed to different thoughts. Water that was the focus of people holding thoughts of love had crystalline structures when frozen that were more elaborate and beautiful than those that formed when focused on by people holding negative thoughts.[3] The idea that thoughts have a specific frequency, or vibration, is not new. Different thoughts produce different brainwave states, which are measured with electroencephalographs (EEGs). Many believe the change in the crystalline structure of the water indicates that the energy of thought, the force measured in an EEG, is absorbed by the water molecules, changing the bond angles. Regardless of the mechanism, the experiment opens the possibility that physical structure can be changed though conscious intent.

Biological Information Codes

Subtle energy carries information in the form of vibration to organize matter and the force needed to do it. Information is transmitted as frequency and coded onto energy carrier waves. If this seems unlikely, consider radios. The information you hear on your radio is made of frequency that is coded onto radio waves, transmitted from the station, and received and decoded by your radio. Consider your cell phone. The conversations you have are coded as frequency on microwaves, transmitted through the server, and received and decoded by your phone.

All technology is based on biological mechanisms, including encoding information on carrier waves. Consider information carried on sound waves to your ear, transformed to mechanical vibration, and then transmitted via neurons to the brain, where it's analyzed. Or light waves received in your eyes. You may be surprised to know that communication between your cells also occurs through vibration that is decoded by cell-signaling molecules called kinases. The use of vibration to transmit information also exists in your energy structures.

Subtle energy is also called vital life force because it creates the difference between a body being dead or alive. All the systems of a body can be in working order, but without the force of vital energy and its life organizing information, the body dies. Anyone who has been with someone at the moment of death knows of the release of life force.

Life is an interface between energy and matter. Frequency coded on subtle energy creates the energy template of your aura, which organizes your physical body through your energy structures. The system is interactive and you are in exchange with other worlds and dimensions. It could be said that you are a sensor, filtering information from other dimensions to the physical world and sending information about the physical world to other dimensions.

Chapter 7

HUMAN ENERGY SYSTEMS

For many thousands of years, many different cultures across multiple continents have developed ideas of what human energy anatomy looks like and how energy "organs" function. Tibetan monks, Native Americans, Indian Vedics, mystics, and present-day metaphysicians have all developed systems of healing, meditation, and consciousness expansion based on these structures. The structures they describe and techniques they've developed are surprisingly similar. The names and descriptions of the structures in this book are from three sources: the Indian Vedic system, Asian medical systems, and metaphysicians of the 1900s.

There are many books and Websites about energy structures and you may already know all you need to on the subject. If this is new territory for you, the information here is very basic and meant to provide a foundation. If you're curious for more, look into some of the books recommended in Appendix B.

Energy structures maintain the organization of your physical body, including emotions, thinking patterns, and sensations. The easiest way to change a physical pattern, whether in your body or in the circumstances of your life, is to first change the configuration of your energy. Here is a brief description of what the energy structures are.

The Interacting Energy System

The energy structures of the aura, chakras, and meridians are described as separate "organs" of energy; however, that's an oversimplification. In reality, they inter-penetrate and interact with each other. They occupy the same space; their vibration within that space distinguishes them as separate. Each structure is in constant interaction with all other energy structures and, as one changes, all undergo corresponding change. The arrangement is holographic in nature.

Through your energy body, you interact with different dimensions and spiritual realities. Broadly speaking, spiritual frequencies are broadcast as vibrations on streams of energy, which are received in the aura, filtered through different layers, and fed into the chakras. The chakras process information and make it available to your bodymind through the meridians. The chakras are energy transducers, stepping down higher levels of energy to lower frequencies that can be fed into your body without overwhelming your physical circuits. Think of plugging an American hair dryer meant for 110 volts at 60 hertz into a British system that transmits 240 volts at 50 hertz and blowing the circuits of your hair dryer. Frequency coming into the aura has to be transformed downward to a level the body can receive without blowing the circuits of the nervous system and then digested into useful information for the bodymind.

From the chakras, energy/information is distributed into the meridians, the nervous system, and the endocrine glands. The meridians supply information and vitality to every cell in your body. The endocrine system uses vibration to direct metabolic activities, and the nervous system integrates the frequency into your level of awareness. Together, your physical body and energy structures form the vehicle of your consciousness.

The transmission of energy and information goes both ways. Subtle energy flowing through meridians collects cellular information that is transmitted back to the chakras. The chakras also collect information from your thoughts and emotions, and everything is radiated outward through the aura, transmitting the quality of your being. In this way, your vibration impacts the world and attracts people and situations into your life. Energy meditations will help you become aware of what you are taking in and what you are transmitting out. Through this process you become conscious of what you create.

The Aura

The aura is a field of luminosity that surrounds people, animals, plants, and objects. It's the radiation of life force that permeates all things. The human aura has been described as a "luminous egg," as it radiates in an emanation that is wider at the bottom than at the top. The total emanation extends an average of 3 feet out from the body, although it can be much larger, depending on different factors. Much has been made about the size of a person's aura being related to his or her spirituality, because your aura will expand with higher frequency. However, the size of the aura often relates to the function that is being performed, rather than spiritual development, and spirituality is best assessed through the clarity and frequency of energy being emitted. The aura can be pulled in when you are integrating information or protecting yourself, and extended outward when you are expressing yourself or seeking information.

The aura contains the energetic template that holds the ideal for this life experience. Through frequency and resonance, it sets up the conditions of your physical, emotional, mental, and spiritual life. It was developed out of the experiences of your past incarnations and holds your purpose and path in this life. It changes during your life as you grow and develop. The consequences of your choices are reflected through the qualities of denseness and light, geometric patterns, and flow.

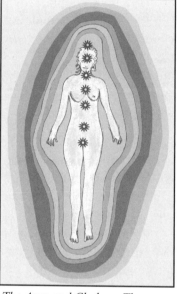

The Aura and Chakras. There are seven layers of the aura, with seven corresponding chakras that penetrate the physical body.

Thoughts, emotions, and intentions are non-transparent areas in the aura and become magnetic forces attracting people, situations, events, and conditions. You may have heard this referred to as the law of attraction. The more awareness you have of energy processes, the more you can consciously create your circumstances and claim your spiritual identity.

There are seven layers, with the first layer very close to the body and the seventh the farthest away. Each layer has a specific frequency expressed as a different color; the farther from the body, the higher the frequency. Each layer maintains a specific function: spiritual, mental, emotional, and physical.

The layers of the aura are grouped together into four auric "bodies," with each body containing one or more layers. You can think of this as you would the systems of the body, each system being comprised of a set of organs. An auric body is the totality of consciousness and awareness that guides each person's life. The auric layers are where this totality of awareness interfaces with the physical. Each layer of the aura has a chakra that feeds into the physical body. A person's aura changes in color, density, clarity, shape, size, and content in response to his or her experiences and development.

The 7 Layers of the Aura

The Hindu system describes the aura as having seven layers; however, clairvoyants today see at least another five layers bringing in higher frequencies that are guiding spiritual evolution. This book reviews the basic seven layers. Information on additional layers can be found on the Web and in books, such as Barbara Marciniak's book *Bringers of the Dawn* (Bear and Company, 1992).

The aura is constantly changing in size, shape, color, and density, depending on your state of being, activity, emotions, and thoughts. Although the levels are thought of as hierarchical, in fact they're interwoven with each other and are in constant exchange. The size of each layer is different in different people, depending on which layer is more developed and used more by that individual. The sizes given here are averages. Each layer is equally important in the evolution of consciousness.

Level 1: The Etheric or Physical Layer

The Etheric layer extends about 2 inches beyond the physical body and follows its physical contour. It extends internally as well, enveloping your organs and cells as if it were Cling Wrap. Electromagnetic activity, as measured by electroencephalograms (EEG) and electrocardiograms (EKG) and pictured in Kirlian photographs, is reflected in this layer.

The Etheric layer is bluish-white in color and looks like a web of laser beams or energy lines. The color can vary from light to deep blue. The web-like energy pathways are the template for the physical body. Energy pulses along the web in different geometric patterns. The activated patterns are in constant motion, reflecting the physical body's response to its internal and external environment. In many ways it looks and behaves remarkably like the activation of neural pathways in the brain, changing with every thought, memory, and feeling.

The Etheric layer is associated with pain and pleasure. Blockages in this layer reflect as illness. Energy patterns hold the memory and sensations of past pain and trauma, and these old patterns can be reactivated during stress. By the same token, memories of health and pleasure are also stored here and can be accessed as a healing resource.

Activating healing patterns of energy in this layer initiates change in the physical body. Returning the Etheric layer to its full flow of energy supports physical health and removes old patterns of dysfunction.

< The Path of Energy >

Level 2: The Emotional Layer

The outermost reach of the Emotional layer is about 3 inches from the body and, as the name implies, holds the template for your emotional constitution. You may not think of yourself as having a fixed emotional response to life. However, essentially you are wired to feel the world in a certain way based on experiences in previous lives. The emotional layer is less fixed than the physical and responds more fluidly to changes in your emotional state. It doesn't have a set color. Emotions reveal themselves as different colors, densities, and movement. Emotional trauma and emotional immaturity are dark, thick clouds of dense energy. They can be any color, depending on their content. Emotional clarity and higher vibration emotions such as love and compassion express as multicolored areas of intense brilliance.

Level 3: The Mental Layer

The Mental layer extends approximately 8 inches out from the body. It's typically seen as bright yellow, although the quality of color depends on the energy being expressed. Thought forms made from your intentions, beliefs, and attitudes are seen as configurations of energy appearing in the aura as three-dimensional geometric structures.

Your thought forms vibrate with energy received from the Emotional layer of your aura, and the connection creates features in the pattern of the flow of energy. Thought forms that are fed with emotional energy are increased exponentially in their magnetism and power. The interaction between your emotional layer and mental layer attracts situations, people and life events.

Level 4: The Astral Layer

The Astral layer extends as far as 12 inches away from the physical body and contains kaleidoscopic color. It is the transitional layer of the aura. The first three layers manifest in the physical world, and the last three layers stream higher spiritual ideals into the first three; the Astral layer is the bridge. It generates the frequency of love, which opens the door to higher vibrational realms. Without love, spiritual frequencies cannot be grounded into your energy network. The Astral level can free you from the constraints of your physical body. It is the doorway to the out-of-body experience called astral projection.

< 82 >

Level 5: The Etheric Template Level

This layer extends as far as 2 feet from the body. Like the physical Etheric layer, it's visualized as a grid. It surrounds all the inner layers and has linkages to each, binding them all together.

The Etheric Template is the blueprint of the perfected human. It holds the ideal of health and function on the physical plane. The first layer, the Etheric layer, holds the blueprint of your physical body as expressed in this life—a reflection of the learning goals and contracts that you were born with. The Etheric Template layer holds the perfect human potential. Drawing energy from this level into the first layer helps activate patterns for healing. When you connect with this layer you're activating divine grace.

Level 6: The Celestial Light Layer

This layer extends about 2 1/2 feet from the body and has a shimmering, opalescent quality and color. It's the seat of spiritual knowledge connecting you to higher understanding and wisdom. Here lies the realization that "we are all one." Spiritual experiences often originate in this layer, including the experience of unconditional, universal love.

Level 7: The Ketheric or Casual Layer

The ketheric layer extends about 3 feet from the body and is gold-silver in color. It is a web-like outer casing. It deals with the spiritual reality of nature and contains your purpose and path. This layer receives frequency from the highest spiritual plane.

The Functioning of the Aura

In your everyday life you're continually flooded with streams of energy. Frequencies you resonate with activate different parts of different layers within your aura, forming unique patterns. These patterns stimulate emotions and thoughts and direct your actions and reactions. Higher frequencies stimulate your capacity to love and expand your awareness; lower frequencies stimulate your fears, both conscious and unconscious. Both levels of frequency are important for your growth. You can't move beyond your fears if you don't know what they are. Frequencies you don't resonate with simply reflect off as though your aura were a shield.

The aura is magnetic in nature and draws experiences toward you. Although everything can be an avenue for growth, sometimes people hold on to low level frequencies that no longer serve. Regular clearing of the aura helps release low-level frequencies, allowing you to take inventory of your issues. In this way, through awareness and release, you can grow and move beyond your current limitations.

Clearing the aura attracts and anchors spiritual frequencies and activates specific energy patterns that support the expression of your spiritual identity. Meditations to strengthen and clear the aura are the *Spiral Pillar of Light* and *Queen Nefertiti's Headdress*.

Chakras

The chakras can be seen within the luminous field of the aura as vortices of swirling rays of light. Although there are hundreds of chakras in the body, there are seven main centers that are associated with the layers of the aura. Each chakra projects like a funnel out into the aura through front and back emanations, except for the chakras located at the base of the spine and top of the head, which project downward and upward, respectively. The chakras originate in a column of light called the Hara line. Chakras are organs of development and guide spiritual evolution. They help you assimilate experiences and provide context, meaning, and avenues for growth.

The seven chakras are each associated with a major nerve plexus, an endocrine organ, and an area of the body. In addition, each correlates to a specific level of consciousness and stage of development, which is expressed as a color, sound, emotion, and developmental challenge. Author and metaphysician Carolyn Myss explains the chakras as a progression of personal identification.[1]

The chakras digest the information coming into the aura, feeding it to the corresponding nerve plexus and endocrine organ. At the same time, changes in your bodymind are reflected outward through the chakras into the aura. Each chakra receives and processes a primary source of energy that radiates outward into the aura on undulating rays, often depicted in paintings as flower petals. There is an increase in frequency from lower to higher chakras, represented in pictures as an increase in the number of petals.

Anthropologist Carlos Castaneda, author of *The Teachings of Don Juan: A Yaqui Way of Knowledge*, describes swirling rays of light in the aura as "fibers" of light.[2] The fibers, which seem to be associated with the chakras, have two functions. They serve to anchor you in the world, attaching you to a frame of reference and creating continuity. They are also sensors. Unattached fibers extend into the world, feeling and sensing the subtle energy emanations around you. The more fibers that are attached, the more secure you feel. The more fibers that are free, the more free attention you'll have to explore your environment, people, new ideas, concepts, and even dimensions. Life is a constant interchange between security and freedom.

The chakras are an interactive system and, as you develop one chakra, it assists the growth of the rest. As one chakra changes, all the chakras shift so that growth happens simultaneously throughout the system.

The Table of Chakras: Quick Reference on page 89 provides a list of chakra qualities and functions. Be aware that different aspects of the same function show up in different chakras; it is an interacting whole. Different cultures have variations of these associations. This is an amalgamation of a variety of approaches which may or may not be the same as how you perceive things. Always trust your own sense of the truth.

1st Chakra/Root Chakra

The Root chakra is located near the base of the spine at the coccyx, relates to the physical layer of the aura, and is associated with the sacral nerve plexus and the adrenal glands. The energy of this chakra radiates in four spokes or petals that alternate the colors red and orange. The conventional color association is red.

As the name implies, this chakra connects to the Earth, providing grounding and forming your foundation. It also sends vital energy up the spine, energizing all the chakras. It is the seat or storage site of dormant, spiritual energy called Kundalini.

The Root chakra processes information from the etheric level of the aura and helps maintain the vitality of the physical body. It determines the quantity and quality of your physical energy that is available to engage life. It relates to survival issues, your will to survive, and your desire to live in the physical world. According to Carolyn Myss, the first chakra is the part of your identity that links you to your culture, or tribe. Ideally, it creates health, prosperity, security, and dynamic presence.

Practically, this chakra deals with issues of shelter, security, nourishment, subsistence finances, medical needs, and standing in the community. With a strong, balanced root chakra, you will face problems with confidence and practicality and have a powerful presence, radiating vitality and physical well-being, plus have strong community ties.

If you have a blocked or weak Root chakra, you may feel tired and unmotivated, physically depleted, and powerless to confront problems. You may spend a lot of time worrying over finances or job security. You may also feel ungrounded and unfocused.

2nd Chakra/Sacral Chakra

The second chakra is located above the pubic bone and beneath the naval in the area called the Hara. The second chakra shares the sacral nerve plexus with the Root chakra. Its endocrine association is to the reproductive organs. It has six petals or undulations that disperse the creative, solar principle and is traditionally associated with the color orange.

The second chakra processes information from the Emotional layer of the aura. This doesn't mean that it handles all of your emotions. Each chakra processes and expresses emotions related to the issues of that center. The second chakra governs *how* you process and express your emotions, reflecting your level of emotional maturity and emotional intelligence. This center senses other people's emotions and provides you with information from the emotional fields of those around you.

The second chakra deals with the creative impulse including reproduction. It relates to sexuality, sexual love, sexual attraction, and relationships in general. When this center is balanced, you will have healthy sexual relationships, be a strong family or community member, express yourself creatively in the world, and have clear emotional boundaries with other people. If this energy center is imbalanced, you may have sexual problems or have poor emotional or sexual boundaries. You may suppress your emotions, mistake other people's emotions for your own, or project your emotional motivations on to others. In addition, you may have disharmony within your family and feel creatively stifled.

3rd Chakra/Solar Plexus Chakra

The third chakra is located in the space beneath the chest bone between the left and right halves of the lower rib cage. It relates to the solar nerve plexus and to both the pancreas and adrenal glands. It's pictured with 10 petals representing the 10 undulating radiations, and the traditional color is yellow. It processes information from the mental level of the aura.

The third chakra is the center of personal identity and ego. It deals with issues of personal power and governs planning, decision-making, and manifesting your goals. It typically relates to issues regarding your soul expression through your career and ambitions. It relates to knowing your unique place in the universe, having impact in the world, and expressing your unique gifts. The ultimate issue in this chakra is living as your authentic and empowered self. In addition, this center deals with clairsentience or inner sensing. It is a major psychic center, receiving information from the world and people around you. Trusting your gut is both the challenge and gift of this center.

If your third chakra is balanced you will be able to motivate your dreams into reality. You will have a clear mind with the ability to understand complex issues. You will be able to envision intricate, long-term plans, execute them with determination, and make decisions easily. You will have a strong, intuitive sense that guides you and be able to work cooperatively with others, maintain self-control, and have a fulfilling career.

If this center is unbalanced, you may seek to control others. You may be either dominating or submissive, play power or mind games, have a hard time making your plans a reality, or have a disempowered place in your work and/or relationships. Because you lack trust in your intuitive guidance, you have a hard time making decisions and often decide based on your fears rather than your dreams. You may lack confidence and have low self-esteem. You may lose your temper easily.

4th Chakra/Heart Chakra

The Heart chakra is located in the center of the chest and relates to the cardiac plexus and thymus gland. It processes information from the Astral layer of the aura. It has 12 rays of energy undulations that distribute the energy of unconditional love through the entire system. Its color is emerald green.

The fourth chakra is the energy center for love, the transformational emotion. It's the bridge between the lower three personal centers and the upper three spiritual centers. Love is the bridge that holds everything together and integrates opposite polarities. It's also the link between body, mind, and soul. This center deals with issues of forgiveness, self-validation, self-worth, compassion, harmony, self-acceptance, and empowered relationships.

When this chakra is opened and balanced, you will express compassionate neutrality, have positive self-esteem, be able to easily forgive others, and have an overall expression of centeredness and peace. If you have a block in this chakra, you may have lost touch with what you love and what brings you joy. You may feel unworthy and have a hard time forgiving yourself and others. You may become critical and hard to please.

5th Chakra/Throat Chakra

This chakra is located in the center of the neck and throat. It relates to the nerve bundle called the star ganglia, and the thyroid and parathyroid glands. It expresses its energy in 16 spokes of blue and silver. Its color is cobalt blue. It processes the Etheric Template level of the aura.

This center deals with speaking your truth and aligning with divine will. It uses sound to manifest ideal reality and inspire creativity. It works closely with the second chakra, which embodies creativity. When the Throat chakra, the third chakra, and the second chakra are all balanced and open, there is nothing that can't be accomplished. This chakra deals with information and communication, knowing your true voice and expressing your inner joy. The Throat chakra also relates to psychic levels of communication. It governs clairaudience (inner hearing) and channeling abilities.

If your fifth chakra is opened and balanced, you communicate well with others, know your own heart, listen to your inner guidance, and speak your truth. People enjoy you because you honor your path and theirs. Issues relating to blocks in the fifth chakra include confusion, poor communication, not listening to your inner voice, and projecting your will above the will of the divine. You may hear voices and wonder if you're losing your mind. You may strive for spiritual understanding, yet feel blocked in achieving it.

6th Chakra/Third Eye Chakra

The sixth chakra is located in the center of the forehead, slightly above and between the eyebrows. It radiates 96 undulations, divided into two groupings of 48 each. Its element is light, its color is indigo, and it relates to the pituitary and pineal glands. It processes information from the celestial level of the aura.

The sixth chakra is the energy and information center for clear seeing and clairvoyance. It relates to the ability to see your life path and know your self as part of a spiritual community. It is the seat of intuition, imagination, and clear thinking. The ability to vision from this center directs the rest of the chakras. The third eye also relates to seeing the whole picture without judgment.

When your sixth chakra is balanced, it is easy to see to the heart of matters. Your intuition guides you and you are able to see solutions that benefit everyone. Your intellect is sharp, and your understanding of spiritual reality is clear. If you're blocked in the sixth chakra you may be blind to the truth, intellectualizing without using your intuition, and you may get stuck in limited judgmental thinking.

TABLE OF CHAKRAS: QUICK REFERENCE

Chakra	Keyword	Color	Musical note	Endocrine association	Motivation	Themes
1st Base	Abundance	Red	Low octave "C"	Adrenal glands	Security	Survival Life/death Finance Security Culture Service
2nd Sacral	Creativity	Orange	"D"	Reproductive organs	Intimacy	Sexuality Creativity Family Change Partnership
3rd Solar Plexus	Power	Yellow	"E"	Pancreas and adrenal	Goals	Manifesting Career Empowerment Building Cooperation Self-expression
4th Heart	Love	Pink/ Green	"F"	Thymus	Unity	Forgiveness Self-worth Self-love Acceptance Compassion Unconditional love
5th Throat	Communication	Cobalt blue	"G"	Thyroid	Truth	Self-expression Truth Divine will
6th Third Eye	Vision	Indigo or violet	"A"	Pituitary	Purpose	Oneness Psychic perception Inner truth Divine inspiration
7th Crown	Divine Wisdom	Purple or white	"B"	Pineal	Wisdom	Higher consciousness Spiritual connection

7th Chakra/Crown Chakra

The Crown chakra is located on top of the head. Its color is violet and, as does the sixth chakra, it governs the pituitary and pineal glands. It has 972 undulations. Although the primary color is violet, the rays are opalescent, reflect all colors, and are often seen as white. It processes information from the Ketheric layer of the aura.

The seventh chakra is the energy center for higher consciousness, higher mind, and higher knowing. It's your connection to your complete spiritual identity. The Crown chakra also brings in inspiration and bliss.

When balanced, the seventh chakra provides direct connection to your own higher spiritual knowing and connection, as well as your inner wisdom. When this center is blocked, you might be looking for answers outside of yourself and become dependent on leaders, gurus, or masters. Equally, you might turn away from spirituality, focusing on the material plane as the only reality.

Meditations for the Chakras

The *Chakra Clarity* and *Chakra Fibers* meditations work directly with clearing and exploring the chakras. The *Five-Hearts Open* and *Winged Disk* patterns activate specific chakras, sending their energy through the meridian system.

Meridians

Meridians are channels in the body that transmit subtle energy as vital life force coded with the information necessary for function at a cellular level. They receive energy from air, food, and water, combining it with ancestral energy and the information brought into the aura and processed through the chakras. In the meridians, subtle energy is fully interfaced with the physical body. They assist mental and emotional development. Each meridian processes and distributes information from a particular emotion and developmental challenge.

Most of the meridians travel up and down the body in parallel pathways. They are energy "arteries," supplying all parts of the bodymind with life force. Points along the meridians that are closer to the surface of the body and able to be interacted with are called acupoints, and are the focus of acupuncture and acupressure treatments. In Traditional Chinese Medicine (TCM), there are 12 organ meridians and five extraordinary meridians, often called Strange Flows.

All meridians are grouped in pairs of yin and yang partners. Yin and yang refer to complementary polarities necessary for physical creation. According to this theory, everything in the universe manifests through the interaction of yin and yang and the energy they create.

The yin meridians are integrative and deal with inspiration; the yang meridians are active and deal with manifestation. There are six paired yin and yang meridians. Each pair is associated with a specific elemental energy force. In general, the yin meridians generate emotions and the yang meridians distribute the information and energy of the emotion. Here is a quick reference to the 12 meridian associations.

QUICK REFERENCE TO THE MERIDIANS

Element	Meridian	Association
Earth	Yin—Spleen Yang—Stomach	Self-care, nourishment, mental energy, thinking, worry, satisfaction
Metal	Yin—Lung Yang—Large Intestine	Boundaries, letting go and taking in, grief, happiness, old patterns
Water	Yin—Kidney Yang—Bladder	Ancestral energy, vitality, survival, fear, faith
Wood	Yin—Liver Yang—Gall bladder	Planning, supervising, decision-making, anger, depression
Fire	Yin—Heart Yang—Small Intestine	Joy, optimism, over-joy, shock, love, sadness, seat of the spirit, directions from the divine essence
Supplemental Fire	Yin—Pericardium Yang—Triple Heater	Protecting the heart and maintaining the flow of heart energy through the bodymind

Meditations for the Meridians

The *Circle of Life* pattern directly activates and balances the meridians through the Central Channel strange flow. *Five-Hearts Open* and *Winged Disk* also send chakra energy into meridian pathways.

Evolution and Energy Structures

Your energy structures have two functions: to maintain your vehicle on this plane of existence and to guide your spiritual evolution. Some energy structures are more engaged with the second than the first. Evolutionary energy structures awaken and release high frequency energy as you begin to expand. Although the entire system is geared to evolution of your soul and awakening your spiritual identity, these structures activate as you grow.

The Nadis

According to Hindu beliefs, the subtle body contains more than 70,000 subtle energy channels called nadis that transport vital life force to all parts of the subtle and physical bodies. Nadis that exist in the physical body seem to be the same as the meridians of Chinese medicine. Nadis in the aura intersect to form the matrix, or template of the subtle body that holds the physical in form. Several thousands of nadis intersect through the chakras.

Three main nadis, the Ida, Pingala, and Sushumna, flow along the spinal column and have a special and unique function in spiritual evolution. They maintain the smooth flow of energy between the chakras, connect the Base chakra to the Crown, maintain communication between all the chakras, and assist in the rising of Kundalini. The path of the three nadis is depicted in the symbol of the caduceus.

The Ida and Pingala nadis run in spirals along the spine, weaving in and out of the chakras. They are associated with the two hemispheres of the brain. The Ida is yin, reflects the moon, and corresponds to the right side of the brain; Pingala is yang, reflects the sun, and corresponds to the left hemisphere of the brain. The third primary nadi runs straight from the center of the Base chakra through all the chakras to the Crown.

When Ida and Pingala are clear and free-flowing, they rise to the Crown and then descend back to the Base chakra, where they activate the spiritual energy of Kundalini that lives there. Kundalini then rises up the Sushumna pathway, elevating consciousness into the higher planes when it reaches the Crown chakra.

Kundalini

The subtle energy that makes up the human energy field has been stepped down from higher frequencies to a fairly dense, observable level. Many people can see human energy fields and most people can feel them. However, embedded in the root chakra is another frequency of subtle energy: the very fine, high-frequency, and powerful vibration of our higher spiritual identity that carries the seed for spiritual awakening. This energy is called Kundalini.

The name Kundalini means serpent power. Kundalini is the germ of consciousness that is each person's spiritual essence. It "sleeps," coiled like a snake, in the sacrum until a person has accumulated enough life force to activate it. This usually coincides with having developed sufficient awareness to advance spiritual enlightenment.

Awakening Kundalini is a double-edged sword. Ultimately it brings enlightenment; opening the doors to spiritual understanding, psychic ability, and higher states of consciousness. In doing so, it can cause disruption as it brings to the surface all the issues that still need to be transformed. As it rises, it wakes old traumas that need healing, and can cause physical discomfort and disturb psychological balance.

When your Kundalini rises, it lifts out of your sacrum and travels upward on the central Sushumna nadi, which runs through your chakras. As it rises it activates and awakens each chakra. When it reaches the Crown chakra, Kundalini opens you to mystical, divine union. Advancement up the spine to the Crown doesn't usually happen in one sitting. The progression can take months or even years to complete.

Awakening Kundalini can happen naturally as part of your soul evolution. Depending on your spiritual awareness, when it awakens organically, it often begins to rise around the time of menopause for a woman and sometime in a man's 50s. Kundalini energy is high-powered and challenges the circuits of your nervous system. The sensations can be quite pronounced and not always comfortable. The more conditioned your nervous system is to carry higher frequency, the easier this transition is. As Kundalini prepares to rise, you might feel electric pulsations or vibrations emanating from your sacrum and shooting down your legs. It's often confused with restless legs syndrome and can cause insomnia, mood swings, and anxiety. It can also feel like alternating burning heat and icy cold.

Once Kundalini begins to rise, it purifies the chakras as it passes through. Any unresolved issues are magnified, providing an opportunity to transform them. If issues are not resolved, they manifest externally as challenges that will allow you to further your development as you resolve them. Spiritual enlightenment is not for the timid. You cannot experience Kundalini without doing the work required for your soul growth.

When Kundalini encounters a chakra with unresolved issues, it may rise to that level, then descend again to the sacrum until the pathway is cleared. People often experience back trouble or other physical complaints at the level where Kundalini is blocked from rising. Most people don't progress organically past the third or fourth chakra unless they actively engage the development of their awareness and intention through spiritual practice.

Many people train in spiritual practices to gently awaken Kundalini and guide its progress through the chakra system. Training prepares the nervous system to handle higher-powered energy, reducing the physical discomfort and psychological disruption that can accompany Kundalini rising.

Kundalini can be prematurely activated through trauma, which can result in serious psychological and psychic damage. Spontaneous triggers can be a severe crisis, a bad drug trip, an automobile accident, or any trauma that jars a person's awareness out of his or her physical body. This type of displacement can lead to a nervous breakdown and damage to the energy structures themselves. In the 1960s and 1970s, people were experimenting with mind-altering hallucinogenic drugs in an attempt to raise their consciousness. Though the drugs did open avenues of perception, they also caused profound and long-lasting damage to many people's psyches and energy structures.

You may be wondering why anyone would purposefully activate Kundalini. The truth is, humans are wired to seek enlightenment. Our spiritual identity demands it. The power of Kundalini is enormous and, when it is activated, your vibratory level will increase dramatically. Although this can cause disruptions in your everyday life, on the other hand, Kundalini integrates, harmonizes, and uplifts all the chakras. Awareness is elevated and consciousness expanded. As difficult as it can be, raising Kundalini and opening our spiritual identity is the reason we are here.

Weaving the Nadis is a gentle practice to clear the nadis and prepare your nervous system for the flow of Kundalini. If Kundalini begins to rise and you're having difficulty, activating the *Weaving the Nadis* pattern and the *Circle of Life* pattern can reduce discomfort and help you access the inner tools you need to clear the chakra issues. Meditation and Kundalini yoga are two good avenues of additional support.

Hara Line

There is a vertical line of energy that runs from the Earth through your chakras, creating a column of light in the central core of your being. In her book *Light Emerging*, Barbara Brennan calls this the Hara line.[3] The Hara line connects you upwardly to the sky and downwardly to the center of the Earth. It's both grounding and uplifting, keeping you balanced, focused, and anchored in this life while at the same time allowing you to access spiritual domains. According to Brennan, the Hara line activates intention and connects each person to the tasks and goals of this incarnation. In essence, the Hara line holds the design of our life purpose and path.

Activating your Hara line will assist you in remaining calm, grounded, and focused. It will help you hold and carry intent. It opens your awareness to higher spiritual realms while keeping you grounded in your physical body. Many of the difficulties encountered in spiritual work can be avoided if the Hara line is actively engaged. Pitfalls may include getting caught in the traps of your ego, losing your grounding, or damaging your energy structures by raising Kundalini too quickly. Activating your Hara line will also help you avoid being psychically damaged through living in this world.

The energy in the Hara line is formed of light filaments structured in geometric patterns that emit high-frequency musical tones. These sound patterns are coded information that provide direction from within. Information in the Hara line is reflected in the chakras. When your Hara line is aligned and connected with Earth and sky, drawing energy into it activates the light filaments. When this happens, your energy structures are enlivened and aligned to higher consciousness. Some people are able to actually hear the music, some only hear high-frequency pitches, and others hear internal tapping.

The *Earth and Sky* meditation directly activates the Hara line, whereas the *Spiral Pillar of Light* and the *Circle of Life* energize it.

Higher-Dimensional Chakras

In addition to the seven main chakras of the traditional system, many psychics and clairvoyants see more chakras developing above the head and below the feet. These chakras are said to be an evolutionary development guiding the connection to higher-dimensional realms. Some are described as being inside the layers of the aura, whereas others are outside and connected through the Hara line.

According to Hindu philosophy and the Theosophists, the seven layers of the aura and the seven chakras correspond to seven dimensions of reality to which humans have access. The development of chakras forming outside the layers of our aura might imply that we are being anchored into higher dimensions of the universe.

In her book *Earth: Pleiadian Keys to the Living Library*, Barbara Marciniak revealed that humans have 12 chakras in their energy system. While channeling the Pleiadians, information was divulged that the original human DNA was comprised of 12 strands of coded information as opposed to the current two. In her book, Marciniak writes that each of the 12 strands was connected to one of the 12 chakras.[4] The original DNA pattern, she claims, was left in the human cells as light encoded filaments.

The *Spiral Pillar of Light* and the *Living Matrix* will help you align and connect with the higher dimensional chakras.

Chapter 8

EARTH AND CELESTIAL LIFE FORCE

The Earth—even the Universe—is alive, is part of a holographic totality, is conscious, and has both an energetic and physical reality. It may be challenging for you to think of the Earth and other celestial bodies as conscious, yet that is the conclusion currently gaining momentum in quantum physics. As strange as it may seem, this is a living universe that is conscious and shares an energetic essence.

Chapter 6 demonstrates the theory that the vibration of specific frequencies creates the geometry behind nature. Vibration impacts how molecules bind together and demonstrates the interdependent nature of life. Earth is our mother in more ways than one. Not only are our bodies made from the physical substance of the Earth, but the forms we take are based on the energy matrix of the planet as well. We are in physical exchange with the Earth through the air we breathe, the water we drink, and the food we eat. Our bodies are maintained on the substance of the Earth, and our energetic body is created, fed, strengthened, stabilized, and developed from within the energy matrix of the Earth. Connecting with the Earth supports our health, energizes our being, and empowers creative living.

The Schumann Resonance is the name given to low-frequency electromagnetic waves of energy that flow between the surface of the Earth and the ionosphere. Although it fluctuates within a given range, the frequency of the Schumann Resonance is basically 7.8 Hz, or cycles per second. The waves are excited by the lightening discharge between the positively charged ionosphere and the negatively charged Earth.

The Schumann Resonance has been described as the heartbeat of the Earth, a tuning fork that all life on the planet is entrained to. In humans, exposure to high amplitudes of the Schumann Resonance induces alpha brainwave rhythms and stimulates altered states of consciousness. Marie Jones and Larry Flaxman, in their book *The Resonance Key*, suggest that sacred geometry and structures of ancient megalithic sites are tuned to the Schumann Resonance and magnify its effect.[1] We can assume it was harnessed for use in the sacred ceremony, healing practices, and spiritual pursuits the sites were built for.

Earth Consciousness

Ancient cultures respected the Earth as a living being. They knew that human life was an interdependent part of the larger whole of the planet. Although the scientific definition of life doesn't fit what science knows about planetary bodies, in the 1960s Dr. James Lovelock, PhD, proposed the first scientific theory for the Earth as a living system. His theory, called the Gaia hypothesis, proposed that the Earth was composed of complex, self-regulating, interactive systems that acted in concert as a single organism to optimize conditions for life.[2]

What the Indigenous people knew and what guided their actions can be summed in the quote alleged to have been spoken by Chief Seattle: "Man did not weave the web of life. He is merely a strand of it. Whatever he does to the web, he does to himself." This quote has been used as a call to environmental awareness and a call to respect for Native American rights. However, it has a third application as well: It's a call to holographic awareness—to acknowledge that each person's individual transmission is reflected in the whole. Every thought, every behavior, every action of each person creates the fabric of Earth consciousness, the vibration of our collective frequency. We might wonder if the Schumann Resonance is a reflection of this combined vibration, not only of humans but all sentience on the planet, including plants, animals, and the elemental spirits of nature.

Living Energy Systems of the Earth

The Earth essentially has the same energy structures as humans. It has an aura, chakras (also called vortices, sacred sites, and power spots), and meridians that are referred to as ley lines. These structures function to transmit information from the larger universe through the Earth to all the individual life forms. In this activity, the Earth receives energy transmissions from other planetary bodies and, according to the ancient Maya, from spiritual dimensions as well. The Earth's aura also transmits the collective frequency of the planet out into the universe, providing information about the inhabitants of this planet. Humans are part of a conscious feedback system to the Universe, helping direct the evolution of the whole.

The energy structures of the Earth act to transduce higher frequencies downward, making them more accessible for human interaction. Indigenous people were aware of Earth energy structures and geared ceremony to utilize the inherent power at specific locations. Ancient Mayan codices (books) revealed that temples were built on sites of higher Earth energy, called k'ul, to increase the sacred power in the buildings. Ancient megalithic sites such as Stonehenge and Avebury in England also seem to have been built with the same awareness of Earth energy.

The Aura of the Earth

The Earth's aura is an energy field that streams energy to and from other celestial bodies. Clairvoyants describe the field as having multiple layers that, as with the human aura, receive and translate frequencies into the Earth's chakras, then transmit them across the planet through the meridians. Collective emotions and thought forms show up in the Earth's aura as clouds or vapors of energy with various colors, shapes, and densities.

Bruce Cathie, a retired airline pilot from New Zealand, mathematically determined the existence of an energy grid that surrounds the planet.[3] Cathie's calculations suggest that this grid maintains the harmonic frequency of the planet, which he suggests provides the matrix for physical form. He claims "that the whole of physical reality was in fact manifested by a complex pattern of interlocking wave-forms."[4] We might consider the matrix Cathie has mapped to be similar to the first layer of the human aura—the grid that maintains our physical health. The difference is that the Earth grid holds the blueprint for every species on the planet.

There are many grids around the planet similar to the Cathie grid. Another such matrix, the Currie grid, is a regular pattern of lines crisscrossing the planet with gaps of about 3 meters between the lines. Where the lines cross, individuals receive positive effects for health and well-being. Another well-known grid is the Hartmann grid, a series of north-south and east-west lines that alternate positive and negative current. Where these lines cross, harmful health effects occur.

Another interesting theory about Earth energy fields comes from English biologist Rupert Sheldrake, who hypothesized a species specific informational field he called the morphic field that maintains the evolutionary knowledge of a species. Information gained by one member of the species is available to all individuals within the species through morphic resonance. The morphic field allows for the inheritance of acquired knowledge, something that cannot be genetically transferred.[5] The theory explains research of learned behavior in rats, Blue Tit birds, and other species. According to the Website *www.co-intellegence.org*, with regard to rat experiments Sheldrake states, "If rats are taught a new trick in Manchester, then rats of the same breed all over the world should show a tendency to learn the same trick more rapidly, even in the absence of any known type of physical connection or communication. The greater the number of rats that learn it, the easier it should become for their successors." This concept has become known as the "100th Monkey" effect, and in humans it has been suggested that, once an idea is in use by enough people, called critical mass, it will create change.

The Earth's aura stores the frequency of all emotions, thoughts, ideas, beliefs, actions, and behaviors of every individual. Frequencies that are fed by large numbers of people with great emotional intensity will have high amplitude. People tune to different frequencies with their beliefs. Tuning in to high amplitude frequencies stored in the Earth's aura can be either highly beneficial or quite frightening, because higher amplitude does not necessarily mean higher frequency. High amplitude means many people believe it and it is easily accessed. A low-frequency belief with high amplitude is seen in its worst form as mob mentality.

In its positive aspect, spiritual practices and group meditation/prayer are enhanced every time another person tunes in and heightens the amplitude of power available to all. The benefits can also be seen in scientific investigation. Often when problem-solving, a person accesses the knowledge of others working on the same problem. Without knowing it, scientists from different countries share information through the Earth's aura, and simultaneously derived inventions are common. In short, there is an energetic think-tank going on with everyone who is working on the same problem. As with the 100th Monkey, when enough people tune in, all people are influenced by the ideas contained. This is referred to as "an idea whose time has come."

Earth Chakras

Energy streaming into the Earth through the Earth's aura is grounded into the planet through the Earth's chakra system. As the human body has seven major chakras, the Earth is also thought to have seven key chakras, also known as power sites.[6] In addition, there are thousands of minor chakras that occur whenever lines of energy, or ley lines, cross and create a vortex. Vortices have been considered sacred sites by Indigenous people for the beneficial energy they exude. Megalithic stone circles such as Stonehenge have been constructed on vortices as have temples built by the ancient Chinese, Tibetans, Mayans, Hindis, and Egyptians.

Indian guru Sai Baba claims there are 70,000 minor sacred sites across the planet, along with the seven major centers. According to Robert Coon, the major chakras are: the Root chakra—Mount Shasta in California; the Sacral chakra—Lake Titicaca in Peru; the Solar Plexus chakra—Uluru and Kata Tjuta, the red rock of Australia; the Heart chakra—Glastonbury, UK; the Throat chakra—Great Pyramid at Giza in Egypt. The Third Eye chakra is considered to be mobile by Coon, though others say it is Kuh-e-Malek Siah in Iran, and the Crown chakra is Mount Kailas in the Tibet Himalaya Mountains.[7]

There is immense power in sacred sites that can add a significant power boost to energy practices, meditations, or ceremonies conducted in energy vortices. Since these areas ground higher frequencies from celestial realms, when accessed they can help you expand your consciousness. Meditating at the planet's seven key chakra sites can cleanse and purify your own chakra system and help both personal and planetary healing. The Mayan legends claim that people everywhere are being awakened by the ancient sites and stimulated to remember their spiritual identity.[8]

Although many people don't have the ability to travel to sacred sites, fortunately time and space don't limit the ability to connect, which can be accomplished by sustaining the image of a particular site while meditating. You may find that focusing on photographs can help focus your intent. More important than going to the places that have been labeled as power places, or where sacred structures have been built, is finding your own place of personal power. You will find exercises to help align to Earth energy and find your personal power spot in Chapter 14.

Earth Meridians

Energy and information stream through the subtle body of the Earth in pathways called ley lines that are comparable to human meridians. Intersecting ley lines create vortices of energy roughly analogous to acupoints that create the Earth chakra centers. Similar to meridians, ley lines have either yin or yang qualities. They function as information highways and translate the frequencies from the chakras and aura into useable biological energy. Energy vortices can have either health enhancing properties or are detrimental to health, depending on the interaction of the intersecting pathways. As in meridians, these pathways can become blocked or damaged. They can also be influenced by human intention.

The ley lines that occur beneath the Earth's surface are not the same as the grids around the planet, just as the meridians in your body are not the same as the grids in the Etheric and Ketheric layers of your aura. In China, energy pathways undulate across the landscape and are called dragon currents or dragon paths. Interpreting their influence forms the basis of the art of feng shui. Buildings and communities, layouts of houses, and the timing of events employing the art of feng shui are designed to be in harmony with the dragon currents. The ancient Maya built temples and pyramids to align with celestial energy coming onto the planet through the pathways of k'ul that traveled from other planets and continue in pathways through Earth.

The term *ley line* was coined by Alfred Watson in his book *The Old Straight Track*, in which he demonstrated that straight lines connected sacred sites in geometric patterns across the landscape of England.[9] It has been theorized that these straight paths were man-made lines that connected power spots and channeled Earth energy. The original description of man-made ley lines was distinct from the undulating pathways of natural Earth energy in Chinese and Indigenous teaching. Over time the term *ley lines* has become synonymous with pathways of energy and is used to denote both man-made straight lines and natural curved lines that move energy across the planet.

Earth energy feeds the meridians in our bodies. In Chinese medicine, the acupoints in the fingers and toes are called the "warp and weft points," representing where our bodies are pinned onto the loom of life and woven into this life's experience. The toes are bound to the meridians of the earth and the fingers are bound to celestial energies. Consequently, humans are suspended between Earth and sky. The ancient Maya also believed the fingers and toes linked us to the Earth and sky and that we have 13 joints in the body that are portals to specific harmonics in the galaxy.

Meditations to Connect With Earth Energy

Your connection to Earth energy is innate and natural; you are alive and therefore connected. However, surrounded by modern technology and immersed in low-level electromagnetic fields from power lines, WiFi, and so on, your entrainment with the Schumann Resonance can be weakened, decreasing your vitality and possibly resulting in lack of mental focus. The *Earth and Sky* meditation strengthens the links in your body between Earth and celestial energy; *Circle of Life* creates a smooth flow of energy along the meridians. *Queen Nefertiti's Headdress* helps align your aura with higher frequencies and with the aura of the Earth. The *Living Matrix* directly weaves you into the matrix of Earth and Celestial energy.

Using the activations not only helps you smooth the flow that runs through your body from the Earth and sky and access high-amplitude, high-frequency thought forms, their use also increases your projection of positive energy into the Earth's aura. Your contribution helps make a higher vibration for everyone.

Sacred Geometry

Sacred geometry is the ancient study of the forces behind and within form and the underlying unity behind creation. Every natural pattern is built with a combination of one or more of the same foundational geometric shapes, including the sphere and the five platonic solids (tetrahedron, hexahedron, octahedron, dodecahedron, and icosahedron). These basic geometries are combined according to particular ratios that shape all the various forms of matter.

The specific ratios and geometries repeat throughout nature: the spiral of pinecones, nautilus shells, sunflowers, DNA, and galaxies; the structure of crystals, beehives, and snowflakes; and the fractals of ferns, tree branches, and leaves. All the life forms we know emerge from geometric foundations that have been termed sacred geometry.[10]

By far the most well-known of the sacred geometry ratios is the Golden Mean Ratio of 1.61803, derived from the Fibonacci sequence. Discovered by Italian mathematician Leonardo Fibonacci, this sequence is generated by adding the previous two numbers in the sequence together to form the next. It begins as (1,1,2,3,5,8,13,21,34,55), so 1+1 is 2, 1+2 is 3, 2 + 3 is 5, 3 + 5 is 8, and so on. When any number is divided by the one before it, the result is always 1.61803. The Golden Ratio produces the Golden Mean Spiral seen in the nautilus shell, sunflower, pinecone, galaxies, and so on.

The vibrational quality of the Golden Mean is said to give it communication properties that resonate with higher realms, increasing the power of prayer. Another spiritually significant shape that incorporates the Golden Mean is the hemisphere seen in the domes of mosques and synagogues.

Hemispheres are energy emitters, carrier waves of sound frequencies, according to French dowsers Leon de Chaumery and Antoine de Belizal.[11]

In chemistry, the geometry of a molecule is determined in part by the amount of energy held in the bonds between the atoms. When more energy is added, as when a molecule is heated, the bond angles change, as does the geometric configuration, to accommodate the additional energy. When the molecule has reached the maximum amount of energy it can hold, it breaks apart, releasing all the energy held in the bonds and making it available for other purposes.

Sacred geometry works in a similar manner: Geometric forms of nature entrain vital energy, which powers life. The principles of sacred geometry can be consciously incorporated in buildings, art design, symbols, and sacred sites to entrain energy and empower intention. This is the basis for symbols such as the Cross, the Star of David, the pentagram, and so forth. Some symbols entrain energy; others move energy.

Esoteric traditions have incorporated sacred geometry in the construction of temples and sacred structures to enhance their use. For example, the Great Pyramid at Giza was constructed such that the ratio of the height of the pyramid to the width of its base is the Golden Mean. It has been found in churches, temples, mosques, and synagogues, entraining and amplifying spiritual energy while promoting health, expanding awareness, and increasing connection to spiritual realms.

Geomancy

Geomancy is the modern name for observing Earth energy and designing human actions in relation to these flows to increase and amplify their beneficial effects. Discerning energy flows can be accomplished by direct intuition, kinesthetic body awareness, and inner sight, or through devices such as dowsing rods and pendulums. Using principles of geomancy, the ley lines of the Earth can be influenced to change direction and even to change their course.

Today's modern lifestyle typically means living indoors encircled by technology, separated from Earth energy flows, and inundated with artificial low-level frequency that interrupts the reception of the Schumann Resonance. This produces interference, resulting in feeling disconnected. The best way to reverse this is to spend time in nature, restoring connection to natural cycles. As people choose to reconnect and align with life enhancing energy flows, they resonate with the Earth and become part of the information system. Native American, the ancient Chinese, and other Indigenous cultures have maintained that humans form the connection between Earth and sky. To the geomancer, this position is both a source of power and a responsibility.

The essence of geomancy is right relationship to the Earth. How we use the Earth, how we walk on this land, how we position ourselves on the planet in relation to Earth energies, what we connect with, and what we transmit, all impact the flow of energy and vibration of the planet. Modern geomancy responds to the Earth on visible and invisible levels, and takes into account the interaction between spiritual and elemental beings—the Devas and Nature Spirits that reside on the planet with us.

Many people feel called to assist in the cleansing of the Earth's aura and the planetary grid system. The *Pyramid Power* meditation is specially designed for this use. If you are drawn to the practice of geomancy, the *Five-Hearts Open* meditation will help sensitize you to the energy of the Earth, allowing you to feel more clearly how to position your home, gardens, and activities. There are exercises in Chapter 14.

Nature or Earth Spirits

Everything in nature has a spirit, a biological intelligence able to interact between the energetic and physical realms. There is a long history of cooperation between humans and Nature Spirits. Modern-day examples are best seen in the intentional communities of Findhorn in Scotland and Perelandra in Virginia, United States.

The Findhorn community was founded in the early 1960s in Northern Scotland by Eileen and Peter Caddy and Dorothy Maclean. All were involved in a spiritual practice of meditation, when Dorothy began to receive inner information during her meditations encouraging her to sense and connect with the forces of nature.

Thus began a daily exploration that guided the community in co-creating with nature. Using meditation as the forum for communication, they contacted and worked with the "over-lighting" beings of different species. Over-lighting beings are the consciousness within nature that holds the archetypal design and the blueprint for a particular species' highest potential. The result was 40-pound cabbages and other exceptional garden feats born out of rocky soil in an inhospitable climate. Findhorn has spearheaded the resurgence of interest in and cooperation with the spiritual essence of nature.[12]

Perelandra was founded by Machaelle Small Wright in the 1970s. It is a nature research center that seeks to empower individuals by providing the tools to cooperatively engage the intelligence in nature. Machaelle believes that in cooperation with nature, we can find the solutions to reverse the ecological damage to the planet. She also believes in the power of one; each individual can create dynamic and purposeful change. She willingly shares the techniques to communicate with Nature Spirits and the specifics that she has learned in her books and workshops. She also makes flower essences for healing and spiritual growth.[13]

Nature Spirits are powerful guides and allies. They exist in many different forms, and have many different names and functions, from the elementals that maintain physical forms to the Devas who are the over-lighting spiritual essences of plants, holding the blueprint for the highest potential of each species. Like subtle energy, the existence of Nature Spirits has been acknowledged in most cultures. According to the Website Crystal Links, in Jewish literature they were called Shedim. The Egyptians called them Afries, Africans called them Yowahoos, and the Persians called them Devas.

The term *Deva* comes from Sanskrit and means the "radiant ones," or "beings of brilliant light." Although conversing with Nature Spirits was fairly commonplace in many societies, today people are surprised when cooperation with the spiritual essence of nature results in the ability to grow phenomenal crops and solve ecological problems.

Fundamentally, beneath the forms of nature is a spiritual essence that has consciousness and with which we can interact. Connecting with this intelligence through meditation and intent with respect is important and empowering. Inviting their support in your energy practice can enliven your ability and create more successful outcomes. Some exercises for connecting with Nature Spirits can be found in Chapter 14.

Celestial Energies

The Earth is in constant exchange with other bodies in the solar system and galaxy, providing a mosaic of energy influences. An example on a physical level is the Northern Light phenomenon, which occurs when the Earth receives boosts of energy from the sun in electromagnetic waves. The influx is received and dispersed along the Van Allen belt, a torus-shaped path of energetically charged particles held in place by the Earth's magnetic field.

Another example is the effect the moon has on tidal waters and on people's moods and energy structures. Less obvious are the effects of the movement of planets in our solar system, the path of the constellations across the sky, and our solar system's orientation to the plane of the galaxy. Each celestial influence interacts across the entire range of physical to energetic reality, and every physical expression has a corresponding energetic manifestation affecting emotions, psychic abilities, levels of awareness, and so forth.

The ancient Maya provide a unique and magical perspective into the cosmos. Looking through the lens left behind in the codices they wrote, we see a world where everything is connected by lines of force—where planets move across the sky magnetizing conditions on Earth as they pass. Alignments between celestial bodies open portals allowing energy to flow from one place to another. Even the human body is intimately linked to the cosmos with 13 key places in the galaxy directly coupled to the 13 key joints in the body (neck, shoulders, elbows, wrists, hips, knees, ankles).

High-frequency or spiritual energy is often referred to as celestial in origin. Spiritual energy received through the Third Eye and Crown chakras is often thought of as related to the heavens and residing among the stars. Though this is a useful metaphor, it's a misnomer to call higher spiritual energies "celestial." We probably do so because the word higher takes us upward. It's more appropriate to call spiritual energies higher-dimensional or multidimensional energies. They don't exist "up there"; they exist right here, simply at a faster rate. In this category are personal guides, angels, ascended masters, departed loved ones, or any number of energy beings that we interact with on a daily basis, often without realizing it.

Although all the meditations will assist you in more clearly interacting with spiritual energy and beings, *Nefertiti's Headdress, Mystic Triangle, Pyramid Power,* and *The Living Matrix* are specifically designed to access higher frequency and provide connection to dimensional consciousness. Chapter 20 has more detailed information and exercises.

Chapter 9

DECIPHERING THE LANGUAGE OF ENERGY

Developing energy awareness requires paying attention. Your body is gifted with everything you need to interpret the flows of energy you live within. Paying attention to what your body is telling you and understanding its messages are skills you know but may have forgotten. This chapter is a guide to remembering.

Chapter 6 demonstrated the theory that subtle energy is a carrier wave for information that organizes both the physical and energetic bodies. It organizes your physical structure, your health, your circumstances, and even your actions and thoughts. As was discussed earlier, subtle energy, and the information it carries, is received through the aura, metabolized in the chakras, and distributed through the meridians. The essence of energy awareness is becoming aware of the information your body is receiving from the energy around you and how you're interacting with it. You're sensing energy all the time; it's just happening below the level of your conscious attention. Your gut feelings, instinct, and hunches are all based on energy information. Becoming more aware of the process will allow you to create a more intentional life.

Sensing Energy

To sense energy, you need to pay attention to what you feel. What is your base normal, and what happens inside when that changes? Your senses are geared to receive information along a range of frequencies. The same senses you use to see, hear, smell, and palpate are stimulated by subtle energy.

Your body tells you about energy through physical sensations, perceptions, moods, emotions, gut feelings, and intuition. All of these modes may be activated at the same time, or any combination may predominate. Everyone has had the experience of reading the "vibe" of a situation when walking into a room. Typically, physical sensations are the first signal most people receive and recognize relating to subtle energy perception. Your body responds and gives you feedback on all types of energy encounters. For example, you may notice physical sensations such as your hair standing on end, goose bumps, and electric tingling when you cross the path of a ley line. When you elevate your internal frequency and/or Kundalini rises, you might feel the tremendously powerful, physical sensations of vibration in your sacrum, heat rising up your spine, and shaking in your legs. This might occur with strong perceptual changes, including the ability to see energy.

Paying attention to your body is your first lesson in energy awareness. Here are some tips on what to pay attention to.

Physical Sensations

Your body translates energy interactions into sensory experience. You may feel a range of sensations such as tingling, vibration, heat, cold, excitation, goose bumps, hair standing on end, skin crawling sensations, pain, burning, the movement of air across your skin, nausea, butterflies in the stomach, a sense of being dropped, heart racing, and more. Physical sensations *without a discernible physical cause* warrant attention, especially when combined with other signals noted here.

Changes in Perception

How your brain processes energy information can cause changes in perception. You may feel as though you're watching the scene around you from a distance. You may suddenly notice that one object in your vision becomes very large as everything else fades into the background. The sounds around you may fade away, making room for hearing outside normal range. You may have a heightened sense of knowing, focus, or mental acuity. Often, people experience altered states of consciousness where they have access to psychic information such as visions, instructions, guidance, and so forth. You may see colors around people or objects, or see color streaming between people. Equally, you may hear musical tones of extraordinary clarity. Many report seeing flashes of light, movement in the corner of the eye, and misty outlines of shapes and scenes.

Commonly, people first experience a heightened awareness of physical sensations that cause them to be more attuned to their body wisdom.

Shifts in Mood

Energy information may stimulate feelings that seemingly have no correlation to what is happening around you. You may suddenly feel calm and peaceful in the face of difficulty, or conversely you may feel apprehension for no reason. You may feel detached or even go into a trance-like state. Changes in mood that correspond with feeling physical sensations frequently represent shifts in energy.

Gut Feelings and Intuition

The vibe you get from a person or place is based on the internal processing of energy information. What is unique about gut feelings and intuition is our certainty of their validity without logical input. There's a sudden, immediate awareness of truth that will not be silenced. Gut feelings often have a strong emotional component that is unrelated to what is happening on the surface exchange. You may experience a strong attraction or repulsion to a person or place for no discernable reason. You may have a strong sense of recognition even though you've never met the person or been to the place before. Your mind might be telling you one thing and your body another.

For example, you may want to enter a business arrangement that makes a lot of sense to you, but you feel agitated and reluctant to move forward. It may simply be that your body is telling you to take a closer look at the details before committing. Or it might be that everything is great but the time line is off. Conversely, think of a time when you just knew everything was ready and it all moved forward with synchronistic events and flow.

Emotions

Emotions are the language of energy. It's not a coincidence that the chakras correlate to specific emotions. Emotions are the body's way of decoding energy information for conscious processing. Although the majority of energy information is beneath conscious awareness, emotions bring energy interactions into direct awareness. We often consider emotions to be either good emotions that elevate us, or bad emotions that we have to avoid or release. Actually, all emotions have important energy functions. We don't need to avoid or pursue them; we need to accept them, listen, learn, and act accordingly.

Inner Visions

As your body receives energy information, the information may be translated into images that form in your inner eye. This is often called *clairvoyance*, meaning clear vision. Rather than seeing energy with your physical eyes, you see energy as an image that forms in your mind's eye. Always pay attention to these images when sensing energy, and explore them. Can you feel what you see in your mind's eye with your hands? Does the image cause goose bumps along your body? Your body will verify information you're receiving through one or more perceptual modes.

Dreams

Dreams often reveal a lot about energy reality. Pay attention to the messages, symbols, feelings, and metaphors in your dreams. Especially important are the exceptionally vivid, lucid dreams that feel as real as waking awareness. Also note recurring dreams and the messages they contain. With practice you can plan assignations with your spiritual guides and mentors, and travel to dimensions of higher knowledge during your dream states.

Emotions: Translations of Energy

Once you've started paying attention, the next step is to understand what it all means. Your emotions are your key to translation. They are a direct link between your body, your mind, and the energy being processed in your chakras. Emotions have two essential functions: They provide information and the energy to mobilize your intention.

Every emotion provides direct and immediate information. It's either telling you what is happening around you right now or where you've gotten stuck in your processing. Then it provides you with the energy to act. The first person to articulate the link between emotions, the body, and energy, was psychoanalyst Dr. Wilhelm Reich, the father of body-centered psychology. His ideas were further developed by Alexander Lowen, father of a form of body-centered psychotherapy called Bioenergetics, and Barbara Brennan, founder of the Barbara Brennan School of Healing.

Emotions inform us that something important is happening. At the same time, physical energy is activated, providing the ability to respond. For example, a person walking in the jungle gets attacked by a tiger. The man's energy field transmits information about the tiger and its intent moments before the man is aware the tiger is present. The Root chakra processes this information and generates the emotion of fear. The fear tells the man he's in danger as his body is flooded with adrenalin. Survival instincts are activated and he has extraordinary strength to fight the tiger or flee. In this example, the function of fear translating energy information into conscious awareness and action is not difficult to understand. But what happens to the man after he successfully escapes the tiger?

It's easy to imagine that every time he takes a walk in the jungle, he feels fear. Every turn of a leaf causes his heart to race as adrenalin floods his system, even though there's nothing to be afraid of at this time. The emotion is no longer telling him of present danger; it is telling him that he has not integrated his past experience. He will continue to experience fear until he processes the event. Avoiding it or trying to release it will not work and will only suppress it, driving it deeper into his psyche. For example, on the surface the message may have been to be careful in the jungle. However, there are deeper layers that now motivate his present fear. Perhaps in the moment that he faced the tiger, unresolved issues around death came to the forefront. His issues of mortality, what happens after death, how prepared he felt to die, or what unfinished business he had left may have been activated. If he does not finish processing those issues, he will continue to feel fear every time the memory of his past experience is triggered. His fear is informing him where he is stuck in his process. It's also telling him the encounter with the tiger was not an accident; it was a wake-up call. The experience itself brought to the surface issues he needed to examine.

If the man processes his fear and integrates the issues, he will no longer be afraid in the jungle. He will be able to walk free of fear, aware of the sounds and sights around him, and respond appropriately to what is actually present. Though the awareness of danger from past experience will keep him alert, he will be free from fear because he has integrated the deeper issues inherent in the event.

As with fear, all of your emotions provide information. If you don't like the emotional states you're living in, you need only to accept them and explore their messages to change them. The more you pay attention to and process the information, the clearer you become and the more your emotions tell you about your present instead of your past. When you live in the present, you're free of self-judgment and are centered and grounded. You are available to respond to life, based on real-time emotions rather than replaying unfinished business.

The Body's Revelations

Living aware in the present moment is achieved by embracing your emotions, listening to their message, and integrating the issues from your past. The problem is that, as humans, we don't like being uncomfortable. We judge difficult emotions as being unworthy, and we think having them means we're unenlightened. Consequently, instead of learning about the energy your emotions are translating, you might suppress them and avoid feeling them. How this is accomplished is quite fascinating.

Emotions happen in specific body segments that correlate to the location of the chakras. Roughly the segments are ocular, oral, neck, chest, upper abdomen, lower abdomen, and pelvis. When you don't like an emotion, you avoid feeling it by tightening the muscles in the segment, decreasing the flow of chi, breath, nerve conduction, and circulation into that area. This decreases the feeling of emotion as the segment becomes numb and closed down. The repressed emotions are stored in patterns of muscle tension. This process is called emotional or muscular armoring, and it not only prevents you from feeling the emotions you want to avoid, it prevents you from feeling all the emotions generated in that segment.[1] Side effects of emotional armoring include:

- No longer feeling any of the emotions generated in a specific segment, including enjoyable emotions. (If you block grief, you block joy as well.)
- The occurrence of pain and physical dysfunction in the segment as contracted muscles develop trigger points, compresses organs, and the area is isolated from the flow of chi, blood, and therefore nourishment.
- No longer living in the present; living in past trauma, re-creating the same scene again and again.
- Living with hyper-vigilance and emotional control with lowered mountains and shallower valleys.
- Losing the capacity for spontaneity and joy.

When you avoid experiencing your emotions, you lose the capacity to feel. The messages your emotions would give you are lost, and you're no longer awake, aware, and alive in the present moment. With emotions shut off, the ability to respond to real-time situations is diminished. Uncovering repressed emotions requires releasing muscle tension and feeling the emotional content. This is where skilled bodyworkers and massage therapists can be invaluable.

EMOTIONAL ASSOCIATIONS

Emotion	Surface Message	Chakra and Segment
Anger	Your boundaries have been breached. There is obstruction in your path.	Solar Plexus chakra Upper abdominal segment
Healthy Pride	You have grown and developed. You belong.	Solar Plexus chakra Upper abdominal segment
Fear	You are not safe.	Root chakra Pelvic segment
Shame	You have interfered in a significant way in someone else's path. You have disregarded your own boundaries.	Second chakra Lower abdomen segment
Guilt	You have breached someone else's boundaries.	Heart chakra Chest segment
Joy	You are part of a bigger purpose.	Heart chakra Chest segment
Sadness	You have lost something of value.	Heart chakra Chest segment
Grief	The configuration of energy in your life is incomplete.	Heart chakra Chest segment
Jealousy	You have undervalued some part of your life, you don't value yourself, or you don't know your own worth.	Solar Plexus and Second chakras, mixed Upper and lower abdominal segments
Satisfaction	The knowledge that you have stretched and grown.	Both Solar Plexus and Heart chakras Upper abdominal and chest segments
Embarrassment	You are locked in judgment.	Whole body event
Love	This is a transcendent emotion. You are complete, whole, where you're supposed to be, and part of an intentional universe.	Heart chakra Chest segment To a lesser extent, all chakras and segments
Ecstasy	This is another transcendent emotion. You are one with the universe.	Both Crown and Third Eye chakras Orbital segment To a lesser extent, all chakras and segments

When Wilhelm Reich originally proposed that emotions are generated in the body, it created a great deal of controversy. Even though most people agree that emotions are felt in the body, the assumption has been that they are generated as a chemical reaction in the brain. The work of Dr. Candice Pert, explained in her book, *Molecules of Emotions*, has substantiated the idea that emotions are body events.[2]

Although everyone is different, the preceding chart provides emotions, their surface function/message, and the segment of the body they're found in. Only you know the deeper meaning your emotions have. Adding your insights related to the chart in a journal and personalizing it for yourself may be helpful when you get to Chapter 11.

Chronic Pain and Illness

Unresolved muscle tension and unresolved emotions can eventually disrupt healthy flow to such a degree that chronic pain and illness result. This does not mean that all illness has an emotional cause; it means that all illness has an emotional component relating to an energetic reality. In fact, using body tension to contain emotion has significant survival benefits. This is especially true when related to trauma. Some events are so traumatic that without protection from their full impact we would simply crumble. Using muscle tension to dampen emotional intensity can provide time to process slowly. It provides protection from experiencing the full onslaught of pain and only becomes a problem if it becomes a way of life rather than a respite.

It's worth noting that most signs and symptoms of energy can also be signs and symptoms of serious medical and/or psychological disturbance. Always be sure you're not using metaphysical explanations to avoid medical treatment. Case in point: A dear friend of mine went through early menopause at age 38. She did not get a medical check-up because her mother had recently died, and she believed she was moving into the role of matriarch for her family, which she was. Thirteen years later she learned she had a tumor in her pituitary gland, the reason for her early menopause. Although the changing of her family role may have triggered events, there was also a treatable condition she needed to pay attention to. Be sure your signs and symptoms are not telling you about a medical condition needing treatment.

No one knows what another person's path is, what his or her traumas are, and what his or her muscle tension or illnesses mean. No one besides you knows what you need to learn or what you need to do. The only thing we know about another person is that we are each here to grow and to help and support each other. There is no judgment; only you know the "right" time for you, and there are no experts. We are on this journey together, learning as we go.

Emotions and Thought Forms

You may be wondering why, if emotions are so useful, they cause so much trouble! We all know the consequences of unmanaged anger, overwhelming jealousy or uncontrolled fear. Actually, many of us also know the unintended consequence of getting in over our head due to the imbalance of over-joy. The easy answer to this question is that you have ignored the message. Though this may be true, it's not complete. As mentioned earlier, one of the functions of emotions is to provide energy to act on the information the emotion is providing. This is the energy we use to engage life. Whether the energy from your emotions works for you, or against you, depends on what thoughts and beliefs you invest your emotions in (see Chapter 12).

We choose our thoughts from one moment to the next. In fact, before we have a thought, we make a decision to think it. Our thoughts are generated from our beliefs and expectations about the world. Once we have a thought and invest it with emotional energy, it becomes a thought form and is able to direct our life.

Consider getting in a car accident that could have been avoided if the other person had been paying attention. If your belief is that everyone is out to get you, your thoughts about the other person will be suspicious and judgmental. Your anger at having your day disrupted will enliven those thoughts, creating unpleasant behavior. If your belief is that everything offers a learning potential, your thoughts will be aimed at looking for deeper understanding. The energy of your anger will be used looking for constructive solutions to your dilemma. Anger management is less about what happens to us and more about what we believe about ourselves and the world.

Finally, the vital energy you have that supports and motivates you is the result of being a spiritual being. It comes from your connection to your spiritual source. When a person has lost his or her sense of connection with his or her source—whatever he or she perceives that to be—he or she loses vitality and access to inspiration. Excess emotions become an avenue for feeling connected and for generating energy. This is emotional addiction. Exercises to address emotional addiction are found in Chapter 15.

Putting It All Together

As you learn to pay attention, you will begin to notice that certain sensations correlate to certain changes in your internal energy flow. You will begin to notice that when your energy shifts, you experience different states of mind and perception. You may notice that you flow better with the life around you as synchronicity increases, and life-enriching events and situations come toward you.

Through time, the way your body communicates to you will become clearer and clearer. You will develop your own language to decipher your energy reality. The trick is to pay attention!

Part III

Empowering Your Life

Queen Nefertiti's Headdress

< 117 >

Awareness of the flows of energy that sustain and direct life is the first step in consciously using energy dynamics to solve personal and planetary problems. This section of the book provides suggestions for using energy awareness in creating your circumstances, making choices, and developing inner resources.

The exercises in each chapter are based on the 13 activation patterns in Chapter 3. They are not recipes; they're not the only way to use energy skills, and they may not be the best way for you. Each chapter offers a step-by-step process to give you ideas and generate insight. They are adventures in exploring; use them as possibilities and see where they lead you. Use them as they are, incorporate them into techniques you already use, modify them to fit your beliefs, or discard them altogether. Only you know what is right for you.

You don't need to read the chapters in order to be able to use them. Start with the topic that interests you the most. However, if energy skills are new to you, reading Chapter 10, Chapter 11, and Chapter 12 will provide the basics you need to navigate energy terrain safely and effectively.

Each exercise begins with activating one or more of the 13 patterns and ends with closing the activation. To activate a pattern, simply visualize it in its completed form. You don't need to go through the original steps. If you've activated the pattern once, your body will remember it; all you need do is visualize it. To close an activated pattern, simply imagine the pattern dissolving.

Each exercise also starts and ends with grounding, centering and establishing boundaries—skills taught in Chapter 10. Opening this way shifts your awareness internally, marshalling your resources so that you can act with power. Ending this way makes sure that you leave the altered state of your meditation and are fully present in everyday reality. Making this a standard in your energy practice will improve your results dramatically.

Approach your practice as a grand adventure. Open yourself to change, surrender old concepts and ideas, and be willing to step into something new. Rich vistas will open before you with unimaginable rewards!

Chapter 10

Developing Personal Power: Grounding, Centering, Presence, and Creating Boundaries

Personal power is not about political, economic, or social clout. It isn't about having authority over other people. It's not the power of self-importance used to intimidate or manipulate others to increase your superiority. It isn't even about getting everything you want in life. Personal power is the ability to live authentically in each moment. It's the ability to remain calm, loving, compassionate, and resolute, regardless of opposition; it's standing in the integrity of your essence before any circumstance and holding your intention with clarity. Personal power is the key element needed to expand your consciousness and create a life of meaning and joy. It is a pre-requisite for mastering energy skills.

There are four basic components to building your personal power: grounding, centering, presence, and maintaining boundaries. As you become more empowered, you become more successful at using energy skills, and as you become more successful, your personal power continues to grow. It is a self-perpetuating cycle.

The three most useful activations for the practices in this chapter are the *Spiral Pillar of Light*, *Earth and Sky*, and *Circle of Life*. Engaging these activations on a daily basis will increase all four elements of personal power. More importantly, engaging them when facing life challenges or to counter confusion and stress can change your life.

As you progress through this book, if the energy practices are not activating the changes you want, come back to this chapter and practice building personal power. It is the key to energy mastery.

Grounding

Grounding means being connected to the Earth, thus increasing your strength and the amount of energy your system can manage. It improves your ability to stay balanced. When you put your attention on the Earth, that's where your energy flows and the Earth's energy flows back into you. This allows you to share in the Earth's strength. Walking is a good example of how this happens. You may think of yourself as being weighted down by gravity. The strength to move a leg forward may seem to come from your muscles; however, your ability to move forward actually comes from your ability to push off the ground—to have a solid, firm contact that pushes you away like a spring board. Anyone who has gotten caught in quicksand or walked through a bog knows that the strength of your muscles isn't enough to move you forward. The force of the Earth pushing against you is the other half of the equation. In this regard, grounding is your access to power and strength.

Let's look at how grounding facilitates your personal power. Grounding:

- Stabilizes your energy field, balancing excess charge in the same manner that the grounding wires function in an electrical circuit. Grounding your energy helps you manage energy surges and keeps your energy focused.

- Restores energy when you are depleted. Much in the same way that the roots of a plant bring nourishment to the leaves, grounding replenishes your field by bringing Earth energy into your body restoring your vitality and increasing your energy field.

- Creates strength and flexibility. Roots stabilize plants against wind and erosion, and in the same manner, being grounded enhances your ability to remain stable, calm, flexible, and full of energy no matter what is happening around you.

- Encourages growth. Another characteristic of roots is that the deeper the root system, the higher the plant can grow. The same is true of people: The more grounded you are, the greater the heights you can achieve. One of the biggest problems people face when starting to work with energy is developing their skills faster than their ability to ground. The result is that they lose their moorings and topple over in the first big wind, or become so charged they can't dissipate the energy and burn themselves out.

- Releases energy that has developed a negative charge. Of course, we know that there is no such thing as negative energy. We also know that energy is a carrier wave for different

frequencies and can transmit other people's thoughts, intentions, and desires, whether helpful or harmful. Sending unhelp-
ful energy into the Earth is one way of clearing yourself. You
don't need to worry about harming the Earth; once energy is
released from its harmful intention, it returns to pure energy.

> Connects you to your body. One of the most important func-
tions of grounding is that it helps you stay solidly connected to
your body, your vehicle of awareness. When you're fully present and embodied, you have more access to the sensations,
feelings, energy flows, and emotions that tell you about the
energy of life around you.

In short, grounding helps you be more connected, responsive, engaged,
energized, and fully present in the moment. It is easy to see that it is an
essential skill in developing your personal power and that connecting with
the Earth is a powerful ally in mastering energy skills.

The best way to become more grounded is to use an adaptation of the
circuit in the *Earth and Sky* activation. Here's the short version.

Simple Grounding Exercise

1. Activate the *Earth and Sky* pattern.
2. As you inhale, visualize energy flowing into your body through the
   top of your head.
3. Breathe this energy through your body all the way to your Base
   chakra.
4. Exhale, and imagine sending this energy out through your sacrum,
   through the Base chakra, deep into the Earth, sending roots into the
   ground.
5. In just a few short minutes you will enjoy the benefits of feeling
   grounded.

Centering

Centering is the ability to bring your attention to the core of your
being, where your path, purpose, and motivation reside. This requires connecting with two primary, internal centers: your spiritual center and your
physical center. In Traditional Chinese Medicine, your spiritual core is
your heart (the home of your spirit or Shen), your personal connection to
your spiritual Source. It is sacred space. Finding your Shen is finding the

"path with heart" for you. Practically, when you're centered, connected to your spiritual Source, and on your path, you have joy in what you do and can access deep reservoirs of love. You are also able to stand resolved and compassionate in the face of obstacles.

Not everyone knows their path and purpose. Being in your Shen helps you feel the connection. You might not know in exact words or vision what your path is; however, you may experience strong compulsions to follow a certain idea or go in a particular direction. When you do, you feel uplifted; when you don't, you feel like you're working against resistance. Train yourself to focus your attention internally to become aware of the sensations, feelings, and energy flows that tell you when you're acting from your Shen. When you're on your path, your internal energy flows freely, life feels like an adventure, and decisions are the result of an inner assuredness. You may not know where the next step is going or what the whole picture looks like, but the step you're taking feels exactly right, and nothing can stop you from taking it. Trust and follow your inner sense of flow in each moment, and if you don't feel it, wait, focus, and listen. You will learn more about using energy for decision-making in Chapter 15.

The second key area is your physical center, the area below your belly button and above your pubic bone. In martial arts and Traditional Chinese Medicine it is called the Dan Tien or Hara. It corresponds to the Second chakra and is where the "Sea of Chi" resides. This is where you store extra energy that can be tapped into when needed. It's the source of unassailable intent that enables you to pursue your path. When you're physically centered, like the Weeble toy, you may wobble, but you won't fall down.

The act of centering is aligning your spiritual center with your physical center through your Solar Plexus or third chakra and thereby bringing all three into alignment. It provides intention and power to your path and purpose. Here's a simple exercise to connect with your core.

Simple Core Centering Exercise

1. Put your right hand over your Hara and your left hand over your heart.

2. If you wish, activate the *Winged Disk* pattern.

3. As you inhale:

   a. Imagine light from your spiritual Source entering the top of your head and collecting in your heart, filling it with brilliance.

b. Imagine energy flowing into your Base chakra from the Earth and collecting in your Hara, filling it with light.

4. With each breath in, let your energy build in your Hara and heart.

5. With each breath out, let the energy between the two centers merge.

6. Continue, and you will soon feel the clear, calming effects of being centered as a star, grown internally, fill your space.

Presence

Your presence is your personal emanation—your projection of yourself into the world. It's the vibe people have when they're with you. You may have a calm and gentle presence, a murderous presence, or any variation in between. Your presence is your ambassador to the world. It negotiates your intent and opens or closes the doors that co-create your circumstances.

Presence informs others of the manner in which your energy is following your mind. If your mind is frenzied and unbalanced, your energy will be scattered and your presence will be insubstantial. If your mind is focused and disciplined, your energy will be coherent and you will be masterful. The quality of your energy is reflected in your presence.

Where you place your attention is where your energy flows. Strong attention comes from disciplining your mind, a practice that increases the strength of your energy field. When you place your attention firmly on an object with no distractions, you develop your presence and it becomes a powerful ally. Your presence can fill into the nooks and crannies of a situation, it can discern truth, it can forge strong alliances, and it can bring meaning and connection, creating better outcomes.

The key skill in developing presence is the ability to hold multiple factors in focus simultaneously. One example of this is staying connected with your inner core while also connecting with elements in the outer world, balancing your attention between your inner feelings and an external person or event. The presence involved with this kind of attention is profound. As a receiver, it is the difference between being listened to and being heard, and the difference between simply being with someone and being connected. Another example is balancing intuitive information with intellectual reasoning. Both work together, one providing energy information and the other providing intellectual reasoning.

Being in the present moment, balanced between the forces of the past and the forces of the future, is one of the most profound examples of this skill. The point of power, the place of decisions, is always in the present moment and the ability to be engaged in the present is the point of personal power.

The Circle of Life pattern activates an energy flow in the shape of a torus, or donut-like array, through and encircling your body. The donut hole of the torus aligns with your cylindrical core and the outer tube expands your personal emanation. Both increase your presence. Here's a shortened version.

Increasing Presence Exercise

1. Center and ground yourself as described.
2. Activate the *Circle of Life* pattern.
3. As you inhale, draw energy up your center line from your Base chakra.
4. Breathe the energy through your physical and spiritual centers, and send it out through your Crown chakra.
5. Allow energy to flow as a fountain out of the top of your head, cascading in an arc around you and collecting in a pool beneath your Base chakra.
6. Keep drawing the energy up, through, and out, forming the torus pattern.
7. With every breath, increase the size of the torus until it reaches the largest radius you can sustain with ease.
8. Notice how your balance, vitality, clarity, and attention are affected.

Creating Boundaries

Your boundary is the place where you end and another begins. There is a profound dichotomy in working with energy. On the one hand, we are all interlinked with each other and energy flows into, through, and among us. We feel each others' energy and influence each others' energy flow. On the other hand, we are each separate individuals with our own distinct energy that is patterned according to our vision, intent, and emotion. The quandary is how to stay connected and flowing with each other, yet maintain a boundary around the energy experiences we want to have versus the ones we don't.

Being able to create and maintain healthy boundaries is the last of the four key elements of personal power. It requires discernment and flexibility. You still are in exchange with others, but there is no confusion about where your space begins and ends. Think of the energy boundary as a semi-permeable membrane, open to other energy that you resonate with and chose to engage and closed to energy that doesn't represent you.

A boundary marks your emotional, physical, and energetic space. Having it ensures your ability to act from your own center and connect to your spiritual Source. For many, this space encompasses their entire aura. For others, it's the space out to the third layer of the aura—the layer that links to the chakra of personal individuation. Healthy boundaries allow independence of thought and action, allowing you to be in exchange with others without losing your personal identity, uniqueness, or autonomy.

When doing energy work, your boundaries ensure that you don't take on another person's energetic condition or fall under someone else's influence. At the same time, it restrains your projections, ensuring that you don't force your own persona on another person or have undue influence. Healthy boundaries demonstrate that you know who you are, have confidence in yourself, are connected to your spiritual Source, and trust and respect other people's path, purpose, and ability.

When you have poor boundaries, the demarcation of your aura may appear either very weak or very rigid, and give rise to several energetic conditions. Your energy fibers can become entangled with other people, impacting your ability to be independent. When you're entangled with another person or group of people, you lose your connection with your center and have trouble walking your path. You have less free attention to explore the world and become less open to new ideas. Entanglement fosters dependency and control. Power issues are forefront; you may be trying to exert undo control over another person, or a group may be expecting you to conform to a set of ideals and beliefs. Either way, independent thought or action is curtailed.

Poor boundaries can result in losing connection with your body. When you abandon your boundaries, or when your space is invaded, the discomfort can be such that it is easier to disconnect from your body than to feel it, especially if you feel powerless to change the circumstance. Once disconnected, you no longer receive the energy information your body provides. This impacts your decision-making abilities, your centeredness, and your grounding. In short, you lose personal power. Effective energy work becomes difficult, if not impossible.

With overly rigid boundaries, you may feel like a victim and become overly protective, or become detached and unwilling to connect with people. Your aura becomes hard and impenetrable, and many of your energy fibers stay coiled up in your chakras. You lose people's input, support, and exchange of energy. Flow is essential to health and function. Without flow you become isolated. Isolation causes physical, emotional, spiritual, and mental health problems. Overly rigid boundaries give the illusion of personal power, yet are as energetically disabling as not having any boundaries at all.

The best activation for defining your boundary is the *Spiral Pillar of Light*. Here's a simple version.

Creating Your Boundaries Exercise

1. Ground and center.
2. Spread your arms straight out from your body and swing from side to side, demarking your personal space. Twist from side to side, bend sideways, and explore your space.
3. Activate the *Spiral Pillar of Light* pattern by inhaling and imagining a pillar of light coming down into, through, and around you to the Earth, encompassing you in safety and peace.
4. Breathe into your core and expand your brilliance, filling your personal space with light.
5. Intend that only input for the highest and best good of all penetrates this boundary.

Becoming Powerful

When you have healthy boundaries, and are grounded, centered, and present, spiritual energy flows into your body through the top of your head and is integrated into your energy structures. At the same time, energy is flowing in from the Earth through your Base chakra and is being integrated into your structures as well. The emanation that radiates from you is brilliantly bright, clear, and strong. There is a definite demarcation between your energy and the energy streaming around you. Your fibers are free, flowing, and curious, exploring the world, people, and conditions fearlessly.

In this state of personal power you have emotional clarity, have connection to the information from your body, and display good decision-making skills. You create relationships with equality, respect, autonomy, creativity, good communication, and joyfulness. You feel the purpose in your life even if you don't have a clear vision of what it is and your spiritual practice is meaningful. You are able to give and receive energy, protect yourself, and become adept at using energy to fully engage life.

Claiming Your Power Exercise

1. Ground, center, and establish your boundaries.
2. Close your eyes and sense your boundary. If you could see it, what would it look like? How far out is it from your body? Is it the same all the way around? Is it weaker in some areas than others? Rigid? Empty? Spiky? Get a good strong image of all aspects of it.
3. What is your energy emanation like? Does it fill all the space within your boundary? Does it radiate beyond the perimeter? What does your emanation convey? How does it interact with your boundary?
4. Activate the *Earth and Sky* pattern and send your energy into the Earth while pulling more in through the top of your head. Allow excess or turbulent energy to discharge into the Earth. Allow strength to fill your body.
5. Notice any changes in your emanation and boundary.
6. Now bring your attention to your center, the core star that is home to your spiritual essence. Allow your essence to shine.
7. Notice any changes in your emanation and boundary. Notice how you feel. Has your level of awareness changed?
8. Activate the *Spiral Pillar of Light* pattern and float within the matrix of your own light.
9. When you're finished, close the activation, ground, center, and establish boundaries.

The best way to master these techniques is to use them. Practice grounding and centering every time you feel unfocused, confused, or overwhelmed. When in conflict, move into your personal power. Start every day with a short meditation; even five minutes is enough. Activate the *Spiral Pillar of Light* and *Earth and Sky* patterns. If you want to increase your vitality, activate the *Circle of Life* as well. The object is to enhance your life by increasing and using your personal power.

Every exercise in subsequent chapters will begin and end with grounding, centering, and establishing boundaries. When you open meditations this way, your personal power will be brought into each exercise. Closing will disengage the activation and bring you back into present time, fully engaged for daily action.

Chapter 11

Sensing Subtle Energy

Once you start developing your personal power, perceiving subtle energy is the next step. Having the ability to sense the flows you're interacting with changes your use of energy skills from ritual to an intentional act of creation. The more your perceptive ability grows, the more effective your energy skills become. Your body has all the equipment necessary; the only things missing are your attention and intention.

How the body receives energy is covered in Chapter 7. How your body reads energy and communicates the information to your mind is discussed in Chapter 9.

Essentially, your energy field and energy fibers act as antennae that feed signals from your environment into your body through your chakras. Your body translates those signals into readily available information, provided you know the language. Energy information is conveyed through physical sensations, changes in audio/visual perceptions, shifts in mood, gut feelings, intuitive knowing, emotions, inner visions, dreams, synchronicities, metaphors, and so forth. The secret is to pay attention.

In general, physical sensations tell you of the presence, amplitude, configuration, and other characteristics of internal and external energy flows. For example, when you connect strongly with another person and feel the flow of energy between you, you may experience physical sensations such as your hair standing on end or goose bumps. When internal energy flows change, you might feel the physical sensations of your muscles relaxing, internal opening and softening, tingling, warmth, and so on. Sensations let you know that energy is present, yet don't tell you very much about its quality.

The quality of the energy you're interacting with is revealed through your chakras, where the information is processed and translated into emotions, perceptual changes, intuition, inner knowing, and so on. In short, your instinct and gut feelings are the end result of an energy process that takes place in nanoseconds, yet feels simultaneous. For example, when sensing a spiritual presence, you may suddenly experience tingling along your spine while your hair stands on end (physical sensations) and while you also feel a rising joy (energy processed through the chakras). At the same time, you sense a presence that you intuitively recognize as your spiritual Source. The recognition of your spiritual Source is the end product of processing the energy information received through your body. This is an over-simplification, yet essentially the process.

Reading energy requires discernment. Every energy interaction is experienced through your personal lens, which has its own bias and is dependent on your degree of energy awareness. None of us is free from the influence of our own experiences, traumas, and issues of self-worth. This may be why all spiritual practices begin with the dictum "Know thyself." As you learn to sense energy, you need to constantly question whether the information is a reflection of you or clear insight. A good starting place is keeping your energy circuits clear.

Clearing Your Energy Circuits

Your physical and energetic bodies act together to receive and translate energy information. Charged areas in your aura behave as attractors, drawing specific types of energy and events toward you. A charged area can be intentional, as when you are working to manifest a desire, or it can be the unconscious result of unprocessed emotions, thoughts, and beliefs. All emotions have function; however, if they're not processed and integrated, they become an unconscious filter in the lens through which you see life and an unconscious director of your actions. Unprocessed emotions are held in both your aura and the cellular memory of your body. Because they are charged with a tremendous amount of energy, bodywork pioneer John Upledger termed them "energy cysts." They are essentially emotionally charged energetic time bombs. Eventually they must be processed and diffused.

When you're receiving energy information and it encounters a charged area in your field, the emotional content will be stimulated. Instead of receiving current information about your environment, you receive information about your habitual patterns that reflect past trauma. To discern the difference, ask yourself which it is: current information about the situation, or stored information about the past. Just ask the question, and then pause and wait for an answer. This seems deceptively simple; nevertheless, internally you know the answer. Within a few minutes you will either receive an insight about your energy encounter or realize that the emotional content is terribly familiar. If the emotion is about you, deactivate it by sending it into the Earth. Then ground, center, and open to receive an accurate read in present time. You can clear old emotional patterns using techniques in Chapter 19.

Keeping your energy field clear can be done using the grounding and centering practices in Chapter 10, and also by activating the *Queen Nefertiti's Headdress* pattern to clear the aura and the *Weaving the Nadis* pattern to clear the chakras. Here's an example of how to do it; although it sounds complicated, after you've done it once, it's really quite simple.

Clearing Energy Circuits Exercise

1. Ground, center, and establish your boundaries.
2. Activate the *Queen Nefertiti's Headdress* pattern.
3. Extend your awareness into your energy field and notice any area that draws your attention. You may be pulled because it feels heavy, dark, charged, unsettled. Feel for the emotion of it. Does it hold fear, anger, superiority, or other destructive forces?
4. Draw the pure energy of love through the wide opening of the headdress with every inhalation.
5. With every exhalation, send energy out the seven striations of the headdress and circulate it along the seven layers of the aura, 360 degrees around the body.
6. Send the energy in each striation, alternately circulating in opposite directions.
7. Allow the charged areas to explode as each layer vibrates at higher and higher speeds. You may experience little pops and sparklers as this happens.
8. Invite higher spiritual energy to enter the headdress; breathe it into the striations of your aura.
9. Breathe energy through the headdress into your center line to fill your core.
10. Spend a few minutes visualizing the seven chakras in your body. Be sure to see/feel them all with equal intensity.
11. With your inhalation, bring Earth energy up your left leg, and weave it in and out of each chakra until it reaches the Crown chakra.

12. Let Earth energy mix with Sky energy in the Crown chakra at the top of your head.

13. On the exhalation, send this energy back down through the chakras, weaving it from one to the next, and then flow down the right leg and into the Earth.

14. Keep this flow moving up on the inhalation and down on the exhalation until the energy flow is smooth and the chakras are balanced.

15. Breathe energy through the headdress into your center line to fill your core, then stream this energy through your core to the Earth.

16. When you feel calm, clear, and grounded, close the activation.

17. Ground, center, and establish boundaries.

Keeping your circuits clear will improve your ability to sense energy and to use it in the advanced techniques you will learn in upcoming chapters.

Feeling Internal Energy Flows

The biggest impediment to feeling energy is the fact that energy is described as inhabiting defined structures. It's easy to make the mistake of thinking energy is an isolated substance in the body. Energy doesn't flow in little tubes, nor is it constrained by boundaries into separate domains. The physical and energy bodies are not separate substances, only separate speeds of vibration. An analogy is that of different currents in a stream: It's all water, just moving more or less quickly, depending on the forces that are affecting it. Energy flow in the body is like a wave passing through an ocean. When you visualize energy as motion, it's easier to feel. Instead of trying to find a structure, you are locating a feeling or sense of movement.

The important thing about working with energy is to know that, like water, you can't push it. You can't "send" energy in the typical way we think of propelling something forward. Your mind has to go first and open the path for your energy to follow. It's an invitation. You can't force anything that doesn't want to move; you can only offer a possibility. Here's a simple exercise to feel and move internal energy.

Sensing Internal Energy Exercise

1. Ground, center, and establish boundaries.

2. Place each hand over any two chakras.

3. Invite your chakras to open to the energy in your hands. Don't send or force energy into your chakras; just offer an invitation by putting your attention on the chakras where your hands are resting.

4. Notice what you feel. Warmth, pressure, expansion, prickling sensations, and a feeling of melting are common. Whatever you feel is exactly right for you.

5. Now imagine the energy in each chakra flowing toward the other and meeting. Once again, just offer the possibility. Notice how this feels. Is there a direction? Does one chakra flow to the other? Do they both flow to meet each other?

6. If energy is flowing from one chakra to the other, amplify it. Imagine energy flowing from one hand and receiving it with the other in the direction of the flow you are experiencing. Continue until the energy stops moving of its own accord.

7. Invite your energy to flow in the opposite direction by imagining energy flowing in reverse from your hands.

8. Continue until the sense of flow has subsided.

9. When you're finished, ground, center, and re-establish your boundary.

Once you understand that you can't force energy to move, it's easier to synchronize with it and invite it to flow. When learning how to feel energy, there's a lot of emphasis on physical sensations. However, the sensations are not what are important; they are only indicators of movement, like seeing a twig traveling in a stream. Whether there is a twig or not, the stream is still flowing. The same is true here.

Don't get discouraged if you don't feel physical sensations. Try not to over-focus on them as proof of the existence of energy or your ability to interact with it. Each person is unique, and how you experience and know energy is known only to you. Eventually you will not need physical sensations to feel energy; the essence of it will simply impress itself on your awareness.

Daily practice of paying attention to your internal energy flows will become the foundation of your library of experiences that guides your energy awareness. As you notice your inner flows, you'll see how they react to your mental and emotional states. You'll recognize how they interact with external events and stimuli. You'll understand that it's not about your mind sending your energy places; it is your energy and attention co-creating opportunities and experiences.

Feeling External Energy Flows

Energy received through each layer of the aura is fed to its respective chakra. However, not all chakras receive information equally. Many people only use their lower chakras to experience the world and are not able to consciously receive information through the higher chakras.

Most people function out of one or two chakras. The centers you primarily receive information through are based on your level of development. An example of two people receiving an influx of the same energy and having completely different experiences might look like this: One receives a sexual rush, while the other receives a rush of love. The energy is the same. The difference is which chakra is more open. One person is more open through his or her Second chakra, and the other is more open through his or her Heart chakra. A third person might feel the same energy through his or her Third Eye chakra and have a spiritual rush. Always investigate what you feel and test it against your own patterns. Most importantly, never assume you have the entire truth—just one perception of a larger whole.

The field around your hands is especially sensitive to energy, and people often use their hands as their primary sensing tool. If you couple what you feel in your hands with an open Heart chakra, you will enter an entirely new level of awareness. The best activations to use to explore your energy senses are the *Five-Hearts Open* and the *Winged Disk* patterns. Here is an example of how to use them to feel external energy flows.

Sensing External Energy Exercise

1. Ground, center, and establish boundaries.

2. Activate the *Winged Disk* pattern.

3. Bring your attention to your Heart chakra and inhale conscious, living light in through your head, down your Hara line, and into your heart, expanding it with light and joy. Let light shine from your heart into the space around you. Become an extension of light.

4. Activate the *Five-Hearts Open* pattern.

5. Focus on your palms, filling them with light from your heart. You may notice your palms tingling and/or becoming hot.

6. Hold your hands with your palms facing each other. Bring them together to about 3 inches and pulse them toward each other. Can you feel them push against each other as you pulse? Pull them apart to about 8 inches and pulse them. Push them together and pull them

apart until it feels as if you are stretching taffy or silly putty between your hands. Compress the energy into a ball and follow the contours of the ball with your hands.

7. Do the same exercise with a plant. Invite the energy of the plant to connect with the radiance of your hands and heart.

8. Move your hands toward the plant, then away, as though compressing the energy around the plant. Walk toward the plant and away, moving in and out of its energy space. You may notice a magnetic repulsion/attraction between your hands and the plant.

9. Your hands are the antennae. As you feel pressure, notice what you feel in your Solar Plexus chakra and chakras. This is where you receive the information your antennae bring in.

10. With light-filled hands, explore the area 3 inches to 3 feet from the plant, feeling for the radiance coming from its core.

11. Notice changes inside your Heart chakra as you connect energetically with life.

12. Notice any body sensations, emotions, gut reactions, intuitions, or insights as you engage the spirit of this plant. You may have a vision in your mind's eye of what the energy looks like.

13. Do this exercise with another person and take turns exploring each other's aura. Feel for the contour and the layers of the aura. See if you find the concentrations of energy that mark the chakras. Notice any pictures that form in your mind's eye. Walk toward each other and back up; see if you can feel when you enter each other's space. Have fun and enjoy.

14. When you're finished, close the activation, ground, center, and establish boundaries.

A more advanced way of perceiving energy is using the chakra fibers of light that are always sensing the world around you. Every chakra has light filaments that stream outward, exploring the world. Some of these fibers are anchored, maintaining the foundation of your reality; others are free to follow the directives of your attention. Most people have an easier time perceiving energy through their Solar Plexus chakra, so this exercise will focus on the solar plexus.

Sensing External Energy With Energy Fibers Exercise

1. Sit comfortably in a chair with a plant placed before you.

2. Ground, center, and establish your boundary.

3. Activate the *Chakra Fibers* pattern.
4. Acknowledge the plant and ask permission to engage and explore it.
5. Focus your attention on your Solar Plexus chakra or whichever chakra draws your attention. With your inhalation, draw light into this chakra.
6. With your exhalation, let light stream outward from the chakra, activating your energy fibers/filaments.
7. Visualize these filaments of colored light softly and gently exploring the plant; feel the contours and connect with the light of the plant.
8. What sensations and information do you feel? What images form in your mind's eye? What intuitive insight do you suddenly have?
9. Extend your fibers to other things around you: the birds, the trees, clouds if you are outside. Notice what you physically, emotionally, and intuitively feel and see.
10. Do this with a partner and explore each other's field.
11. When you're finished, ground, center, and establish your boundaries.

Feeling another person's energy is a natural part of interacting; you are doing it all the time. Observing what happens and what information you receive is part of developing awareness.

Seeing Energy

Usually it is easier to feel energy than to see it. Some people are natural clairvoyants who see energy as easily as they see color or light. Children often have this capacity. They typically lose their ability between the ages of 5 and 8. Although this is partly due to the pressures of socialization, losing the ability is also protective. Being able to see and interact on an energy level without the guidance of informed parents is confusing and potentially dangerous to the development of a healthy psyche. Many who saw energy as a child and lost the ability, find it again later in life.

The best method for strengthening your ability to see energy is to train your mind to perceive information differently. Holographic images are a great way to do this. Have you seen the book series *The Magic Eye* by N.E. Thing Enterprises?[1] They are books of pictures that look to be random lines or simple patterns, but when focused on with a different part of the brain, suddenly burst into complex, three-dimensional pictures. You might remember from Chapter 5 that making a three-dimensional holographic image requires the use of coherent light beams or lasers interacting with interference patterns. Using the *Magic Eye* method trains your brain to be more coherent and retrieve information differently. This will greatly assist your ability to perceive energy.

To see the images you are required to shift your eye focus and let your brain make new patterns. When you do this, there is a distinct feeling in the brain as you access a different part of your awareness. Once you're proficient in seeing the three-dimensional images and can identify the distinct feeling of success, practice using the following technique to see energy.

Seeing Energy Exercise

1. Ground, center, and establish boundaries.

2. Activate the *Mystic Triangle* pattern, opening the triangle in your Third Eye.

3. Hold your hands in front of you at about the distance you would hold the *Magic Eye* picture. Hold them with thumb edges toward you, fingertips of the right hand touching the fingertips of the left.

4. Slightly un-focus your eyes, looking at your hands in the same manner you would a *Magic Eye* picture until you feel the internal shift in your brain.

5. Slowly pull you hands about 3 inches apart, noticing the streams of light that flow between your fingertips.

6. Continue bringing your fingers slowly toward each other and pulling them apart, noticing the changes in energy.

7. Use the same technique of seeing with people, objects, plants, and animals. It is particularly effective when looking at tree tops.

8. When you're finished, ground, center, and establish boundaries.

Many people see energy as an inner vision. When energy information is received and translated by the body, it can become a visual image seen in the mind's eye. Whenever you practice energy sensing or using energy skills, pay attention to the images that form in your mind. Test what you see against what you feel. As with all energy information, use discernment. Rather than take an image as absolute reality, ask what the image has to teach you. As with all intuition, it can be flavored through your own lens.

Energy Pathways

You are part of a network of energy, one of the focal points within a constellation of other focal points: other people, forms of consciousness, and spiritual forces. The energy that is exchanged between these focal points creates the events and opportunities of life. Your energy moves ahead of you, interacting along this network to create the outcomes you seek. Sensing this energy flow helps you create the life you desire, as discussed in Chapter 17.

Energy can be sensed externally through synchronicity, the flow of energy between events. When you notice synchronicity, you're working with time in a different dimension. We define time as a linear progression of measured increments that organize events. Not all cultures see time this way. The ancient Maya saw it as a relationship between cycles with specific qualities that were imparted to the events taking place within these periods. Synchronicity happens when different cycles overlap, opening portals between seemingly non-related events. The result is an increased flow of ideas, excitement, and opportunities. Paying attention to synchronicity keeps you observant of the links between events and the interconnection of the universe. The more synchronicity you notice, the more aware you are of the influences in your life and direction you are taking.

A Beginner's Mind

A delicate balance is required between paying attention to everything you feel, see, and sense while holding no expectations of what they mean. It's easy to get discouraged or over-focus on the signs of energy when what is important is simply opening your mind to possibility. Enjoy yourself and don't take it too seriously. It's innate, and your awareness will unfold naturally as you begin to pay attention. Practice, be patient, and play!

Chapter 12

USING ENERGY PROTECTION

Protection is the last of the foundational skills needed to negotiate energy terrain with clarity, safety, and intent. Although it would be great to live in a world where everyone has the highest level of intent, unfortunately that isn't the way it is. Protective activations help you maintain your personal power during conflict or confrontation, disengage energy you take on from other people that isn't yours, and repel an energy attack from other people or entities. It's a good idea to use energy protection skills when negotiating energy terrain to keep yourself clear and focused on your path.

In daily life, protection skills can help you stay centered and aligned to higher purpose while negotiating tricky contracts, while resolving conflicts, or when confronted with an angry person. To use protective practices in daily challenges, simply activate the *Spiral Pillar of Light* pattern any time you feel stressed, confused, or manipulated. This will not only strengthen your resolve and personal power, it will help ensure your thought forms and uncontrolled emotions don't hurt others. On the other hand, if you feel harmful energy is being used against you, the practices in the rest of the chapter may be helpful.

What Is Disruptive Energy?

Harmful energy falls into three categories: excessive or discordant energy that disrupts your field, conscious and unconscious energy manipulation/attachment, and psychic attack. In addition, energy can become constrained in patterns that repeat through generations. Some call these energy miasmas, and breaking them can shift generational patterns of dysfunction.

Excess energy can cause harm any time your system takes on more than you can channel. This can happen if Kundalini rises unexpectedly and your system is unprepared to deal with it, or when you enter a strong vortex of Earth energy that overloads your circuits. Generally, your natural defenses will keep you from overloading, yet, as with your immune system, there are times when you are in a weakened state. You're especially vulnerable if you're an empathic person who has poor boundaries, when you start employing new skills before you have totally mastered them, or when you have a lot of attachment sites, which will be discussed in the next section.

Energy manipulation happens when a person, group, or system uses energy practices to maneuver another person into acting in a way that is counter to his or her authentic self and higher beliefs. The desire to control or manipulate another person creates energy projections and/or hooks that implant in the person's energy field. Of course this happens all the time in big and little ways: A parent uses manipulation to control an unruly child, governments implant fear and propaganda to manipulate the public, a rejected lover tries to hold the object of his or her desire by wrapping his or her lover within projections of affection. Anytime one person tries to control or influence another, he or she is assuming that his or her idea of what is right is best for everyone.

Energy attacks are by far the most palpable form of interference. Much of the time, energy attacks are unconscious. One person is simply trying to fill his or her needs and doesn't comprehend the energetic nature of his or her behavior. Parents rarely think they are placing energy projections in their child when they control him or her through shame. "Your father would be ashamed of you" is merely an expedient way of getting the wanted cooperation. On the other hand, some people purposefully use energy practices to hurt other people. This is called a psychic attack, and the karmic backlash is severe.

What Is Energy Protection?

Energy protection is a misunderstood skill. It's not a matter of creating a shield against attack; it's about vibrating at a frequency that doesn't allow anything of a lower nature to attach. If you have no attachment or receptor sites in your field, nothing can energetically harm you. Removing your attachment sites is like closing the docking port on a spacecraft; you can't be energetically invaded if you're not available. Although energy attack is very real and can take many forms, you are in control of whether or not you are vulnerable. Recognizing an energy attachment is covered later in this chapter.

Receptor sites are highly charged areas in your field. The charge can be emotions that have not been integrated, such as poor self-esteem, pain, fear, anger, and so forth, or unhealed trauma, beliefs, attitudes, addictions, and thought patterns. Any part of you that works against your higher path and purpose can become a receptor site for lower energy. Emotionally charged areas not only receive energy attachments and are available for attack; they attract them and are often called attractors. Energy practices that clear your aura and raise your vibration minimize both your attractive force and receptivity to harmful energy.

Harmful energy is itself a misnomer. Energy is neither positive nor negative; it has to be directed in its use to be one or the other. You can direct energy to hurt someone else consciously, as with black magic practices, or you can do it accidentally. Sending hate-filled emotions toward another person is an act of energy attack. Although most people strive to be constructive, everyone has, at one time or another, through anger, jealousy, or fear, sent negatively charged energy to another person. Everyone has also been the object of someone else's harmful projections. Protection techniques have the benefit of shielding you from being hurt at the same time that they safeguard you from damaging someone else.

Ultimately, protection is the act of aligning with your spiritual Source or higher ideal. When you are aligned with higher truth, understand with humility your spiritual identity, and are filled with gratitude, your vibration is heightened and nothing can touch you. Grounding, centering, and establishing boundaries are the keys to staying aligned. This is especially true for people who are naturally empathic, as will be discussed in Chapter 18.

Truthfully, no one can be completely clear of dark feelings in every moment at all times in life, and consequently there are times you can be vulnerable to energy attack. This is when techniques of protection are helpful.

Energy Attachments and Influences

There are many different methods of energetically influencing another and, although you wouldn't want to dwell on this, being aware of the possibilities is the first step to eliminating an unwanted presence.

Other people's thought forms, projections, and hooks can be attached to your receptor sites and influence your actions and perceptions. Lower-level entities can also attach to receptor sites. Energy attachments have absolutely no power except that which you give them. Every time you engage an energy attachment with fear or anger, you feed them and make them more powerful. Directly attacking them can also fuel their hold on you. The best approach is to eliminate your receptor sites, which eliminates the attachment, whatever its form. An exercise to do this appears at the end of this section.

If someone is attempting to manipulate you through an energy attachment, you will probably feel the impact without necessarily understanding it. You may feel pulled in a direction you don't want to go, feel obligated to someone without knowing why, or simply be unable to shake someone else's attention. You may feel like you're operating in a fog and making decisions you can't explain. You might start thinking of this person, dreaming of them, or seeing his or her face when you close your eyes. Because energy attachments are pulling you off your path, you will probably resent the attentions of the other person and rebel, even while staying somewhat obsessed with them. You may actively dislike the person, yet feel unable to detach.

Thought forms, projections, hooks, and entities can attach to the aura.

Here's a brief over view of different types of energy attachments and influences.

Thought Forms

Thought forms are intentions powered with emotion that live in your aura. They are structured constructs and are part of the attractive force that generates your experience. Charged areas of past trauma and unconscious beliefs are one type of thought form, as are intentions for manifestation that you have consciously created. However they can also be other people's thoughts that are placed in your aura to manipulate you.

The unique aspect of self-generated thought forms that makes them different from your daily random thoughts is that they don't require your continued attention to exist. You don't have to feed thought forms with continued worry or other emotional energy. Once created, they are independent of your thought process and have a life of their own. Seeking to manifest their program, they grow by finding like-energy to combine with and become more powerful. In doing so they attract toward you the people and events that will help them grow.

Subconscious constructs can be both attractors and receptor sites for lower-level energy. Additionally, you can project your thought forms onto other people. Once implanted in someone else, they combine and make bigger and stronger constructs in both of you. Other people can do the same to you such that it becomes difficult to know whose thought form is whose. Any time you give your power away to someone else, you are combining thought forms. Massive constructs are formed and reinforced through the news, teachers, religious authority, governments, and so forth. Owning and deconstructing or transforming your negative thought forms helps not only you, but everyone around you.

A curse is a thought form intentionally constructed and placed in another person's field to purposefully destabilize them. Curses are programmed to stay through time and may activate only under certain conditions. For example, a curse from an old lover placed on your love life will only activate when you are establishing a relationship. Curses are often difficult to see yet can be quite easy to get rid of, as you will see at the end of the section.

Projections

Projections, as the name implies, are directives and desires that are unintentionally projected into another person's energy field. To some degree everyone is under the influence of some one else's projection: Children try to live up to their parents projections of what they should do or be in the world; spouses are influenced by the projections of what their partner wants in a lover. Many of the negative self-images that people have are the result of conflict between their authentic self and living up to someone else's idea of what they should be.

Interestingly, projections are often used to keep people connected. When you receive a projection from someone else, you're connected to him or her as long as the projection is in your field. For some people, this is the only kind of relationship they know. Though removing projections is liberating, it can also be lonely.

As much as you have received projections from other people, you have certainly sent them as well. Every time you judge someone or think you know what's best for him or her, you're essentially sending an energy projection. If there is a receptor site for it, the other person becomes susceptible to your influence. In order to grow, you need to both remove the projections in your field and also reclaim the projections of yours that you embedded in other people. This will allow you to form relationships based on equality and trust.

Hooks

A hook is essentially someone else's thought form that has hooked into your energy field and is pulling you toward him or her. Hooks are the result of another person's desire for you. This happens most often with a romantic interest; however, it can happen in business partnerships or any type of relationship where one person wants to maneuver the other. Hooks are insidious because they are based on desire and, often, affection. The person sending them rationalizes that he or she is acting for the other person's "best interest." Hooks prey on the part of you that wants to please others; nobody likes to disappoint another, and hooks take advantage of that feeling. (How this relates to patterns of codependence is found in Chapter 16.)

Hooks are rarely an intentional act of energy control, although they certainly can be. Most often, the sender's desire is simply so strong that it latches on to your field. Your fear, perhaps of letting someone down or abandoning him or her, allows it to happen. Hooks are continually being reinforced through the sender's repetitive thoughts and longing, pulling you off center and influencing your behavior.

Couples often have hooks in each other, which can be an unconsciously agreed-on arrangement. Without consciously making an agreement, each person accepts the other's hook and maintains the receptor site that receives it. People do this out of fear, and it is a codependent arrangement.

The difficulty with romantic hooks is that they are often mistaken for love. However, real love carries no agenda other than loving, and hooks always have an ulterior agenda. The other person wants something from you, or he or she wouldn't be hooked into your field. He or she may want your returned love and affection, your agreement to join him or her in a project or business plan, or simply your approval. Every time he or she thinks of you, the hook becomes stronger. Often one person will have multiple hooks in another, each one representing a different aspect of what he or she hopes will happen, what he or she hopes to gain, or how he or she is controlling you. Hooks that come from a third party and interrupt a primary partnership can have devastating consequences.

An initial hook cannot take hold in your field without your opening in some way to the person sending it. Just giving someone your attention in a simple conversation can be enough, especially if you accept an idea or advice from him or her. Once you've received a hook, it can be reinforced without your participation. When someone is hooking into you, every phone conversation, e-mail, or text message is reinforcement. Closing the receptor sites and eliminating the hooks is the only way to be free. You might consider that you have hooks if you feel obligated to respond to another person even though you don't want to, feel unduly influenced by some one else, or continually feel responsible for another's happiness.

Any unfulfilled part of you can be a receptor site for a hook. Maybe you're having a hard spell with your spouse and some one else's attention boosts your ego. Maybe you're feeling financially precarious and a "get rich quick" scheme seems to be the way out. Any time you're feeling vulnerable or unfulfilled and looking for someone or something to save you, you're open to receiving someone's hook. The best protection is to "know thyself," and stay in alignment with your path and purpose. Because hooks rarely augment your path and purpose, if you're in alignment, people will not be able to hook you. A sense that you are being diverted from your path is another indicator that you may be hooked.

When hooks are inserted via an electronic carrier, it has a different quality than those that are delivered on biological carrier waves. In the same way that electromagnetic pollution harms your energy field, hooks carried on electricity cause more damage to your energy field and are more disruptive to your thinking than those that arrive on biological carrier waves. They are much harder to extract. Deleting all electronic messages you've been saving, de-friending people on Facebook, changing your phone number, and so forth are essential if you truly want to disengage the hook.

Energy Vampires

Drugs, trauma, loss, and psychic attack can tear holes in a person's aura, making it difficult to hold energy. If this has happened to you, you may feel depleted and unable to maintain enthusiasm or direction in life.

When you come in contact with a person who has a hole, he or she may latch into you with one or more of his or her energy fibers and use your energy as fuel. He or she comes alive when latched into someone else and deflates when the person leaves. When you're with a person like this, you feel drained by your conversation. Do you know someone who drains you every time you see him or her? This person may have energy fibers latching onto your field.

Another type of energy stealing happens when someone is jealous of you and doesn't want you to get ahead. Subconsciously, his or her fibers can latch on and keep you from moving forward.

If you have a hole in you aura and are stealing another person's energy, then you have forgotten your connection to your Source, which is the only place you can receive an unlimited supply of energy. (An exercise to repair your aura can be found in Chapter 19.)

Low-Level Entities

It would be nice to think that only beneficent energy beings exist, such as guides, angels, and Nature Spirits. Unfortunately, low-level entities also exist. Sometimes these are simply destructive thought forms that have become independent from their original source and are looking for more energy. They seek people with unresolved issues who throw around a lot of emotional energy. They attach and feed off the emotional outbursts. In the beginning they will seem relatively benign, only taking what is being expressed. As they get stronger and as the host gets used to their presence, these entities begin to manipulate their host into damaging behavior that generates ever more emotional turmoil for the entities to latch to.

These types of entities are like parasites hanging onto people and getting strong off excessive emotions of anger, greed, fear, lust, jealousy, and hatred. If you have a receptor site they will stick to you on contact. You can pick them up in bars, gambling facilities, prisons, mental institutions, and other places where people's destructive impulses are unchecked.

Other types of low-level entities can be different energy beings who desire to harm others for unknown reasons. At best this type of entity can be manipulative; at worst they can be involved in psychic attacks that can be quiet frightening.

As with other types of attachments, low-level entities can't impact you unless you have a receptor site or are available through fear to their ministrations. Energy attachments of all kinds are removed the same way: by eliminating the receptor sites and vibrating at a higher rate. When faced with a challenge of this type, go within and face your fear. Bring it into the light and let it become light.

Reclaiming Projections Exercise

1. Ground, center, and establish boundaries.
2. Activate the *Mystic Triangle* pattern and stand in one corner of the horizontal triangle.
3. Call to mind a person you would like to have peace with. You must genuinely want a resolution.
4. Invite this person to join you in another corner of the triangle. Imagine the person facing you, and invite him or her to participate in a healing exchange.
5. If you wish, invite a guide or spiritual being to stand in the third corner of the triangle.
6. Take a moment and look to see if you can locate your projections in this other person. What do your projections look like? Where in the person's energy field are they imbedded?
7. Sincerely apologize for any harm you've caused the person, and ask for his or her forgiveness.
8. Explain that you need to reclaim all the projections you've sent out and ask if they can be returned to you.
9. Allow the person to extract your projections and hand them back to you. As you take them back, give thanks, and release the projections. You might want to bury them, burn them, dissolve them or hand them to your spiritual guide to transform into light.

10. Ask if the person would like to have his or her projections back from you. If you feel the answer is yes, forgive this person for any pain he or she has caused you, find the projections in your field, and return them with grace.

11. When you feel complete, close the activation.

12. Ground, center, and establish your boundaries as you end the exercise.

Removing Energy Attachments and Low-Level Entity Exercise

1. Ground, center, and establish your boundaries.

2. Activate the *Celtic Cross* pattern and stand inside its protective boundary. Use your breath and attention to expand your presence and explore your energy field with your light fibers.

3. Invite the spirit of whoever has sent you a projection, hook, thought form, curse, or other energy attachment to be present. Imagine him or her inside an additional *Celtic Cross* construct, where he or she is completely neutralized and unable to attach.

4. Imagine looking into the eyes of this person with compassion, understanding, independence, and resolve.

5. Remove all the attachments you are carrying that came from this person and offer them back. If the person takes them, ask him or her to give you back any attachments you may have injected into him or her.

6. If the person will not take back his or her energy attachments, wrap them up and leave them respectfully at his or her feet.

7. Activate the *Queen Nefertiti's Headdress* pattern. With every inhalation, imagine each layer of your aura vibrating faster and spinning in alternate directions.

8. Allow the charged areas in your aura to vibrate and spin until they burst and disintegrate. If you have a rattle you can shake it at the charged sites.

9. Imagine interacting with this person with no agenda and with total honesty between you. Activate two *Spiral Pillars of Light* patterns and see each of you standing in your own pillar, separate and complete.

10. Break the connection by offering the person peace.

11. Ground, center, and establish boundaries.

Removing Attachment Sites and Deconstructing Thought Forms Exercise

1. Ground, center, and establish boundaries.

2. Activate the *Spiral Pillar of Light* pattern.

3. Explore your energy field and locate your attractor sites. They may feel like empty spots, dark areas, or blocks in your field.

4. Explore them by asking yourself what you gained by the attachments you received. Some common attractors are: increasing self-importance, gaining energy from the emotional charge, avoiding internal emptiness or unresolved emotions, and using the attachment to manipulate events to your favor. (There are considerably more attractors than this; only you have the ultimate ability to discern the though forms you've created.)

5. Activate the *Queen Nefertiti's Headdress* pattern and imagine shaking the thought construct lose and deconstructing it by vibrating it with energy until it falls apart. You can also use a rattle or other energy tool to help.

6. Establish your presence and, using personal power, take command of your emotional and energetic space.

7. Breathe color and vitality into your field.

8. Replace existing beliefs and patterns with new ones. No one can think your thoughts except you, and no one can attach to your field if you're not receptive.

9. Ground, center, and establish boundaries.

Taking command of your energetic space is essential to maintaining the personal power to consciously create your life. Keeping yourself as clear as possible requires the inner resolve to take responsibility for what you carry. Start each day with ground, center, presence, and establishing boundaries. Keep light, gratitude, and humility in your field with a heart-centered approach to life.

Psychic Attack

Psychic attack is an attempt by one person, or group of people, to inflict harm on another using energy to disrupt the emotional, mental, physical, or spiritual state of the target. Harm can be inflicted consciously, or someone can simply project his or her uncontrolled anger, jealousy, or other emotions without knowing the impact. The more conscious and intentional the attack, the more harm it can cause.

Jealousy, envy, hurt, grief, revenge, and fear are the common motivations for a psychic attack. Using psychic energy to assault another creates a severe karmic backlash on the sender.

You might wonder if you're under a psychic attack if suddenly your life begins to fall apart and things you have worked for slip out of your grasp. You may experience disruption in your relationships and have a hard time understanding what went wrong. Your motivation and sense of direction may founder, leaving you depressed and even suicidal. Physically, you might feel tired and depleted and, in the case of severe attack, feel as though you're having a heart attack.

Psychically attacking someone is a narcissistic act, and the perpetrator often wants you to know that he or she is the cause of your troubles. Your recognition makes the other person feel powerful. Consequently, he or she may project his or her image into your mind. You might have frightening dreams of him or her, or see his or her face watching you in your dreams, in your meditations, and as you fall asleep at night or wake in the morning. The person's face may appear much larger and take on a cruel or evil expression. You might find yourself thinking of him or her obsessively. This is part of the control the person is exerting as he or she works to disrupt your life.

Although there are effective ways to remove yourself from an attack, you have no control over whether the other person stops attacking you. What you can do is stop feeding the attack through fear or anger, and neutralize its effects. A psychic attack has a lot to teach you about yourself. After stopping the attack, examine what you had to gain from this experience. An energy attack is a concentrated opportunity to practice mental discipline. Strengthen your mental ability by refusing to engage the images, emotions, and thoughts that assail you from this person or group. Every time the person's face comes into your mind, replace it with light. Allowing your mind to be used as a projector of images meant to intimidate you makes you complicit. Unknowingly, you may be using the energy rush you feel to fuel your self-importance or to motivate your life.

Sometimes a psychic attack is an initiation that pushes you into a higher level of awareness and energy function. This does not excuse the attack or attacker, but may be part of the attractive force within you that helped create it. Was some part of you wanting to test your prowess? If so, affirm your humility, gratitude, compassion, and inner resolve, and affirm your spiritual path.

Stopping a Psychic Attack

It is actually very easy to stop a psychic attack. When someone resorts to terrorizing another, it's a sign that he or she has no real ability or personal power. Simply acknowledging that a psychic attack is under way removes a considerable amount of its force. Attacks use your fear and confusion to gain strength. When you take this away, the power over you can, in some cases, be completely eliminated.

However, directly confronting your attacker with the desire to overpower him or her will fail. Your energy will be used against you, and you will be fighting yourself. In addition, as soon as you engage on this level, you become a perpetrator of energy misuse yourself and will damage your spiritual connection.

Disabling a Psychic Attack Exercise

1. Ground, center, and establish your boundaries. Connect strongly to your spiritual Source.

2. Open the *Celtic Cross* pattern and stand firmly inside its spinning field of energy. Acknowledge that a psychic attack is under way and, if you know the attacker, name him or her. Make a firm statement of intent that you are safe and in command of your inner space. State that the person has no power over you.

3. Ask to neutralize the other person by placing him or her in a *Celtic Cross* pattern, but don't engage in a battle of wills. If the pattern doesn't activate, move on.

4. Activate the *Spiral Pillar of Light* pattern and clearly establish that any harmful energy directed at you be transformed into love and returned to the attacker.

5. Clearly state that you are not available for the attack and that all the energy sent to you by the attacker is transformed to love and returned. Fill your field with light.

6. Keep your physical space clear and protected using the techniques in Chapter 13.

7. There is nothing more powerful than love. Emanate love.

8. Ground, center, and establish boundaries.

Usually this exercise is sufficient to stop an attack. However, if one persists, activate the *Celtic Cross* pattern whenever you feel the presence or impact of the attacker. You can form the *Celtic Cross* pattern around you and around your entire family. Construct it around your bed at night and around your house, your car, and your work environment. Start every morning and end every day by grounding, centering, and establishing boundaries.

Karmic Backlash

Misusing energy to hurt another comes with severe energetic consequences. This happens in two ways. First, as soon as the person under attack uses protection techniques, the attacker's actions are reflected back on him- or herself, often seeming like a psychic retaliation as light bulbs explode, computers break down, and other challenges befall them. In fact, this is the return of the attacker's own energy. If you have misused psychic energy, it can be hard to tell the difference between being under psychic attack and receiving the return of your own actions.

Secondly, a conscious psychic attack is the act of empowering your undeveloped parts and letting them become external realities. As soon as you do this, you create the need to meet these parts of yourself in external events and reclaim them. Carl Jung called this "integrating your shadow." You cannot avoid the ultimate purpose of your life—to grow spiritually—any more than you can avoid the laws of nature that determine you are born, grow, and die. Whatever you put out will return to you a hundred-fold as you must meet the results of your actions. "As a man sows, so shall he reap."

If you believe the chain of difficulties you face is due to your own karmic return, don't panic. There is a path out. Through grace and forgiveness, you can accept your actions and return light to the universe. You can read more about this in Chapter 18.

Generational Miasma

Patterns from one generation tend to repeat in the next. This can be the understandable passing of knowledge from parent to child that makes generations of lawyers, mechanics, or businesspeople. It can also be the understandable passing of lifestyle practices such as alcohol use, or traits such as honesty and trust. There is another kind of pattern that seems to be beyond the transfer of knowledge or tendency and can be called a generational energy miasma.

Energy miasmas enlist the action of people and principles outside of the control of the person or family that is living the pattern. For example, a man loses his job at the exact time that his wife unexpectedly dies. Neither event seems to be related, nor in his control, yet the same coincidence happened to his father and grandfather. Some families live the same tragedy in different stories, generation after generation.

Energy miasmas are sometimes caused by thought forms or low-level entities that are transferred from one generation to the next. They can skip expression in a generation, only to return two or three generations later.

Some energy miasmas are strange, but not destructive, as when family members who come to the end of their natural life tend to die in the same month of the year. On the other hand, many patterns occur in constellations of dysfunction. If your family has such a pattern, therapy is an essential component in protecting yourself from its effects.

Family constellation therapy is specifically geared to look at these types of patterns from a psychological perspective. Changing the energy construct will help remove the forces holding the pattern in form. Coupling therapy with the exercises in this chapter to deconstruct thought forms and to release attachments will support your freedom.

Chapter 13

CLEARING SPACE

Keeping your home, office, car, and land clear of energetic debris is as important as keeping your mind and psyche clear. The energy in a house or specific geographic area can be imprinted by impressions left behind from previous events. Your energy field responds and the debris magnifies any similar resonance in your field. For example, if you are prone to depression and you encounter traumatic imprints, you can find yourself becoming more depressed for no known reason. On the other hand, have you ever been in a house that felt happy and comfortable even though there was nothing special you could put your finger on? Clarity of energy and positive charge is palpable, just as arguments, worry, and stress can create an ambiance of gloom. Keeping your space clear helps you keep your mind clear, your emotions stable, and your energy uplifted. Most importantly, it allows you to work with fresh input rather than being overshadowed by previous impressions.

Imprints come in all types; they can be traumatic and keep you in turmoil, nostalgic and keep you stuck in the past, seductive and keep you in illusion, or joy-filled and keep you in optimism. Whatever the imprint, the bottom line is that you want to be clear of influence in order to act in freedom rather than from a pre-existing program. Even very positive imprints can carry an agenda that attempts to influence you. Consider the spiritual energy in a church, synagogue, or mosque that can be both uplifting and controlling.

The more intense an event, the more energy is entrained in the imprint that it leaves behind. Battlefields, mental institutions, murder sites, cemeteries, and so forth often carry enormous energetic charge. Sensitive people report an inability to sleep and experience other types of disruption when they are in such areas. Houses built over the sites of traumatic events often carry a residue. Fortunately, nature has mechanisms to erase imprints and restore the natural vitality. The elements of wind, rain, and sun restore the electromagnetic clarity of land, and we can use the same principles to clear our living space.

ELFs, also called ELFEMSs, are extremely low-frequency electromagnetic fields in the range of 50/60 hertz that are created primarily through the generation, transmission, and use of electricity. They have been shown to interact with the electromagnetic emanations of the Earth's field, and there is a suspected association with risks to human health. Where the Earth's natural electromagnetic field is artificially impacted, there is a greater affinity for picking up energy imprints. If you live near a power transmission plant or under large cables, you may want to investigate ELF-clearing technology in addition to releasing any energy imprints. Biofield technologies are designed to eliminate the effects of ELFs and can be found on the Internet. Be sure to thoroughly investigate the company and supporting research before purchasing.

Clearing space is about transformation. Whatever is holding back movement or growth is transformed and released into the etheric space as creative, life-enhancing energy.

Clearing Your Aura

Clearing your space begins with clearing your personal energy space: your aura. Your aura has a magnetic quality and collects energy and emotional imprints in the same way that houses and land do. The imprints can unite with your existing thought forms, increasing their strength, as discussed in Chapter 12, or they can simply become little energy critters adhering to your field. Imprints can be both friendly and unfriendly; either way, they're not yours. Having a clear field augments alignment with your path and purpose. It allows you to have better perceptive ability and assists lucid decision-making free of unintended influences. It also enhances your ability to receive clear energy information and deepen your spiritual and energy practice.

Clearing your aura before doing any energy work is basic. It's also a good idea to clear your field on a daily basis, just as you clean your body. This doesn't have to take a long time; simply visualizing any of the appropriate activation patterns in Chapter 3 for a few seconds is very effective. In addition, the practices to increase personal power in Chapter 10 are techniques that clear and enhance the energy field, and Chapter 12 explains how to keep your field clear of thought forms and attachments.

When practicing the following exercise, you can shorten it by reducing the number of activations. Rotate the activations in a daily practice of cleansing to keep your practice lively.

Daily Energy-Clearing Exercise

1. Ground, center, and establish your boundaries.
2. Activate the *Spiral Pillar of Light* pattern and allow your aura to expand in light.
3. Further energize your field with the strength of the Earth and the freedom of the sky by activating the *Earth and Sky* pattern.
4. For a deep cleansing, activate the *Chakra Clarity* pattern and visualize each chakra full of clear, brilliant light, free of emotional residue that creates thought forms and attachment sites.
5. Activate the *Queen Nefertiti's Headdress* pattern to clear any attachments or imprints in the aura.
6. When your energy feels clear and free of imprints, close the activations.
7. Ground, center, and establish boundaries.

You can also use energy tools to assist your cleansing. Here's a very effective method that you can use alone or in combination with the previous activation.

Clearing Your Field With Energy Tools Exercise

1. Ground, center, and establish boundaries.
2. Shake a rattle all around your body through your entire energy field to move stagnant energy, loosen attachments, and shift thought forms.
3. Light a cleansing herb or tree resin such as sage, sweet grass, or copal, scoop the smoke into your hands, and then wash it through your aura.
4. Visualize light entering the top of your head and filling your central core, filtering out through your entire aura.
5. Establish a higher frequency by ringing Tibetan bells, a singing bowl, a tuning fork, or simply toning "Aum" or another sacred chant.
6. Fill yourself with gratitude and grace.
7. When you feel complete, ground, center, and establish boundaries.

Energetic Detoxification

Toxicity is a serious and often-unrecognized health hazard that can be an underlying cause of many major health issues. The primary source is pollution, both from physical poisons and low-level energy emissions. Heavy metals, pesticide and insecticide poisons, and bisphenol A are the better-known culprits; however, the list is long and distressing. Toxins that overload the liver's ability to detoxify them are collected and stored in tissue, where they eventually cause damage. Most people benefit immensely from detoxification protocols that use saunas, supplements, and diet to help clear toxic residue. Adding an energy detox into the protocol can dramatically improve results and decrease side effects.

On an energetic level, toxins create stagnation and generate a magnetic attraction that accumulates vital energy. Energy that doesn't move loses its vitality and becomes part of the energetic foci that attracts more toxic residue. It becomes a self-generating cycle. Additionally, energy and emotional trauma that have been stored in the body, as discussed in Chapter 9, can also attract toxins, both energetic and physical. When you begin to move energy through your system, old energy foci can be stimulated to release their toxic load.

Use the following energy detox any time you feel that noxious emotions or debris are interfering with your health. When you do emotional process work, clear the aura (as described previously) and use this toxic energy cleansing, too. Adding this to your physical detox protocol is highly recommended. This exercise is not meant to take the place of appropriate medical care.

Energy Detoxifying Exercise

1. Ground, center, and establish your boundaries.

2. Imagine yourself sitting inside a body-sized pyramid with your head at the level of the capstone.

3. Activate the *Pyramid Purification* pattern and visualize Earth energy entering the corners of the pyramid base and coalescing in the center where you are sitting.

4. Invite the energy to spiral up your central core. Be with this image for a few minutes, feeling its effect. Imagine the spiral as a violet flame.

5. Observe that the violet flame magnetizes the energetic and physical toxins in your body, drawing them into its center.

6. Visualize the toxins meeting the flame and incinerating. The transformed energy is released to spiral up your core, through your Crown chakra, and out the top of the pyramid.

7. Maintain your awareness on the purple flame until the flow stops.

8. Bring your awareness back into present time and close the activation.

9. Ground, center, and establish your boundaries.

You can follow any type of detoxification with the use of some simple energy tools. Here are some ideas:

- Brush your skin with a dry brush. Always stroke toward the heart.

- Take a shower alternating cold and hot temperatures for 30 seconds at a time.

- Take a sauna or steam shower followed by a cold splash.

- Take an Epsom salt bath to draw toxins through the skin and stabilize your energy field.

- Take a series of full, deep breaths to stimulate lymphatic flow.

Clearing Your House and Other Spaces

If your space has a lot of people coming through or is used for healing work, it's beneficial to clear it on a daily basis. Otherwise, it's a good idea to get into the practice of clearing your house, office, or special rooms regularly: once a week, once a month, or even once a season or year. Many people use clearing techniques every time they clean their house as part of the cleaning process; other people only clear when it feels heavy, dull, or depressed.

One way to clear space is to simply activate the *Pyramid Purification* pattern and let it go to work. Here is another, more active method. You can use this to clear rooms, gardens, barns, and outdoor areas. To clear land masses you might want to use the Earth-clearing exercises in Chapter 14. When possible, clear energy after you've already cleaned or de-cluttered the space.

Clearing Space Exercise

1. Ground, center, and establish boundaries.

2. Activate the *Five-Hearts Open* pattern and spend a few minutes flowing energy through your hands and fingers.

3. Disrupt the energetic dust bunnies collecting in the corners of the room along with stagnant thought forms. Do this by walking through the room shaking your hand with loose fingers into the corners of the room and imagine stirring everything up. You can add to this by shaking a rattle or sweeping the room with a feather. Move systematically around the room, pausing and giving more attention to areas that seem dense or sticky.

4. Disperse the energy you have loosened by standing in the center of the room and sweeping the room with the energy projection from your hands. Sweep from top to bottom, turning in a 360-degree circle to cover all the space. If you want, smudge the room by burning sage, sweet grass, resins, or other cleansers. Walk around the room sweeping the cleansing smoke into the corners and all the nooks and crannies.

5. Establish a new harmonic to raise the vibration of energy. Stand in the center of the room with your arms lifted sideways slightly away from your side and open the *Mystic Triangle* activation pattern. Focus on the triangle created between your hands and third eye. Radiate love from your Heart chakra through the triangle.

6. To add sound vibration, ring Tibetan bells, singing bowls, or chimes, or chant "Aum."

7. Seal the cleansing by enclosing the room in the *Spiral Pillar of Light*.

8. Close all the activations except the *Spiral Pillar of Light*.

9. Ground, center, and establish boundaries.

To maintain the clean ambiance open windows for at least a short time every day to promote energy flow.

Creating Sacred Space and Sanctuary

Clearing techniques can also be used to create sacred space for your spiritual practice or a sanctuary for soul renewal. According to *Free Dictionary Online*, "sacred space is any space, tangible or otherwise, that enables those who acknowledge and accept it to feel reverence and connection with the spiritual." *Sanctuary* is defined as both the holiest part of a sacred space and a refuge. More than a physical condition, sacred space and sanctuary are states of mind. Any space can be sacred space and provide sanctuary if we intend it.

Creating sacred space generates an ambiance of upliftment and clears attachments to mundane desires. By keeping space consistently clear of energetic imprints and tuned to higher vibrations, you don't have to start from scratch each time you sit to meditate or worry whether you are energetically safe. Your connection to spirit is palpable and tangible. Sacred space maintains spiritual intention clear of lower-level influences, enhancing your ability to quickly enter deep meditative states and increasing the effectiveness of your practice.

Natural areas with strong Earth energy can energize your field and inspire awe and reverence, such as Niagara Falls and the Earth energy vortexes in Sedona, Arizona. Humans can interact with high energy sites to entrain the energy, magnify it, and use it for ceremony, as described in Chapter 14.

Creating sacred space in your home is a matter of intention. First, it has to be designated for spiritual purposes and not used for anything else; otherwise it will become cluttered with random energy. Your designated space doesn't have to be a full room or even a corner of a room. You can designate a special chair, window seat, or tree to sit under. You can declare a single shelf as an altar. Once declared, however, you must respect the space to keep it clear and build energy. Don't set your laundry on your meditation chair or put your keys on your altar.

Once you have a designated area, bring in any sacred objects you want to use. Bring pictures, candles, crystals, a prayer shawl, or any items that carry uplifting energy for you. Keep it simple and meaningful. Create the space in whatever way you're comfortable. Use the clearing techniques in this chapter or any others you know to raise the energy and then seal it using the *Spiral Pillar of Light*. As you regularly use the space, it will increase in energy and focus, deepening your spiritual practice.

Chapter 14

In Concert With the Living Planet

Living in the modern, technological world has inured many to the powerhouse we live on. All around is access to a source of energy so powerful it can provide for all your needs. This is true physically as the Earth supplies food, water, and the power to generate electricity and to heat your home. It's also true spiritually as the Earth maintains everyone's energy structures and supplies the power to fuel intentions.

As discussed in Chapter 8, the Earth is formed from consciousness. Humans and the life of the planet are interlinked and interdependent; your physical body is made from the substance of Earth, and your energy body is formed from Earth energy. In addition, the Earth's aura modulates frequency input from other dimensions, affecting the evolution of consciousness on the planet.

Learning to connect with the Earth will magnify your goals while enhancing your ability to sense and feel energy and to perceive with higher levels of awareness. Connection provides vital life force and supports good health.

Aligning With Earth Energy

Powering your own goals and abilities is only one aspect of aligning with Earth energy. As people begin to accept their spiritual power and to work with nature to solve the environmental crises of the planet, we will take our place as stewards of the Earth. Throughout time there have been groups of Indigenous people who have maintained this stewardship. The best known are the Tibetan Monks of the Himalayan Mountains and the Kogi, Arhuaco, and Wiwa tribes of the Sierra Nevada Mountains in Columbia, considered the Heart of the World. These people have maintained a continued practice of maintaining harmony on the planet through meditation, holding the space necessary to allow the rest of humanity to learn how to be spiritual beings in physical bodies. Aligning with Earth energy will assist you in preparing for the stewardship that is all of ours.

The best way to explore your connection is to link with nature in love and respect. One powerful way to do this is to activate the *Five-Hearts Open* pattern while using the activation/celebration pattern *Dancing with the Elements*. These two practices can open your feeling/sensing capacities to link to the powerful flows moving through, into, and around the planet. Other ways to connect include establishing your power spot and connecting with Nature Spirits.

Personal Power Spots

Power spots, vortices, or sacred sites refer to the Earth's many energy chakra points as described in Chapter 8. A power spot is a place along an Earth meridian, or ley line, with the capacity to amplify and transform energy. They occur most often where two paths interconnect. In general, they are areas that are believed to possess special access to spiritual energy and therefore promote elevated spiritual experiences.

Although power spots occur along intersections of the ley lines, energy also accumulates in places where Nature is left undisturbed. Waterfalls, mountains, lakes, forest copses, rock ledges, and caves all have special energetic properties. Typically, power spots are associated with areas of striking natural beauty and/or areas of extremes of Nature, as in the Grand Canyon or Victoria Falls.

The idea that different physical locations have special spiritual qualities, or power, is not new, nor is it specific to one belief system. Traditional religions believe in holy sites as do the New Age, Eastern religions, and Indigenous traditions. Power places and holy sites amplify and intensify intention, so whatever is brought—both good and bad—is magnified. Meditating, praying, or performing manifestation in these locations can have a profound impact on the desired result. Consequently, power spots are chosen as the sites of temples, monuments, and places of worship, such as Stonehenge and the Great Pyramid.

Building a structure on a power spot can magnify its influence, especially if geomantic principles and sacred geometry are incorporated as described in Chapter 8. At Stonehenge in Britain, for example, the giant blocks of Sarsen stone are aligned to planetary and celestial events at specific times of the year such as the solstice, augmenting the natural energy of the location with an influx from planetary alignments. The configuration of the stones also incorporates sacred geometry so that the energy is entrained, combining the Earth energy of the location and the celestial energy of the alignment. The result is a sacred site that has tremendous capacity to interact with the creative energy of people to manifest intent.

To create your own sacred site, you will want to identify or choose a power spot. Once you've located your spot, you can enhance its effect by placing sacred objects such as crystals in a geometric pattern. Optimally, you can align the pattern you create with the four directions or the rising sun at the solstices or equinoxes. On the other hand, if you can't get outside or live in the city, you can make a sacred site anywhere, even in a quiet, calm room in your house. You can even interact with the ley lines and draw them toward your power spot to increase its potential. The following exercise is simple, yet very powerful.

Selecting and Creating a Power Spot Exercise

1. Ground, center, and establish your boundaries.
2. Take a walk outside and notice how you feel in different areas. You may already have a favorite spot or be drawn to a particular location for its natural beauty, rock ledges, or arrangement of trees. Circular copses of pine trees are particularly special. You will know when you've found the right place by how you feel. In your power spot you may notice feeling connected, opened, inspired, and full.
3. Ask permission to enter and, if you feel invited, stand or sit in the center of the space. If you did not receive permission, give thanks and, with respect, move to another location.
4. If there is a particular feature, such as a boulder or tree that is the focus of the location, stand or sit there. Activate the *Spiral Pillar of Light* pattern and bring the cone of power down, into, through, and around the entire area, creating a sacred circle of peace, safety, and healing.
5. If you want to, incorporate sacred geometry into the creation of your power spot.
   a. Place the circle inside the triangle. The circle and the triangle are transformative shapes in sacred geometry and can be used separately or together to magnify connection and spiritual continuity. A powerful portal can be created using Joe Crane's geometry of the Gate of Grace. Feel free to use any geometry to which you're drawn.
   b. Using your intuition, place markers around the perimeter of the geometric shape you're using. You can use crystals, stones, poles, or even mounds of dirt to mark the space.

    c. Place large markers in the four directions (or some astronomi-
cal alignment such as the points where the sun rises on the
solstices) and smaller markers in measured increments along
the border, or you can simply place markers at spots that draw
your attention.

    d. Use your inner sense of what feels right to guide you. If it
doesn't feel right, change the arrangement until it does.

6. Use the clearing practices in Chapter 13 to cleanse the area of any
psychic imprints.

7. Invite the Nature Spirits of the location along with your spiritual
guides to be present. Spend several minutes transmitting love. Draw
the ley lines toward your site.

8. Declare your space a sanctuary that transmits peace.

9. Use this place for any spiritual work: to meditate, vision, manifest,
heal, and so forth. It's your sacred space; use it however you feel.

10. When entering and leaving, it's a good idea to seal the boundaries
by activating the *Spiral Pillar of Light*. When re-entering, check
the markers and determine if any need to be shifted. Earth energy
changes with the seasons, sky, and so on; your energy markers will
shift as well.

11. Ground, center, and establish your boundaries as you leave.

It's not always possible to be outside in nature, yet you can still connect
with nature and create a power spot. Chapter 13 provides suggestions for
creating a sanctuary inside your house. You can also create a sanctuary/
power spot inside yourself.

Creating an Inner Garden Exercise

1. Ground, center, and establish boundaries.

2. Take your awareness inside your body and make an intention to
create an inner garden/power spot.

3. Notice which chakra is drawing your attention. Focus on this chakra,
and ask the Nature Spirits and your guides to help you create an
inner garden/power spot.

4. Notice what natural contours are present, then fill the space with
something from each element: plants and flowers, a water feature,
fire, rock and earth, light and airy vistas.

5. Create the garden with several seats: one for you, an over-lighting Nature Spirit, your guide, and any others you would like to invite as part of your council. Arrange them in geometrically significant patterns if you feel you need to. This can be a circle, a triangle, pyramid, star, or other pattern.

6. Dedicate your inner garden to a higher concept.

7. Seal by activating the *Spiral Pillar of Light* pattern. Know that you carry this sacred space within yourself and can access it at any time.

8. Ground, center, and establish boundaries.

Connecting With Nature Spirits

One aspect of developing energy awareness is becoming more alert to the energy beings we share the planet with and how they interact. When they want to communicate, they make their presence known in many different ways. You may smell fragrant flowers when none are around, or feel tingles, rushes, warmth, or a sense of opening and softening. You may see a radiant light in your mind's eye, or suddenly see a face and hear a voice or feel a touch. Some people receive entire messages, either as a complete knowing or a heard message.

Learning to communicate with Nature Spirits is an extension of energy awareness and meditation. It requires an ability to listen to inner messages during your meditations and to couple those messages with bodily sensations that provides authenticity. Although your connection to the Nature Kingdoms will be strongest in a wild, natural setting, access is not limited by space. You are a creature of nature and you carry the connection within. When doing this exercise you can go to your outdoor power spot, a sanctuary you have created in your house, and/or the inner garden you have made in one of your chakras. The key to working with Nature Spirits is to hold them in respect and to trust your instincts.

Connecting With Nature Spirits Exercise

1. Go to your power spot, indoor sanctuary, or inner garden.

2. Ground, center, and establish your boundaries.

3. Activate the *Spiral Pillar of Light* pattern and establish a cone of safety, healing, and connection.

4. Send out thoughts to the Nature Kingdom on a carrier wave of love. Acknowledge that they, not you, are in control of whether they choose to connect.

5. Activate the *Earth and Sky* pattern and feel the power of the Earth flowing up into your body. Feel the power from the sky bringing light. Broadcast your presence gently into the space and give the Nature Spirits time to accept you and become curious.

6. Tell them why you have come, what you want to create, and invite them to join you in co-creative practice.

7. Follow what you feel and be thankful for any guidance you are receiving. You may need to invite the Nature Spirits many times over a long period before you begin to receive direct messages.

8. Pay attention to the animals and insects that join you in your exercise; messages may come symbolically. Does a butterfly keep flying around your head? Is there a pattern in the cloud formations? Do you always see a hawk on the way to or from your meditation spot?

9. When you begin to receive information, ask questions. Present the Nature Spirits with problems and wait for solutions. Be sure to act on the information you are given or explain why you can't. This is an important step in building trust. You should never act on something that feels unethical or wrong to you, and fortunately Nature Spirits will not ask you to do something harmful or wrong. If you receive such a message, question the source and do some clearing exercises. (See Chapter 12.)

10. Invite the Nature Spirits to leave the garden and join your daily energy practice, manifestation, healing, gardening, problem-solving, and so on. Be sure to ask if they need anything from you.

11. Release the connection and give thanks when you are finished. You will sense when they are ready to leave as the vitality of the exchange will start to fade.

12. Ground, center, and establish boundaries.

Powering Your Practice

Using your power spot, internal or external, as sacred space for your meditation practice will dramatically improve your results. You can further your success by connecting to ley lines. These powerful sources of energy can boost your psychic ability and empower your manifestation and healing practice.

Ley lines are the supply pathways of the planet, distributing information and vitality. In the past Shamans or holy men of Indigenous tribes used ley lines for traveling across the planet. Through the energy pathways they were able to access information from faraway places and to send information outward to harmonize the planet. The Tibetan monks and the Kogi, Arhuaco, and Wiwa Mamas (Elders) may still use this practice. Today, ley lines are being used to transmit frequencies for planetary healing.

Connecting With Ley Lines Exercise

1. Ground, center, and establish boundaries.

2. Activate the *Earth and Sky* pattern.

3. Using your breath, feel the energy of the Earth flow up into your body. Send your energy down beneath the surface of the soil.

4. Activate the *Five-Hearts Open* pattern. Feel the chakras of your feet come alive and penetrate the ground.

5. With your breath, send the light from your feet deep into the Earth. Imagine light sifting through the soil, creating a path from you into the Earth. As you descend deeper, feel the denseness of the ground you are descending through.

6. Picture the ley lines as pathways of energy traveling underneath the surface of the Earth. Imagine the energy from your feet weaving through the ground to meet this path. You may be able to go straight down, or you might have to turn to the right or left to find the lines of force. You will know that you've reached them when you suddenly feel "plugged in." You may feel a surge of energy fill your feet, causing them to heat, tingle, and pulse.

7. Send love and light into the ley line and imagine it flowing around the planet, joining all others who are operating in love.

8. Once your feet have found the ley lines, send the fibers of your Base chakra into the ley line, too.

9. Activate the *Celtic Cross* pattern and use it as a protective filter as you invite Earth energy from the ley lines into your body. The *Celtic Cross* will ensure that only high-frequency energy is invited inside your body. With your breath, pull energy up into your feet and into your Base chakra, letting it stream upward through your body.

10. Focus your energy on healing, manifesting, or increasing psychic ability as follows:

a. For healing: Activate the *Winged Disk* pattern and focus the energy from the ley lines into your heart. Allow the energy to cascade down your arms and into your hands.

b. For manifesting: Using the manifestation practice in Chapter 17, focus the energy in your second, third, and fourth chakras, letting it join the rainbow bridge surging into your future reality.

c. For psychic ability: Activate the *Mystic Triangle* pattern and open the triangle in your third eye. To use this to journey, re-mote view, or telepathically communicate, focus your attention on the third-eye triangle as the energy in your feet travels along the ley lines. Send the energy anywhere you want to go. Pay attention to the images you receive in your mind's eye.

11. Close by once again sending love into the Earth through the ley lines, intending it to go where it is needed most. Give thanks and express gratitude.

12. With your breath, pull your energy back into your Base chakra and feet. Close any activation patterns you have been using.

13. Ground, center, and establish boundaries.

Cleansing Earth Energy

Although spending time in nature keeps your energy field charged and clear, locations in the Earth can become a repository of low-level energy, as discussed in Chapter 13. Imprints from past traumatic events can remain behind and impact health throughout the area; plants don't grow well and animals even tend to avoid the site. People who live in such locations become depressed and lose vitality.

The Earth has its own detoxification methods using sunlight, wind, rain, and moonlight to cleanse and clear events. However, some areas, such as the sites of devastating battles or any place where there has been a huge loss of life, carry so much emotional charge they begin to attract low-level energy and can even become a repository for lost spirits. This creates a block in the energy flow of the ley lines, and eventually the ley lines will reroute around the site. Cleansing such areas transforms them and allows the natural cycles to effectively recharge them. After they've been cleansed, the ley lines will return to normal flow.

You can use this exercise to cleanse an ancient battlefield or graveyard, to un-block an Earth chakra, or to cleanse the entire planet. It is powerful to do alone and is exceptional when done in concert with others. Because the blocks in the Earth and the thought forms in the Earth's aura are reflective of human projections, as you cleanse the Earth you can focus on issues for individual people as well.

When working with a group, remember that in meditation you are particularly open. Be sure to protect yourself from taking on any projections or thought forms coming from a member of the group. You can do this by aligning with a high vibration of love or activating the *Celtic Cross* pattern.

Cleansing the Earth Exercise

1. Ground, center, and establish boundaries.

2. Activate the *Pyramid Purification* pattern and imagine the pyramid placed over the area you're cleansing.

3. Activate the *Spiral Pillar of Light* pattern and surround the pyramid with a column of safety, healing, and love.

4. Hold the image of the pyramid over the spot in your mind's eye. If you're working with another person or group, see the variations that follow this exercise.

5. Invite the Nature Spirits to assist in the process and ask if there is anything they would like to add.

6. Visualize all the pain, anger, fear, trapped souls, and trauma stored in the area flowing into the base of the pyramid via the ley lines as well as streaming through the Earth's aura. Imagine the pyramid acting as a vacuum, sucking up all the old imprints.

7. Focus on the violet flame in the center. Energize the flame and feed it with love.

8. Visualize the imprints and emotional debris being consumed by the flame and transformed into rainbow-colored light. Watch the rainbow light flow out the apex of the pyramid as love, filling the Earth's aura.

9. Allow the process to continue until the flow ceases, then close the *Pyramid Purification* pattern.

10. Invite golden light to descend through the *Spiral Pillar of Light* to infuse the area, revitalizing the Earth.

11. Imagine the area reconnecting with the ley lines and reentering the harmonic of the planet.

12. Give thanks to the Nature Spirits and close the activation.

13. Ground, center, and establish boundaries.

Variation 1 (for two people)

1. Sit facing each other in cross-legged position, making a square with the lines of energy projecting straight out from your knees. The four corners of the pyramid are formed where you are each sitting.

2. Imagine a four-sided pyramid rising up from the square you create together. The apex of the pyramid is at the level of the third eye.

3. Activate the *Spiral Pillar of Light* to encircle both of you.

4. Connect with each other through the fibers of your chakra, and build love and acceptance between you.

5. Hold the intention of creating purification for a specific place, issue, person, and situation, and imagine the area or concern in the center of the pyramid.

6. Invite the Nature Spirits to assist in the process and ask if there is anything they would like to add.

7. Visualize all the pain, anger, fear, trapped souls, and trauma stored in the area flowing into the base of the pyramid via the ley lines as well as streaming through the Earth's aura. Imagine the pyramid acting as a vacuum, sucking up all the old imprints.

8. Focus on the violet flame in the center. Energize the flame and feed it with love.

9. Visualize the imprints and emotional debris being consumed by the flame and transformed into rainbow-colored light. Watch the rainbow light flow out the apex of the pyramid as love, filling the Earth's aura.

10. Allow the process to continue until the flow ceases, then close the *Pyramid Purification* pattern.

11. Intend that the energy is released from its negative pattern and is transformed into unconditional love, feel it flow out into the aura of the planet.

12. While cleansing the Earth, feed anything that needs purification to the flame: reputations, relationships, careers, illness. All things are returning to love.

(See *www.thepathofenergy.com* for illustration.)

Variation 2 (for four people)

1. Using the basic idea in Variation 1, create the base of the pyramid as a square created from the placement of four people, each sitting on a corner. The pyramid rises up out of the square to the level of your higher chakras.

2. Help to strengthen the stability of the planet by using this powerful construct to cleanse the Earth of destructive human-based activity.

3. Hold the intention of being of universal service.

4. Invite the Nature Spirits to assist in the process and ask if there is anything they would like to add.

5. Visualize all the pain, anger, fear, trapped souls, and trauma stored in the area flowing into the base of the pyramid via the ley lines as well as streaming through the Earth's aura. Imagine the pyramid acting as a vacuum, sucking up all the old imprints.

6. Focus on the violet flame in the center. Energize the flame and feed it with love.

7. Visualize the imprints and emotional debris being consumed by the flame and transformed into rainbow-colored light. Watch the rainbow light flow out the apex of the pyramid as love, filling the Earth's aura.

8. Allow the process to continue until the flow ceases, then close the *Pyramid Purification* pattern.

9. Acknowledge that we are all responsible for every destructive thought or emotion on the planet. We are all part of the matrix of pain and part of its healing as well.

10. Be open to any changes in the construct that are necessary for the intention being held.

Variation 3 (for larger groups)

1. Create a multi-faced pyramid with a corner for each person.

2. Envision as many sides to the pyramid as there are people who want to participate.

3. Proceed as in Variation 2: Help to strengthen the stability of the planet by using this powerful construct to cleanse the Earth of destructive human-based activity.

4. Hold the intention of being of universal service.

5. Invite the Nature Spirits to assist in the process and ask if there is anything they would like to add.

6. Visualize all the pain, anger, fear, trapped souls, and trauma stored in the area flowing into the base of the pyramid via the ley lines as well as streaming through the Earth's aura. Imagine the pyramid acting as a vacuum, sucking up all the old imprints.

7. Focus on the violet flame in the center. Energize the flame and feed it with love.

8. Visualize the imprints and emotional debris being consumed by the flame and transformed into rainbow-colored light. Watch the rainbow light flow out the apex of the pyramid as love, filling the Earth's aura.

9. Allow the process to continue until the flow ceases, then close the *Pyramid Purification* pattern.

10. Acknowledge that we are all responsible for every destructive thought or emotion on the planet. We are all part of the matrix of pain and part of its healing as well.

11. Be open to any changes in the construct that are necessary for the intention being held.

Chapter 15

FACING CHALLENGE AND CLEARING LIMITATION

The world is experiencing a paradigm shift that is changing the way people think, interact, and identify reality. Old ways of doing things no longer work to solve global problems—problems unlike any we have seen before. Personal and planetary solutions require flexible thinking, freedom from polarized emotions, compassion, open-minded wisdom, and the ability to stay balanced through wild fluctuations. This time offers an unprecedented opportunity for using energy skills.

Difficulty and challenge can be the results of destructive thinking, fear- and ego-based decisions, and conditioned patterns. They are also a road to growth. Unfortunately, embracing the power of positive thinking has sometimes brought judgment and blame to people undergoing difficult times. People with difficulties are judged less spiritual, as if the more spiritual you are, the fewer problems you will have. The truth is that difficulties are not a measure of your spirituality. They're not a punishment or a reward. They are not a reflection of your value or what you offer the world. Whereas they may be the result of negative thinking, on the other hand, they may also be the means you've set up on a spiritual level to achieve a set of objectives that you've chosen to accomplish.

Although your thoughts and attitudes attract and create your life, you don't have absolute power over the outcomes; after all, you are not the ultimate force in the universe. You act in concert with others, physical and non-physical, to co-create reality. You do, however, have one absolute power: You can choose to grow. You can choose to use whatever you're confronted with to make yourself more, rather than let it make you less.

When faced with a challenge, approach it as a call to growth. Find the truth hidden in the situation and ask how you can express that truth. What quality or inner resource do you need to develop? Maybe it's a quality such as courage, perseverance, forgiveness, compassion, unconditional love, or determination. Maybe it's a new ability such as flexible thinking, learning a new skill, or adapting an old skill to new uses. This chapter will help you engage the underlying energetic reality behind the conditions you're facing. If you can shift your energy by developing inner resources and aligning with your spiritual essence, your circumstances are freed to change as well.

Obstacles and Limitations

You were probably conditioned to think that all of your problems are hindrances. Yet limitations and obstacles have the power to stimulate growth. Obstacles are interruptions in the flow of energy from one event to another. Energetically, you're connected to the people and situations around you. The stream of energy that flows through people and events forms ever-changing patterns. Ideally, the energy you feed in is magnified and returned, allowing for growth and development through inspiration and interaction. When it isn't, you encounter limitation.

Sometimes difficulties and limitations are a reflection of karma; the result of past mistakes or opportunities that were passed by. They can be the result of what you've attracted through your attitudes and beliefs. Sometimes they're patterns from childhood conditioning. However, dwelling in the past and over-analyzing past situations won't give you the key to changing the future. Neither will stuffing your emotions into a box.

The point of power is always in the present moment. What you have to learn from the past is embedded in the emotional matrix of what you feel right now. Engaging your feelings in the present and making new choices provides the doorway to changing dynamics. Your emotional patterns provide the information of where growth needs to focus and the energy to fuel change. There's a saying: "What you feel, you can heal." In this case, what you feel, you can shift. Use your emotion to stay connected to your growth edge.

As much as limitation and obstruction can be reflections of thought patterns, they can also be protective adaptations for survival. As a spiritual being, your core self cannot be harmed. No matter what terrible circumstance you endure, your spiritual essence remains intact. However, mental and physical survival requires that you adapt your reactions and ways of thinking to minimize external threat. You may look at your defense structures as mistakes, but they are not; they are life-saving choices.

The problem is that, although each adaptation protects you, at the same time it also takes you farther away from living according to your spiritual essence. The more adaptations you make, the farther away you move from your true self. Adaptations helped you survive, yet they are not who you are. If you define yourself by your adaptations, you will diminish the quality of your life. Rather than fighting them, or endlessly analyzing them to find their meaning, thank them for their service, change the pattern that holds them in place, and connect with your spiritual identity.

An obvious example is that of a person who grew up with an abusive parent. In order to survive, the person adapts his or her behavior and accepts a series of limiting beliefs, such as "the world is not a safe place," "I am worthless," "love is too painful," and so forth. These attitudes and beliefs initially protect the person from an abusive circumstance, but later, when the circumstance no longer exists, these thoughts and beliefs become a liability. Through resonance, they continually attract similar circumstances. The person must re-identify with his or her spiritual core.

When facing an obstacle or limitation, ask "Is this helping me or hindering me?" Once you know which it is, you can move forward. If it's helping you, is it protecting you from yourself or someone else? If it's hindering you, what inner resource do you need to develop to let it go? Just because an adaptation has served you, it doesn't mean you have to keep living it out. It was a choice, and you can choose something else.

Energetically, choosing a new path requires re-anchoring your fibers to a new reality and clearing your energy field of old patterns. Because energy follows your mind, what you believe is reflected in where your energy fibers are anchored. It can be incredibly hard to make changes when you're solidly anchored in the adaptations that became your limitations. For example, if all your fibers are fully attached to the job you are in, it becomes very hard to open your mind to other possibilities. If you want to leave a job, start school, end a relationship, commit to a new project, and so on, changing your energy attachments will make it easier.

Sending light fibers to anchor in the solution is like sending an emissary ahead of you to negotiate on your behalf. Once you detach your energy from limitation by affirming your spiritual essence, new possibilities appear. How this happens won't necessarily be how you imagine.

If limitations are pushing you to develop new resources, look at your situation right now. What inner resource will help you overcome this challenge? Do you need a new skill? Do you need courage? Do you feel defeated at the first obstacle you face and need self-confidence? If there is a quality that will help you through, begin to practice it in daily life. For example, if you need better communication skills to save a relationship, get the help you need to learn how to communicate and then practice by communicating more clearly every time you interact with a person. When it comes to communicating in your relationship, you'll have the skill well developed.

You may rail against your limitations, feeling they keep you from realizing your dreams and being the person you want to be. Remembering that the person you want to be is an expression of a quality, not a circumstance, you can be that person right now. The best way to do this is to align with your new self. Who would you be if you had no limitations? How would you behave? What would be important to you? When you immerse yourself in being your new self, you open the door to becoming. Firmly attach your light fibers into the future and let your future be a magnet drawing you forward.

Consider this: In every religion and spiritual path, there is one prime directive: Love one another. It's so simple that we overlook that it is the point and purpose of being alive. That one sentence reduces everyone's purpose to the same thing: increase love in the world. Growth becomes clearing from within everything that chooses not to love over loving. How is your limitation an expression of a lack of love?

Clearing Limitations Exercise

1. Ground, center, and establish boundaries.
2. Activate *Queen Nefertiti's Headdress*. Stream light through your aura and visualize the release of limiting patterns.
3. Activate the *Chakra Fibers* pattern and explore the energy links you have to your limiting circumstances. Here's how:
   a. Picture one of your limiting situations.
   b. Observe the energy flowing from you to the situation. Is there one fiber flowing to it or more? How thick are they? How much light is in them? What colors? How much energy and what is the quality of energy flowing through? Is it fast, slow, chaotic, focused?
   c. Notice the quantity and quality of energy that flows from the situation back to you.
   d. Ask your spiritual center if this energy exchange represents your path and purpose. You don't need an answer; simply ask the question and notice how you feel.
   e. Bring your attention to your inner core and the flow of energy along your Hara line.
   f. Invite the energy fibers that are attached to your limiting situation to detach and come back into your chakra. Connect them to your core.

g. Thank the limitation/situation/pattern for the growth it has offered and assert that you no longer need it to grow. Its job is done.

4. Imagine yourself as the person you would be without limitation. Invite your energy fibers to explore this image and anchor it. Feel energy flowing to you along your energy fibers firmly linked to your new situation. Be the new you. See the new energy configuration, feel it and send energy through it.

5. Ground, center, and establish your boundaries as you go out into the day, renewed. Make choices through the day that support the flow of energy into your new situation.

Here are two illustrations of what can happen when you shift the energy, or not.

Example 1: Brie

In a past life, Brie had a position of great power and wealth. Losing himself in gluttony and lust, he abandoned his spiritual essence, and caused pain and hardship to many hundreds of people. In this life, his higher self imposed external limitations on his excesses. He was born into a limited financial situation with few opportunities. In essence, he was protecting himself from hurting more people while he learned the art of mental discipline. His circumstances offered protection from his weakness. They also forced him to extend his energy in ways that taught him to use his mind constructively.

As you might expect, Brie spent many years in this life focusing his energy on changing his circumstances. He discovered and used programs of positive thinking to initiate change and tried to hypnotize himself out of his limiting beliefs. However, his idea of life without limitation was one of ease and excess. He visualized himself with yachts, women, and the ability to have whatever he wanted. This was not in alignment with his path and purpose and created inner conflict so that every attempt to change backfired. His energy fibers were anchored in the objects of his ego desires and at odds with his true self.

Transformation came in a flash of intuition. He understood that his vision of an easy life didn't serve him. It didn't create satisfaction. Withdrawing his energy from the endless get-rich-quick schemes, he examined where his joy came from and remembered that as a young child he had loved painting pictures to make other people happy. It could be said his karmic path was the path of beauty.

Brie stopped focusing on eliminating his limitations through positive thinking. In fact, he stopped thinking about his limitations at all and invested his energy in bringing beauty into his neighborhood through a local art initiative. He changed the constellation of his life by developing friendships and activities that brought meaning and joy to him and others. The limitations he lived with no longer defined his identity and lost their importance. Because they were no longer needed to curb his excess, they disappeared and his finances dramatically improved.

The key? He stopped focusing on himself and started being a positive change in the world.

Example 2: John

John had tremendous opportunities in his life and was relatively successful, but he wasn't happy. He felt he worked too hard and wanted "free" money—money that he didn't have to work for. He believed that having money without working would allow him to be free, and having freedom would allow him to give more to the world and be able to bring joy to people. In reality, John could give to the world and bring joy to others regardless of his external circumstances. He could bring joy to people exactly where he was; he could even do it in his work environment while he worked.

John wasn't being truthful. His reason for wanting freedom was to be able to experience his own joy. As long as he felt he didn't deserve joy, he felt guilty for wanting it and was in internal conflict. Because he didn't have a truth to anchor his light fibers to, he couldn't create change. Unfortunately, he still hasn't learned that being in his joy will open his service to the world. They are the same.

Loss and Change

Change, even when positive, is challenging. Withdrawing energy from one point of attachment and refocusing it elsewhere requires flexibility of mind and heart. It takes courage and self-trust to let go of the familiar and link with something new. Successful change happens when your fibers link into your new situation and receive strong flows of energy. As long as you have an energy gain, you will connect more and more strongly.

Traumatic loss is devastating, and grief is one of the hardest emotions to contend with. When you lose someone, your constellation of people is shifted and the flow of energy disrupted. Loss of someone you love, through death, divorce, or otherwise, creates trauma to your energy structures.

Attachments can be violently severed, leaving leaks in your field, and damage to your fibers. Consequently, you may not be able to reattach elsewhere, becoming depleted and depressed, and losing direction.

As difficult as grief is, it does have an energetic function and is a necessary stage in adjusting to loss and change. Grief is a pure emotion. Its ravaging force breaks through defense structures and reveals truth hidden beneath layers of adaptation, convention, and rationalization. It travels along the damaged fibers and the fiery intensity burns away the old. It helps you release past bonds and realign to the future. It's cleansing force helps heal and prepare you to re-attach elsewhere, forming new constellations of energy exchange.

As powerful a cleanser as grief is, it can get stuck. This can happen to you if grief becomes your way of keeping connection to a lost love. In this case, instead of being cleansing, grief becomes limiting. Maybe you stay connected through grief because moving on feels like betrayal, or perhaps you're simply afraid to move forward. Your continued attention on your memories is maintaining an energy bridge to the past. A more fulfilling connection would be to link with this person's spiritual essence in the present whether he or she is alive or has passed over. As harsh as it seems, holding on to grief is a choice, and mental discipline is required to let go. You can adjust the following exercise to reconfigure your energy in any situation. Instead of a person, let go of a situation or belief; then anchor to something new.

Assisting Grief, Clearing Fibers, and Reconfiguring Energy Exercise

1. Choose a time when you're not rushed with other constraints and settle in a quiet, private, and sacred space. Use your power spot if you have one.

2. Create a personal sanctuary by clearing the space. Add a memento of the person you're grieving (a picture, personal object, letters), or simply light a candle to represent the person's spirit.

3. Ground, center, and establish your boundaries.

4. Ask the person to join you in spirit, knowing you are safe and protected at all times. If you feel vulnerable, activate the *Celtic Cross* pattern.

5. Notice the energy attachments that flow to the memory of this person. Feel his or her condition. Does he or she take energy or give you energy? Are the fibers strong, weak, and vibrant, or battered, tattered, and worn?

6. Let yourself feel your grief fully and completely. Don't hold back. Give yourself permission to fully embrace all of your feelings. Don't be afraid of the depth of your feelings; you have time and you will come back.

7. As you grieve, allow the pure fire of the pain to burn through any residual emotions you carry: longing, despair, resentment, envy, or any emotion you still hold on to. Let yourself feel with no judgment. You may be surprised to find many contradictions in the array of feelings you have. Simply allow them all.

8. Speak whatever words you need to say to this person.

9. With love, call your fibers back. Visualize light flowing into them, repairing the tears and staunching the bleed of energy.

10. Affirm your connection to the spiritual essence of this person, and allow your light fibers to link with this essence. You are never truly separated from anyone you love; even when he or she is on the other side of the veil we call life, you are always connected.

11. Send love along this fiber to the spirit of this person. Receive his or her love in return. Feel it enter your body along this fiber. You receive strength and help any time you wish.

12. You are free to connect with new people forming a new energy network. You can still hold this person in spirit without limiting additional connections.

13. Know this: Love is never lost. No love you give or energy you spend is ever lost, regardless of how it appears on the physical level.

14. Say goodbye to the way things were and welcome a new type of connection into your life. Give yourself permission to start the process of re-networking.

15. Ground, center, return to present, and establish your boundaries before ending.

Decision-Making

Decision-making is easy when your choices are aligned to your goals and desires and take into account the resources at hand and the necessary action steps. Decisions are difficult when you focus on what you want and ignore your existing resources, or refuse to look at all aspects of the problem. When you deny the truth of your circumstances as well as the forces that created them, decisions can become overwhelming.

You have everything you need to make the best decision possible. All you have to do is listen to your body. Are you putting off making a decision because you feel resistance? Resistance is your body's reaction to the vibe of the situation. Instead of resisting your resistance, honor it; it's telling you something. Perhaps you don't have all the information you need and more time is necessary. Making a decision without enough information will leave you uncommitted to the outcome and undermine your success. For the best outcome, you need to be 100-percent committed to the action you take. Any residual doubt will act against you. This doesn't mean to do nothing; it means do more to find the answers you need to move forward, fully committed to an outcome.

Sometimes resistance is warning you of opposition that you need to prepare for, or that going forward will damage your integrity and you will lose part of yourself in the decision under way. Sometimes it's alerting you to old programs that you need to change. In all cases, your subconscious is joining you in making an ultimately beneficial choice.

When you feel resistance, for what ever reason, examine your feelings and discern the message before taking action. You'll know when you've received the message by how you feel. Your resistance will dissipate, and you'll have energy and direction. This may lead to an immediate decision or to an action step you need to take first. As you move forward, the path will feel more open, and you'll notice synchronicity and flow.

Maybe you're tormented by a decision you have to make and none of the options are what you want. Sometimes the options you have don't match your identity. You simply can't see yourself in any of the projected outcomes. This may be a call to think outside of the box and find an as yet undiscovered option, or it might be a call to self-examination. Is your self-identity aligned with your higher path and purpose or with your ego? Did you get where you are because of a series of unrealistic decisions based on fulfilling your ego? What do you need to shift internally in order to shift things externally?

Clarifying Decisions Exercise

1. Ground, center, and establish your boundaries.
2. Fully immerse yourself in the situation as it exists right now. Feel all the intricacies, fears, hopes, dramas, motivations for change, safety issues, and everything else that is part of the situation.
3. While immersed in the situation, ask yourself: Does it drain you or excite you? Does it arouse passion, anger, jealousy, or other strong emotions?

4. Activate the *Weaving the Nadis* pattern and allow your energy to smooth.

5. When you feel clear and free of distracting passions, name the options before you, and try the following:

   a. Fully immerse yourself in option A. Imagine yourself making the decision and carrying out each of the steps involved in this path. Does thinking about it give you energy or take it away? Imagine every obstacle you will have to overcome and every benefit you will receive. See your life in five years if you proceed along this path. Does your future give you energy when you see it or take it away?

   b. Do the same with each subsequent option.

   c. Ask yourself which scenario gives you the most energy. Not which is easier, but which one mobilizes your internal energy? That's the one you want to follow. It may take more energy to do it, more hard work and perseverance, yet it gives you back more than you put in. The others may require less of you, yet leave you empty.

6. Examine your feelings. If none of the options gives you a clear energy boost, what gets in the way of you receiving energy? Fear of loss, fear of success, fear of failure? Make the decision to decide and act; you will soon see if you need to adjust your direction or modify your plan.

7. Commit to movement. Sometimes any action is better than none. When faced with either stagnation or making an ill-timed action, act. However, do it with a flexible mind set and be willing to change your direction as needed.

8. If you're not connected to your spiritual essence, activate the *Mystic Triangle* to assist the connection. The decision you need to make might be impacted by your self-importance or poor self-esteem, the result of not honoring your essence.

   a. Stand with your arms spread slightly away from your side, palms forward.

   b. Imagine a triangle forming between your third eye and the palms of your hands.

   c. Re-identify yourself; let go of restriction and receive connection with your true self.

   d. Hold your situation gently in your mind's eye and allow new information, options, or insight to enter your awareness.

9. Ground, center, and establish boundaries as you return to daily awareness.

10. Take a moment to write down whatever you have received and list the action steps you need to take.

Stress: Trauma, Drama, and Addiction

Emergency situations, confrontation, deadlines, and emotional trauma trigger a physiological stress response. Your body is flooded with chemicals that gear you for fight or flight. It can also overwhelm your system and put you into shock. Appropriately responding to crises requires staying present, and being intellectually aware of events, people, and what is needed, while staying in your body, connected to your feelings, impressions, and intuition.

Use the practices in Chapter 10 on a daily basis to prepare you for using them during an emergency or crises. Train yourself to immediately open the *Spiral Pillar of Light* and *Earth and Sky* patterns in any challenge. You don't need to go into a meditation. Simply breathe and vision the pattern; your energy will shift accordingly. Breath is your key to staying connected on all levels. If you can remember to breathe, you will remember to stay grounded and centered. Use this resource when going in to a negotiation, involved in confrontation, or facing a life-endangering emergency.

Do you live in a state of perpetual crisis? Emotions and stress have a key element in common: Both provide energy. As explained in Chapter 9, emotions provide both information and the energy to do something with the information. Stress also creates an energy boost in the form of adrenaline, which raises your blood pressure, activates your muscles, and sharpens your mind. In the short term, this response is life-saving. However, as a long-term reaction it is health-destroying. Addiction to the energy boost from stress and emotion can keep you in turmoil.

People become stress addicts when they need the high adrenaline life to feel alive. Relaxation feels like coming down and, as does any drug addict, stress addicts get edgy, restless and irritable until the next adrenal fix comes along. These people are workaholics, exercise junkies, or worse; they subconsciously create one emergency after another to keep the high going. Eventually, they crash.

One reason for stress addiction is to avoid uncomfortable emotions. It's far easier to keep on running than to stop and discover that you have no joy in life or that your primary relationship has no real connection and is merely a convenience. The second reason is the loss of connection to your spiritual Source—the connection that provides the juice of life. Without it, there is little energy to motivate you. The body seeks sources for energy and finds stress an easy answer.

Emotional addiction is a close cousin to stress addiction. Emotional scenes are generated to provoke reactions that heighten energy. Getting your energy this way quickly turns you into a drama junkie, where ever-more dramatic expressions are needed in order to keep you fueled. Relationships are battlefields with few true connections. People have a hard time trusting you because they don't know when your next explosion and energy grab will happen.

Whether you're addicted to emotional drama, stress, alcohol, or drugs, the problem is essentially the same: You've replaced your spiritual connection as the source of your energy with a substitute. Overcoming this takes mental and emotional discipline. As you re-pattern your energy, you must also be dedicated to changing your actions. Change must always take place on both the energetic and physical levels.

Releasing Addiction Exercise

1. Ground, center, and establish boundaries.

2. Imagine yourself engaged in your addictive behavior. Notice the energy rush you receive. Allow scene after scene to pass your mind's eye. Let as many scenes flow through as come to mind. When you feel yourself having to reach for more, stop.

3. Where in your body do you receive the energy? What part of you feels alive? What do you lose by connecting to life this way?

4. Clear your addictive patterns by activating the *Pyramid Purification* pattern. Visualize all the old patterns being drawn into the pyramid and being transmuted in the violet flame in its center.

5. Activate the *Spiral Pillar of Light* and the *Earth and Sky* pattern and pull energy up into your core from the depths of the Earth and down into your core from your star, your spiritual Source. Breathe through this pattern and send energy through your body.

6. Imagine yourself in one of the situations where you would normally engage in addictive patterns. Instead of creating a drama or emergency, imagine behaving calmly and receiving your energy boost from the *Earth and Sky.*

7. Acknowledge your spiritual connection to your source by activating the *Living Matrix* pattern and affirming your interconnection with the whole. Breathe light through your body. When you feel fully alive and spiritually connected, release the activation.

8. Ground, center, and establish your boundaries.

Transmuting Karma

Karma is called the law of cause and effect. In physics it's said as "Every action has an equal and opposite reaction." In religion it's stated as "As you sow, so shall you reap." As shown with Brie earlier in the chapter, the conditions in your life—where you were born, to what family, and in what situation—are determined by your past karma. Karma is not a cosmic score card of retribution; it's a teaching tool. Once you've learned what you needed to learn, the situation is free to change.

Transmuting karma is done by recognizing your error, changing your behavior, and forgiving yourself and others. When someone harms another, he or she is operating from the illusion that we are separate beings. Forgiveness is the bridge between the illusion of separation and the knowing that we are all one—that one person's pain is everyone's pain. Simple forgiveness is the most powerful way to transmute karma. It recognizes that the people in our life are working in concert with us to provide opportunities for growth.

One of the mistakes people make in using the law of karma is to judge another person by his or her circumstances. Circumstances do not define or reveal a person's soul. The quality of what a person offers—his or her success on his or her spiritual path—is not determined by material conditions. You are not a better person if you've manifested a BMW instead of a Ford, nor are you worth less than someone else who has fewer problems. Many people choose to incarnate in poverty situations, enduring hardship for the sake of a larger plan. Bob Randall, one of the stolen generation of Aborigine children in Australia, is a good example. He used his circumstance to deliver a powerful world message of love and interconnection.

Karma is misused when suffering and cruelty are ignored because the person's situation is regarded as "his or her karma." In ignoring someone's need, you learn a lot about your own lack of compassion and spiritual connection, and nothing about the karma of the other person. To transmute your karma, activate the *Pyramid Purification* pattern and, as your past actions are burned in the violet flame, release love, compassion, and forgiveness into the world.

Chapter 16

Dynamic Relationships

The moment you walk into a room, you're in contact with everyone else who is present. Even as you enter a party and look for someone you know, your energy fibers are exploring, contacting, and assessing. What they find is fed into your body to become part of your gut feelings and intuition. Although you are a self-contained energy system, you are connected to others and in perpetual exchange. The degree of exchange depends on the depth of relationship and connection.

Relationships provide meaning and context to life. Through interacting with others, including humans, animals, and spiritual beings, we know ourselves better and see ourselves more clearly. Much of the information we receive comes from our subconscious energy connection and is illustrated in our language. Metaphors describing emotional relationships also express mirrored energetic interactions. For example, when you are "attached" to someone, you're referring to an emotional bond that also describes your energetic condition: being linked together through energy connections. After an emotional trauma, you might say "he or she broke my heart" or "my heart is bleeding." Although the words reflect your emotional feelings, they also describe the energy impact of trauma; your Heart chakra fibers may well have been torn, and are indeed broken and bleeding (leaking energy). Emotions and energy speak with the same metaphors because emotions are the body's translation of energy reality. Becoming aware of the energy dynamics between yourself and others is fascinating and helps create lasting and loving connections.

Energy Interactions

There are three primary ways people exchange energy. The first is simple resonance; one person raises or lowers another's vibration through the strength of his or her frequency. Being around people who raise your vibration is stimulating, exciting, and healing. Being around people with a lower vibration can be depleting. You can raise your own vibration, or maintain it when around lower vibrations by connecting to higher frequency emotions such as love and joy, or by connecting to the frequency of higher consciousness as discussed in Chapter 20. Some people have incarnated especially for the purpose of holding higher frequency. They are like light houses, sending out a beacon for others.

Energy exchange can also occur as streams that flow from one person to another. Barbara Brennan, author of *Light Emerging: The Journey of Personal Healing*, calls this exchange "bioplasmic streaming."[1] Essentially, any time you put your attention on another person, you're streaming energy to them whether he or she is physically present or far away. This energy can be uplifting for the receiver, as when you think loving and supportive thoughts, or destructive as when you project judgment and criticism. Strongly formed and consciously projected destructive thoughts become projections in another person's field, as discussed in Chapter 12. Even loving thoughts can become hooks in another's field when sent with an agenda such as wanting the other person's love and attention beyond what he or she chooses to give.

The third type of exchange happens through the energy fibers that emerge from the chakras. Links between the chakras are formed by people who have a strong connection to each other. They occur between chakras of the same level; the Heart chakra of one person links with the Heart chakra of another, and so on. How many and which of the chakras are coupled depends on the type of connection. An employer and employee may have only one chakra tie, whereas a parent and child are bonded through all their chakras.

Respect and Boundaries

Relationships that feature equality and good boundaries are ones that can grow and develop. Equality occurs when the needs of both partners are held with equal respect and compassion. Each person's happiness depends on both people getting what they need rather than one person getting what he or she needs at the expense of the other.

Having healthy boundaries is essential to set limits that maintain your well-being and engender respect. When you're strong, grounded, and centered, you're more likely to respect other people's boundaries, making you a safe person to be close to. Contrary to what many think, having a boundary does not inhibit intimacy. Rather, it acts like a semi-permeable membrane; loving connections are welcomed, whereas destructive connections are turned away. Relationships are not about losing your sense of self or individuality, and strong boundaries foster loving, equal, and trustworthy relationships.

Without a strong boundary you may do things that are not part of your core in order to win approval, make more money, be loved, and so forth. This susceptibility reduces your trustworthiness and invites imbalance. On the other hand, an overly developed boundary becomes impermeable and keeps all energy out, limiting interactions and causing isolation. Use the *Spiral Pillar of Light* in your personal interactions and notice how much more present, confident, and kind you become. If you feel you're losing your individuality or autonomy in your relationship with a lover, boss, or family member, revisit the practices in Chapter 10 and reconnect to your core.

Romantic Connections

When two people have a deep, loving union, all their chakras line up and link together. Their energy fields merge and their personal boundaries become more permeable, allowing for greater exchange and fostering trust. As the relationship grows, the couple's energy structures co-join and their internal pathways of energy connect. When two people with strong boundaries and identities have a complete energy link-up they develop a depth of intimacy that has no comparison. It's as though they see through the same eyes and feel with the same nerve endings, sharing personal safety few people experience. Fully formed connections of this nature are rare and quite precious. You may have heard of them referred to as a soul mate, twin flame, or high level relationships.

High-level romantic relationships are not luck or happenstance. They're painstakingly developed, if not in this life, then in a past life. Although the energy connection between two such people happens naturally, it can be deepened using energy awareness exercises and meditation.

Energy-linking exercises can be used between true friends as well as in romantic connections as long as the practice is approached with respect. As you explore your combined energy circuits, you're opening yourself in very deep ways. However, with good boundaries, you don't need to worry that you will lose your individuality, be invaded, invade someone else, or receives someone's "negative energy." The truth is that every time you make a strong connection with someone, you're exchanging energy with him or her. Becoming aware of it doesn't make it more harmful than when you were not aware. Trust that you have good energy filters, and that nothing stays with you that isn't yours and nothing leaves you that belongs with you.

The following three exercises progress in the degree of intimacy involved. The first and second exercises can be comfortably explored with friends. The third is usually most comfortable with a primary partner. Perform the exercise with people you're close to and with whom you enjoy exploring. It may seem like an oxymoron to establish boundaries before merging with another, but with strong boundaries you can choose what to open to and what not to. Also, you may enjoy practicing the techniques in Chapter 17 and Chapter 18 while engaged in linking energy. (Illustration of exercises can be found at *www.thepathofenergy.com*.)

Linking Exercise 1

1. Sit back to back with your partner on the floor in cross-legged position or on two stools. Feel the warmth of your partner spread into you as you lean in to each other.

2. Ground, center, and establish your boundaries.

3. Activate the *Celtic Cross* pattern to filter the energy moving between you.

4. Relax into each other and feel supported even as you are supporting your partner. What else can you let go of?

5. Release tension and melt together.

6. Activate the *Chakra Fibers* pattern and bring your attention into your chakras. Notice the energy flowing through your back between each of your own chakras and your partner's chakras.

7. Breathe in, pulling energy into your chakras. Breathe out, sending energy to your partner.

8. Synchronize your breathing to reflect this in-and-out flow of energy between your chakras.

9. Send love and light, and receive love and light.

10. Notice what you feel, see, and experience.

11. After a few minutes, return your attention to your body. Gradually lean forward, away from your partner. Notice how far apart you are when you stop feeling the energy connection. Can you maintain awareness of the connection even across the room?

12. Ground, center, and establish your boundaries as you close this exercise.

Linking Exercise 2

1. Sit facing your partner in cross-legged position, or in chairs, knees touching.
2. Ground, center, and establish your boundaries.
3. Greet your partner with a bow to honor the divine within.
4. Activate the *Spiral Pillar of Light* pattern or the *Celtic Cross* pattern to maintain a filter.
5. Each of you activate your own *Circle of Life* pattern using the internal energy flow of the pattern like this: Energy builds up your internal center line, spills out your Crown chakra, and flows in a fountain over the top of your head, raining down all around to be collected under your torso and sent back up through your Base chakra along your center line once again.
6. Once you've established the flow, with respect and in the utmost love, invite your energy to flow together.
7. As you and your partner come into sync, be with the energy flowing up the center line of both of you, out the Crown chakra, down around you both, and then back up.
8. As energy flows along this pathway, notice how you feel in your body, what you see in your mind's eye, and what emotions you experience. Share this with your partner.
9. When the energy slows, let it return to individual flow patterns. Notice your energy flowing up your internal center line, out your chakra, forming a fountain over the top of your head, and so on.
10. When each of you feels complete with the exercise, bow to each other and offer thanks.
11. Close the activations.
12. Ground, center, and establish your boundaries as you disconnect. Share your experiences.

Building Intimacy Exercise

1. Sit facing your partner on a mat or on stools with your knees touching, or sit with arms and legs wrapped around each other.
2. Ground, center, and establish your boundaries.
3. To deepen the energy connection if you are on a mat with crossed legs, try sitting inside the circle of your partner's legs as he or she sits inside the circle of your legs. Wrap your arms around each other if not already sitting that way.

4. Press foreheads and honor the divine within.

5. Individually activate the *Circle of Life* pattern using the external pathway of the body. The energy flows up your spine, over the top of your head, and down the center line of the front of your body, circling under your torso and rising up the spine again.

6. Merge your pathways. There are two variations how this happens and the depth of your connection will determine which one is more natural for you.

   a. Invite your energy flows to link. Energy rises along your spine, crosses over to your partner, and flows down his or her front center line, crossing back under you to rise up your spine. At the same time, your partner's energy is rising up his or her spine, crossing over the top of his or her head and flowing down your front center line. A variation of this link is for the energy to flow up the spine of one partner and down the spine of the other partner.

   b. The more intimate variation utilizes the inner pathway of the *Circle of Life* pattern. Invite energy to rise up the center line of one partner, out the Crown chakra, and over the top of the head to the Crown chakra of the second partner. The energy will then flow down the center line of the second person, out the Base chakra, and into the Base chakra of the first person. If the two partners are male and female, the energy usually flows up the female and down the male.

7. Once the circuit is flowing, activate the *Chakra Fibers* pattern and invite the fibers of your chakras to explore your partner's as your partner explores yours. Notice how each of your chakras connects with each of your partner's chakra of the same level. Notice the strength and quality of each connection. Allow anything that needs to change to be adjusted.

8. Observe what you see in your mind's eye, feel in your body, and experience emotionally. Let creative impulse direct the energy.

9. When the energy flow subsides, share your experiences with your partner.

10. Close the activations.

11. Ground, center, and establish boundaries as you disconnect.

All of these exercises can be done at a distance. Time and space are pliable in the realm of energy, and distance is no object. Set an agreed time to do the exercises and imagine your partner sitting across from you as you explore the energy links between you. Write down what you experience and compare notes. You might be surprised that your experiences match.

Consciously connecting with another is not a practice you can do without the other person's permission. If you have feelings for someone that are not returned, you must respect his or her boundaries. If you use your will power and intent to create bonds that are not naturally part of a mutual attraction, your attention will become hooks and projections in the other person's field. In short, you will be engaged in a type of psychic attack, albeit unintentional. Always connect energetically with permission and awareness.

Imbalance in Relationships

Regardless of the type of association, a healthy relationship is character-ized by each person giving and receiving equally. This is true in romantic partnerships, employer-employee relations, and everything in between. A fulfilling connection promotes personal growth for both people. Many rela-tionships, however, are based on unequal input and require rectification.

Losing balance almost always occurs as the result of uneven growth. Sometimes one aspect of a person grows at the expense of another, such as the intellect growing at the expense of the heart, causing difficulties in relating to others. Or sometimes one partner grows when the other doesn't, or one partner grows at the expense of the other. Another imbal-ance is one person unduly influencing the other through domination or passive-aggressive behavior. These types of imbalance can include many of the psychic intrusions described in Chapter 12, such as harmful thought forms, projections, and hooks.

One way to start rebalancing is to shift the energy dynamics of the relationship. This will automatically alter your emotions and perceptions. Once you've initiated a change in energy flow it becomes easier to address problems and find solutions. As with all things, moving the energy is only half the job. Making the necessary adjustments in your lifestyle, work divi-sion, communication, and expressions of respect for each other are the next steps.

Exploring the energy flow along the fibers that are attached to other people is a powerful tool in rebalancing energy. This is extremely effective, especially when done with your partner. However, if your partner is unwilling or unable, you can still work on balancing the energy between you by focusing on your end of the energy exchange.

Fiber-Balancing Exercise

1. Ground, center, and establish your boundaries.
2. If your partner is present, sit facing each other. If you're working at a distance or working alone, imagine your partner sitting across from you.
3. Bow to each other, or to the image of your partner, and acknowledge the divine within.
4. Activate the *Celtic Cross* pattern to filter the energy exchange.
5. Activate the *Chakra Fibers* pattern and visualize the fibers of energy that link the two of you. Look for the chakra(s) with the strongest connection; this often includes the third chakra.
6. Observe the condition of the fibers. First look at yours, then your partner's. Notice your first impressions and feelings, then look at specifics such as how thick the fibers are, how dense, rigid, flexible, or free. How firmly does your fiber attach to your partner? How firmly does your partner's fiber attach to you? Is this comfortable?
7. Observe the energy flow along your fibers. Is it slow or fast? Turbulent, free-flowing, or stagnant? A full stream or mere trickle? Notice how much it supports and feeds your partner. Then notice the same details about your partner's fibers that link with you. Are you both receiving what you need?
8. Assess whether the flow along both fibers is equal.
9. Assess whether or not you want to receive the other person's energy. You can't change the flow of energy the other person is sending; however, you can choose not to receive it or to slow its flow. To do so, imagine placing a valve at the entry point that you can turn on and off, or up and down. If you want, remove the attachment all together. You can change what you receive; what you can't do is take more than is being offered, or seek to change the other person. Stay with this image until the flow is smooth.
10. Decide if the flow of energy to your partner is as you want it. You can increase this flow as long as you don't demand the other person receive it. If you are sending more than you want to send, slow it down. Stay with this until you are sending what you want and the flow is smooth.

11. If you're working with your partner, share your impressions. Try not to force your observations of the other person or be influenced away from your own impressions; just let each person's experience be part of the picture.

12. Focus on unconditional love for yourself and your partner while holding the intention of balance. Observe changes in your fibers and the flow and quality of energy. Continue until the flow has equalized and stabilized in its new state.

13. Take note of what you feel, see, and experience.

14. Bow to your partner, or the image of your partner, and give thanks for the exchange.

15. Close the activations.

16. Ground, center, and establish your boundaries as you end this exercise.

Performing this practice can't ensure that your relationship will become more balanced or even survive long-term. It will make clear what needs to change and allow you to decide whether it's possible to do so or not. If you and your partner decide to do the work to re-establish a solid relationship, doing this exercise on a regular basis can support your intentions.

Co-Dependence

Co-dependence happens when two people are drawn together to complete each other's imbalances. One person in the relationship operates strongly where the other is weak, and vice versa. In the beginning, this is empowering as each partner "borrows" from the other and feels stronger, while at the same time each gives from an area he or she has an excess in. Ultimately, if both people don't develop their weak areas, the relationship becomes draining as each person loses his or her boundaries and the two become energetically enmeshed.

A common, co-dependent imbalance happens to people connected through the first chakra of physical safety and the third chakra of personal power. This imbalance can be part of a parent-child or employer-employee relationship as well as a marriage with traditional male/female roles. In this pattern, one person gives up the development of his or her personal power (third chakra) in exchange for safety (first chakra). The other partner happily provides safety in exchange for feeling powerful. Ultimately, one feels underappreciated, the other feels used, and both feel victimized. In this arrangement, any attempt of one partner to grow happens at the expense of the other.

Another common, co-dependent pattern in love relationships is a second- to fourth-chakra imbalance where one partner provides the sexual energy of the second chakra (usually the male) and the other partner provides the heart-centered energy of the fourth chakra (usually the female). At first, each person feels complete, as his or her empty chakra is filled by the other, but eventually each feels drained. The woman complains that "he is unemotional and unfeeling" and she does all the caring. He complains that "she has no sexual interest" and "it's all up to him." Each is drained by the other person drawing energy, the same exchange that was originally empowering.

Co-dependent relationships are based on avoidance. Not able to face the healing and growth that must take place in order to develop, the person avoids the problem by linking up with someone who can fill the missing element. Although each partner rescues the other, what's missing are equality and healthy boundaries; consequently there is no depth of connection.

If you are in a co-dependent partnership, you can initiate change by developing your entire chakra system. Use the Fiber-Balancing Exercise (page 192) to assess which chakras are linked in dominant or weak patterns. Then use the *Chakra Clarity* meditation to work with each of your chakras, developing your own inner resource and strength.

If you have a true connection with your partner, when you become more independent your partnership will strengthen. Then you can stay with each other and build your relationship out of joy, rather than need. On the other hand, if your partnership was based on need only, as you both grow you may realize that it's time to part. Try to part company with genuine care for the other person, knowing he or she served a purpose for you, as you did in return. It's also possible that you may grow while your partner does not. In this case, the relationship will become harder and harder for you to sustain, and you will have to make a difficult choice of whether to stay and stagnate, or leave.

Enable vs. Support

Another challenging imbalance happens when a partner, friend, business associate, or child is involved in self-destructive behavior that sabotages opportunity and growth. This behavior can be mild, as in being perpetually late for deadlines and thus losing jobs, or devastating, as in drug and alcohol abuse. In a relationship with a self-sabotaging person, it can be hard to know how to be supportive without enabling the destructive behavior.

A self-destructive person can fall into a downward spiral and lose the ability to maintain energy. As things degrade, the person becomes a vortex, drawing in other people and unintentionally ensnaring them. The person then lives off the energy field of those who help, becoming an energy vampire, as discussed in Chapter 12.

Support is growth-oriented. Enabling sustains the continuation of self-destructive behavior, allowing the person to avoid growth. Oftentimes the enabler is co-dependent, obtaining self-importance or purpose from helping. Energetically, the connection can look like hooks from the self-destructive person into the enabler and like projections with waves of streamed energy from the enabler to the self-destructive person. There may be a strong fiber link where the enabler is supplying energy through one or more chakras. Although a complete withdrawal of energy may cause the self-destructive person to spiral, a shift needs to happen or both people will collapse.

If you are an enabler, you may need to practice the protection exercises in Chapter 12, the Fiber-Balancing Exercise (page 192), or the Extracting Energy Fibers Exercise (page 196). Also, professional help may be necessary. This doesn't mean to withdraw your love and support. It means to develop your boundaries, practice protection, and learn to support the person in developing his or her own energy instead of loaning yours.

Growth-oriented support is clean, with no agenda other than love itself. The biggest gift you can give a person is to trust his or her path and support his or her essence. Every judgment and criticism adds weight to the person's problems. Don't imagine that the person doesn't see his or her own failures; he or she does. The best thing you can do is to screen every thought with this question: Does this thought help or hinder this person? If the answer is that it hinders, choose to replace that thought with love.

Betrayal and Endings

Nothing is worse than a relationship ending through betrayal. The grief of loss is compounded by extensive damage to the chakra fibers that were once linked together. The damage is severe because energy fibers are literally ripped and severed, leaving tears in the aura and leaks in the torn appendages. Because these fibers contribute to stability and orientation, the sudden disruption can leave the person disoriented, confused, and disconnected. Physically, the person becomes drained and nutrient-deficient, often provoking underlying physical problems such as muscle spasms, migraines, and even cancer.

Techniques to repair chakra fibers were introduced in Chapter 15 (in the "Overcoming Grief" section) and are further covered in Chapter 19. However, even when using these techniques, damage can take years to heal, depending on how deep the connection was and how much of the person's identity was involved. Without work there will be permanent scars in the energy field and psyche. Damage of this nature needs to receive healing attention on all levels: energy healing, physical support such as nutritional balance and massage, and psychological-spiritual counseling.

One of the reasons overcoming betrayal can be so difficult is that your fibers were never consciously disconnected and some may still be linked to the person who left. Even though the quality of energy now being exchanged may be anger and revenge, it still constitutes a connection. Consciously removing the energy links between you will greatly enhance your healing efforts. This exercise can be used to finalize connection between ex-partners, regardless of how they parted.

Extracting Energy Fibers Exercise

1. Ground, center, and establish boundaries.

2. Activate the *Celtic Cross* pattern, and invite your spirit guides to be present and help.

3. Bow to the image of your partner and recognize his or her inner divinity. Explain that you are releasing his or her energy fibers and retracting your own.

4. Activate the *Chakra Fibers* pattern and focus on your chakras. Where is your attention drawn?

5. Notice the fibers that connect you and your ex-partner. What is the condition of the fibers? What do they look like? How much energy is flowing toward you and away from you? How much hope does this connection have for you?

6. If there's anything you still need to say to your ex-partner, spend a few minutes visualizing your partner and looking into his or her eyes, and then tell him or her what you need to say.

7. Imagine letting go of your ex-partner's fibers, and visualize them being retracted and returned home.

8. Retrieve your fibers, visualizing them being recoiled like a hose being rewound.

9. Pull your fibers into your chakras and coil them into a nest of loving energy. Allow your spirit guides to fill this nest with healing light.

10. Thank your ex-partner, and acknowledge that you are both released and free.

11. If possible, let go of any remaining resentment or anger, forgive, and be free. If not, put these feelings in a container, and ask your guides to hold them for you and help you with them.

12. When you are done, close the activations.

13. Ground, center, and establish your boundaries.

Conflict Resolution

Resolving conflict can be very difficult, especially with the strong polarization going on today. This method works on bringing you and the person with whom you are in conflict into alignment so that you can discuss your issues. It won't solve your problems; it will simply help reduce the charge in the discussion. This is also excellent to use if you are estranged from a person and want to reduce any acrimony. You can use this during conflict resolution mediation, negotiations, divorce settlements, and so forth to clear unnecessary emotional charge.

Conflict Resolution Exercise

1. Ground, center, and establish boundaries.

2. Imagine that the conflict you are in with this person resides as a vibration in your aura. Using your intuition and energy senses, locate where in your aura your part of this conflict resides.

3. Using your intuition and energy senses, scan the other person's aura and locate the area holding the vibration of conflict. If you're not sure, trust your gut instinct.

4. Visualize the area in your aura being joined with the area in the other person's aura via an energy link.

5. Invite the two areas to find resonance with each other. No energy has to be exchanged; this is a balancing due to changes in vibration.

6. When you are finished, disconnect the link.

7. Ground, center, and establish boundaries.

Forgiveness and Relationship Healing

When two people are finished with their relationship, forgiveness is the final act of letting go. It releases anger and the desire for revenge, forces that appear to want closure but actually serve to maintain connection. In a state of forgiveness, the Extracting Energy Fibers Exercise (page 192) is very effective for closure.

On the other hand, when two people have been through difficulty and decide to stay together, forgiveness builds a bridge across the chasm of separation. One of the misconceptions of soul mate or high-level relationships is that they have no problems. In truth, the closeness of these connections provides a depth of safety that allows the couple to work through deep karmic patterns and difficulties. No relationship is free from the need for growth.

Forgiveness and trust are not the same. Trust is built on a solid energetic connection. You can understand why someone has hurt you, can forgive his or her actions, and still not trust that he or she won't hurt you again. Consider a wild animal in a cage: You can understand why it is behaving aggressively and feel compassion for the animal, yet you wouldn't put your hand in the cage without protection. A person becomes untrustworthy when he or she is driven by non-integrated emotions. Staying together may depend on whether or not either or both of you have a real desire to do the emotional work necessary to be trustworthy.

If you and your partner are in conflict and want to stay together, there are two essential energy practices that can help, aside from the Conflict Resolution Exercise (page 197). First, create a sanctuary (as described in Chapter 13). Agree that in your sanctuary you are both safe. Neither will attack the other in word, deed, or attitude. Agree that while in this space you will not discuss your difficulties. You have all the rest of the world in which to talk about your problems; in your sanctuary, just be together in love. Let it be a place where you remember the true feelings that hold you together, not the difficulty that tears you apart. Respect this space and never violate it. If you find you can't maintain a sanctuary or that one of you doesn't want to create it, you may need to re-evaluate if you have the true desire to solve your issues.

Next, reframe the context of the issue. You and your partner need to be on the same side. It sounds contradictory to be on the same side with someone with whom you're in conflict, but both you and your partner want the same thing: a better, stronger, more loving, and fulfilling relationship. Be together in facing the issues that provoke separation. Instead of fighting

< 198 >

with each other over an issue, stand together against the issue. This simple reframing reminds us that if both partners don't win, neither does.

Relationship-Healing Exercise

1. Create or enter your sanctuary.

2. Choose an item that represents the conflict you and your partner are having, or write down all the details of your differences on a piece of paper. Put them in a container such as a basket or bowl.

3. Sit next to each other and place the container across from you.

4. Ground, center, and establish your boundaries.

5. Bow to each other and acknowledge the divine within. Invite your spiritual guides to be present.

6. Start with each person making a statement of affirmation, such as "I believe there is a path we can walk where we both get what we need" or "Our health and happiness are increased when we both get what we need."

7. In a short statement, explain how you feel in the situation of your relationship. Then listen to you partner explain how he or she feels. Don't interrupt each other. Even though you've both said how you've felt before, this time listen without judgment, reactivity, or guilt.

8. Pretend you are the other person. Immerse yourself in the feelings your partner has expressed and, using empathy, be him or her in the situation. Imagine what you would need to get to the other side of the issue. Have your partner do the same.

9. Write down what you felt and understood when you pretended to be your partner, and put it in the container along with your partner.

10. Visualize light filling the container. Allow your energy to stream into the container. Turn the issue over to your highest and best good.

11. When the flow is complete, see/feel what has changed for you.

12. Ground, center, and establish boundaries.

13. Take a break from your issue. Wait a full 24 hours before talking about it on any level. During this time, take control of your thoughts and every time you find yourself thinking about the issue, replace your thought with this affirmation: "I release the situation to the highest and best good for all."

14. When you revisit the discussion, start by sharing how you felt when you walked in the other person's shoes.

Energy awareness can help rebuild a relationship that has broken down from neglect or betrayal. However, repairing a relationship isn't something you can do alone. Both people must want to rebuild; you alone cannot do it for another person.

Using energy awareness in relationships is exceptionally fulfilling. Partners who include this level of engagement delve into the deepest parts of each other and commit to a path of shared intent. However, as with all energy techniques, respect and permission are paramount.

In the midst of the hard work and self-development underway, take time to simply love and honor each other. The following exercise is a wonderful reconnection.

Expanding Love Exercise

1. Sit opposite your partner in chairs or in cross-legged position.

2. Ground, center, and establish boundaries.

3. Active the *Spiral Pillar of Light* pattern creating a circle of safety, healing, and light that surrounds and supports both of you.

4. Place your right hand on your partner's Heart chakra while he or she does the same to you.

5. Cover your partner's right hand with your left hand.

6. Look into each other's eyes.

7. Activate the *Winged Disk* pattern and breathe light into your heart. Feel it expand.

8. Send energy from your heart down your right arm, through your hand, and into your partner's heart.

9. Receive energy from your partner into your heart.

10. Let the energy circulate and grow as your love expands and joy fills your entire being.

11. Honor the divine within each of you. You may find yourselves laughing as you engage each other in this way.

12. When the flow slows and feels complete, close the activations.

13. Ground, center, and establish boundaries.

Chapter 17

CREATING AND MANIFESTING YOUR VISION

There is an inherent contradiction between knowing you create your own reality and doing so in concert with others. Using manifestation skills, the power of positive thinking, and the law of attraction can teach you to mobilize energy; however, you are not acting alone. Creating your circumstances happens through interactions with other people and with more realms than those that you see and feel in the physical. You're engaging other dimensions and perceptions of reality.

Life is a creative process, and your visions are manifesting around you all the time. Manifestation in its most obvious form consists of having an idea, marshalling resources, and making the idea reality. This threefold principle of creation exists in everything, from the couch you're sitting on to the conditions in your life. Using subtle energy principles works the same way. Some people think using energy skills to manifest is somehow manipulating spiritual forces. In fact, spiritual forces are never more present than in the ordinary activities of life. Becoming aware of how you're directing those forces is accepting responsibility as a spiritual being.

Tools of Manifestation

Changing external conditions starts with changing yourself. If you want new conditions, you must be a new person generating new thoughts. Otherwise your creative power is channeled into the same manifestations over and over. Honestly, how many times a day do you catch your mind circling around the same series of thoughts? How many times do you react with the same hurt feelings? Taking charge of how you think is essentially taking charge of your life. Some teachings claim that only 10 percent of a person's thoughts are original; the rest are ideas that circulate through society, directing the creative force. Are the thoughts directing your life your own, or are have they been drummed into you from a parent, significant other, or society?

Awareness and intention are the keys to change. Everything that surrounds you today is the result of a series of choices—yours and other people's. Each choice is the result of attitudes and beliefs. It's a circular situation; what you believe directs the choices you make, and what you choose creates the conditions you live in, which in turn supports your belief. Without awareness, only radical input such as collapse can shift the cycle in a different direction. It requires imagination—the capacity to see beyond what you know.

Awareness is observation: making connections between your inner world and what happens in the outer world. Intention is the ability to hold an inner vision and invest it with energy. Energy comes from the power of your passion and emotional connection to spirit. Your emotions generate the energy you use to engage the world. The intensity of what you feel feeds the intentions that you hold, consciously or unconsciously. When used consciously, you can manifest your highest ideal. When you unconsciously invest thoughts with emotion, your life is driven by unfulfilled ego demands that create little satisfaction.

Random thoughts with no emotional content have very little power to create. The unconscious thoughts that create life conditions are the repeating thoughts with an emotional charge. On the other hand, if your life is scattered, misdirected, and chaotic, you're probably investing emotion into every random thought that crosses your mind. Manifesting something different requires both paying attention to repeating thoughts and removing the emotional charge. Then you can replace the random thoughts with intentional thinking that you purposefully invest with energy.

Awareness is linked to imagination. Intent is linked to the essence of who you are. Used in conjunction, your imagination is fed from your spiritual essence to vision a better world. Connecting with your authentic self allows you to stand with solid, unshakable intent. This is the source of personal power.

There are hundreds of books teaching how to manifest what you want in life. Some teach how to use magnetism, such as *The Law of Attraction* and *The Secret*. Machaelle Small Wright teaches in her book *Behaving as if the God in All Life Matters*, that your intent can work with Nature Spirits and elementals to deconstruct molecules and rearrange the atoms to create what you need on the physical level.[1] This chapter will not spend time re-creating what is taught in other approaches, as these books are readily available. The methods here can be used alone or adapted and used in conjunction with other practices.

The Principle of Three

Traditional manifestation practices teach that three aspects are necessary to bring something from the etheric into the physical: power from your spiritual Source; intent, which connects you to your source; and the image of what you want to create. The following exercise is a slightly expanded version where spiritual connection is activated and shines its light through a threefold intention.

The elements of the intention are: the situation as it exists, the growth/change you need, and the situation you want. This is roughly based on the Reiki manifestation practice. In Reiki, a triangle is drawn on a piece of paper as the intention is formed. In this exercise, the triangle is formed in your body.

The *Mystic Triangle* meditation activates a spiral energy that magnifies intent. It amplifies the power in your Heart chakra, energizing the vision you create. Your intention creates the template of what you want, your body provides the physical and energetic substance to manifest the template, and your spiritual connection opens the portal. It is fast and easy to use.

Threefold Manifestation Exercise

1. Ground, center, and establish boundaries.

2. Activate the *Spiral Pillar of Light* pattern and connect to your personal Star, your doorway to your spiritual Source.

3. Activate the *Earth and Sky* pattern, and breathe the light from your Star into your core, through your body to the Earth, and back again to the sky.

4. Activate the *Mystic Triangle* pattern and stand with your hands pulled slightly away from your side, forming a triangle between your third eye and your two hands.

5. In your third eye, hold the image of what you want to manifest.

6. In one hand, hold the situation as it currently exists; in the other, hold the internal changes/growth, known and unknown, that you need.

7. Let light fill your heart and let your heart feed the triangle. Maintain this flow of energy from your Source, into your heart, and through the triangular intention until the energy flow subsides.

8. Close the activations, and ground, center, and establish boundaries.

Ninefold Principle of Three

You may have noticed that the Threefold Manifestation Exercise (page 203) actually incorporates several sets of three. Building on groups of three is a significant force in sacred geometry as seen in the very powerful Shree Yantra. *Yantra* is a Sanskrit word that means instrument and is used for symbols that incorporate sacred geometry to entrain and move energy. The Shree Yantra consists of nine crisscrossed triangles. It is said to be able to align cosmic energy and has been used for hundreds of years in Buddhism for healing and manifestation practices.

This next manifestation exercise incorporates the power of nine and three by building on the sacred geometry of the triangle. One triangle is based on intention, alignment, and divine timing, which are each based on three aspects, making four triangles. Within those four triangles are embedded all the aspects of the other five, making nine in total.

It isn't necessary to know them, but for your information, here are the other triangulations. The fifth triangle links the past with the present and anchors your intention into the future, drawing you forward. The sixth merges the energy of your heart, with the power of your solar plexus and the creative juice of your second chakra. The seventh is physical energy linked to an etheric template and energized with spirit. The eighth incorporates the human realm with the realm of nature and the angelic realm. The ninth is the threefold aspect of the divine seen as the father, mother, and son (father, son and Holy Ghost). It sounds complicated, but the only three you need to remember are the first set; the rest are incorporated in the process.

Intention

Intention is the vision of what you want to create. It guides your choices, and forms a bridge between what exists in the physical realm as conditions and what exists in your heart and mind in the etheric realm. Your intention creates a force that works through time to pull etheric reality into physical form. Intention is based on it own triad.

First, your intention must be fully formed, yet loosely held. Many people aren't specific enough in naming what they want to form in intention, whereas others are so specific they leave no breathing room. Your intention needs to be a complete vision, yet available for creative interplay and growth. You don't want to curtail future joy by the limits of your current imagination. What if you outgrow your vision before it arrives in the physical? When you hold your intention loosely, it means you link it to your own evolution.

Second, your intention has to generate energy and that means it must engage your emotions. It must be compelling enough to jazz you. If your intention doesn't engage a high level of emotion, it won't be powerful enough to overcome the momentum of your current direction or any opposition that might arise. When you imagine yourself living your intention, it must excite you, thrill you, and satisfy you.

Third, your intention must be believable; it must be consistent with who you are. If you envision an intention that is unbelievable, you will sabotage yourself. This doesn't mean to settle for less; by all means go for as much as you can energetically sustain. But if you can't see yourself there, you will create your intention with a twist that reflects your disbelief. If anything pulls you back, you need to examine it. If it is a limitation, go back to Chapter 15 and release it. If it's a projection of someone else's dream, go back to Chapter 12 and remove it. Then reframe your intention to reflect your own dreams. If it's an ego-based desire, let it go. Align with your highest expression of unconditional love.

Alignment

The alignment triad of the threefold process resonates with your spiritual essence, your path and purpose, and the highest and best good of all. Alignment removes obstacles. Like a combination lock, the gears of your life click together around your intention when this threefold alignment is present. It opens the flow of your creative energy into the life you ultimately desire.

Divine Timing

No matter how perfectly formed your intention is and how well aligned with higher forces, it can only happen through divine timing. This is not a linear progression where one event advances to the next, revealing your manifestation. Rather, it's based on synchronicity, the bringing together of events that manifest your intention. When all the elements of timing align, the threefold principle of manifestation is accomplished. This triad includes completing the past, living fully in the present, and welcoming the future.

In this process, using the *Mystic Triangle* pattern is a tool for helping you be the frequency of your new self. Spend the time you need to create your intention before using this exercise.

Ninefold Manifestation Exercise

1. Stand facing the sun or imagine yourself standing and facing the sun, with arms held slightly away from the sides, palms forward.

2. Ground, center, and establish boundaries.

3. Activate the *Spiral Pillar of Light* pattern and ask your spiritual Source to bless your manifestation.

4. Activate the *Earth and Sky* pattern to energize your body.

5. Invite the Nature Spirits, guides, and angels working for the highest and best good to be present.

6. Imagine three small triangles: one in the third eye, and one in each palm.

7. In the third eye, place your intention. Feel it. Be it. Become the outcome you are wanting.

8. In the left palm, envision the triad of alignment. Vibrate with your path and purpose, perfectly balanced with the highest and best good of all.

9. In the right palm, imagine divine timing and know that everything happens in relation to everything else. Your time is now.

10. Connect the third eye and palms together to make one large triangle that becomes a portal or doorway into the future.

11. See a bridge between your intention and its future manifestation.

12. Send the threefold energy from your second chakra (creativity), third chakra (empowerment), and Heart chakra (unconditional love) as a spiral into the portal.

13. Vibrate with the frequency of your future.

14. When you feel complete, close the activations.

15. Ground, center, and establish your boundaries.

Partner Manifestations

This meditation can be very powerful when working with a partner. Partner work is covered more fully in Chapter 16.

Partner Manifestations Exercise

1. Sit opposite your partner, or, if you are in separate physical locations, imagine yourselves opposite each other. See yourselves as forming the base of a larger triangle with the apex your spiritual Source.

2. Ground, center, and establish boundaries.

3. Activate the *Spiral Pillar of Light* pattern and ask your spiritual Source to bless your manifestation.

4. Activate the *Earth and Sky* pattern to energize your body.

5. Invite the Nature Spirits, guides, and angels working for the highest and best good to be present.

6. Imagine three small triangles in each of your bodies: one in your Third Eyes, and one in each of your palms.

7. Both of you place your intention in your Third Eye. Feel it. Be it. Become the outcome you are wanting. Project your intention to a point that exists in the space between you. Image the fibers from your Third Eye chakra weaving together.

8. In your left palms, envision the triad of alignment. Vibrate with your path and purpose, perfectly balanced with the highest and best good of all. Project alignment to a point in the space between you and hold in place with light from the palms of your hands.

9. In your right palms, imagine Divine Timing and know that everything happens in relation to everything else. Your time is now. Project Divine Timing to a point between you and hold it in place with light from your palms.

10. Connect the points together to make one large triangle, floating in space between you, that is a portal or doorway into the future.

11. Weave your chakra fibers together and send your combined energy of your second chakra (creativity), third chakra (empowerment), and Heart chakra (unconditional love) as a spiral into the portal.

12. See a bridge between your intention and its future manifestation.

13. Vibrate with the frequency of your future.

14. When you feel complete, close the activations.

15. Ground, center, and establish your boundaries.

Manifesting really isn't difficult; you do it all the time without being aware of it. With consciousness, you can usually manifest change in any area of your life. Create the job you want, bring a relationship into your life, express your creativity, and so forth. There is only one caveat: Avoid selfishness. If your attention is on self-gratification alone, you will become bored and indolent. On the other hand, when using these techniques for service and as an expression of love, the possibilities are endless.

Group Intentions

When people join together in manifestation, they create a circle of intention that amplifies the potential exponentially. People have long used prayer circles to promote healing and positive outcomes. Some scientific studies show a positive correlation between prayer and outcome; others show mixed results, possibly indicating that the parameters have not yet been properly isolated.

One of the most innovative group intention projects underway right now is "The Intention Experiment" conducted by Lynne McTaggart, author of several books, including the best-selling book *The Field: The Quest for the Secret Force of the Universe* and *The Intention Experiment*.[2] According to her Website, she is working with leading physicists and psychologists from the University of Arizona, Princeton University, the International Institute of Biophysics, Cambridge University, and the Institute of Noetic Sciences.

McTaggart's experiments in intention are not focused on making money or creating material gain. Rather they focus on personal and planetary healing, including counteracting the effects of pollution and decreasing the prevalence of violence. (To take part in her experiments, visit her Website at *www.theintentionexperiment.com*.)

We can call life itself an experiment in intention as we are all co-creating planetary conditions. Just as you use energy-protection techniques to ensure that you don't pick up other people's projections and thought forms, be sure to use energy protection when participating in group meditation. It's not that anyone would purposefully harm you, but you want to be clear of other people's influence. You never know what pain or hurt another is carrying that might trigger something in you. It's important to clear your energy field before and after group meditations, not only to avoid taking something away, but also to avoid bringing something to the circle that might impact another. Activating the *Queen Nefertiti's Headdress* pattern is one way to clear your field. Using the *Spiral Pillar of Light* pattern will maintain your boundaries and the *Celtic Cross* pattern can act as a filter, cleansing what comes in.

If you are working with or forming a group for intentional manifestation, try using the group *Pyramid Purification* pattern to amplify your effects. The pattern is ideal for working with Earth cleansing, covered in Chapter 14. However, you can adjust the use by changing the intention. Instead of pulling impurities into the base of the pyramid, pull in old thought forms and beliefs, and transform them into your group-held intention. Here's an example of how to do that.

Creating Group Intention Exercise

1. Spend several minutes in a guided meditation to ground and focus the group as a whole.

2. Create the intention and agree on the period of time you will focus on it ahead of time.

3. Ground, center, and establish boundaries.

4. Activate the *Pyramid Purification* pattern and create a side of the pyramid for each person in the group. Imagine each person sitting at a corner.

5. Activate the *Spiral Pillar of Light* pattern and create a circle of safety and healing around the group.

6. Spend time for each person to clear his or her field and establish his or her individual boundary, ensuring that no one picks up someone else's energy projection. You can guide the group in doing this, or, if people are well versed in energy practices, just allowing time will be sufficient.

7. Imagine a violet flame in the center of the pyramid.

8. Place the group intention in the flame.

9. Call in all the old, outmoded thought patterns that created the condition you are changing, and imagine these energy projections being pulled into the base of the flame where they are incinerated.

10. Envision the energy, released from the old, feeding the strength of the violet flame.

11. Empower your new intention with the pure spirit of the flame.

12. Focus the group on clearly seeing, feeling, and being the intention.

13. Imagine light from everyone's chakras feeding the strength of the violet flame.

14. Stay focused for the agreed on period of time. Use a bell timer if necessary.

15. Close the activations.

16. Ground, center, and come back to present time awareness.

Taking Action

The three steps of creation are having an idea (forming an intention), marshalling resources (investing the intention with energy), and taking action. Many people stop short of taking action, thinking they must wait for their vision to appear. Nothing is further than the truth; action and visioning complement each other. Manifesting requires action for the unfolding of timing that brings events together. Without action, it takes more energy and more time for events to coalesce. If you're feeling frustrated in the process, look and see if there's an action step you can take toward your goal. Just because you're moving energy on the etheric level doesn't mean you don't have to work on the physical level. You do. The difference is that the work you do is informed by your vision, and a path is created through the density of the material world toward your goal.

Chapter 18

DEVELOPING YOUR INTUITION AND EXTRASENSORY PERCEPTION

Psychic ability and intuition are natural extensions of energy awareness. Right now, people are experiencing a heightening of their innate abilities due to the shift that is underway, as we'll discuss in Chapter 20. Have you noticed how often you decide to call someone and the phone rings with that person on the line? Or you know what someone is going to say before he or she actually says it? Perhaps you're having visions of future events or maybe receiving messages from people who have died. As odd as these events seem, don't they also feel completely natural?

The terms *extrasensory perception (ESP)*, *intuition*, and *psi phenomena* (from the word *psionic*) are often used interchangeably because all involve knowing information that is not obtained through the five senses or through logical reasoning. Here are some common forms:

- **Telepathy**: the ability to pass information directly from the mind of one person to the mind of another.

- **Clairvoyance**: the ability to see distant events (past, present, and future) through a combination of mental imaging and felt information.

- **Remote viewing**: the direct knowing of distant events (past, present, and future) through mental imaging.

- **Clairaudience**: the ability to hear spirit voices.

- **Precognition**: seeing the future.

- **Mind-matter interaction**: the ability to influence physical matter with intention, including manifestation work and distance healing.

Some of the techniques in this chapter have been used by the military for the purposes of spying. If you're concerned that using these skills could invade another's privacy, that's a good concern to have. Maintaining integrity is essential. Although it is unlikely that you will be able to see anything you aren't supposed to, when working with energy integrity is the key. At the very least, what you put out, you will get back. In all instances, use these skills with the utmost respect.

Mechanisms and Research

How telepathy and other extrasensory phenomena occur may not be as important to you as the effect they have in your life. Yet breakthroughs in scientific understanding are often the forerunner to changes in paradigm. How science reacts to these phenomena helps or hinders people's ability to accept the changes being experienced. If this is old news, you might want to jump straight to the "Psi Methods" section.

Psi research has been going on for decades. However, in the past it has been governed by the axiom "extraordinary claims require extraordinary proof." In other words, psi research has been held to a higher standard of proof than other forms of scientific investigation. Interestingly, the advent of quantum physics is changing the conversation. What was once considered quackery is now in the realm of possibility as quantum mechanics reveals vagaries in how subatomic particles interact that provides a model for paranormal activity.

Energy awareness has provided many people with direct experience of what quantum physics is revealing. The ability to contact another person through telepathy or to influence events with mental imaging is mirrored in the interactions of subatomic particles. The two primary principles involved are non-locality and entanglement, and go well beyond the exchange of subtle energy. They seem to be expressions of what is possible when a bridge is made into the realm of the hologram. If the universe and consciousness are holographic, then within is access to all information at all levels of reality.

Dr. Karl Pribram, a Stanford neurophysiologist, has researched the holographic nature of memory and believes that the brain stores and retrieves information holographically.[1] Essentially, the brain can decode the holographic information you receive in meditation. Deepening your meditation practice will help you contact the information you wish to receive; access to the information occurs through resonance.

Resonance happens when two or more vibrating objects in the same vicinity come into phase with each other. Resonance is happening all the time: Hearts come into sync and beat together, pendulum clocks come into phase and swing together, and plucking the "C" string on a harp will cause all the "C" strings in different octaves to vibrate. When two vibrating objects come into resonance, they increase each other's amplitude, making each other stronger. In the realm of quantum mechanics, resonance transmits instantaneously.

Non-locality means that subatomic particles influence each other through space. Regardless of how far apart they are, the movement of one is instantaneously communicated to and reflected in the other. Michael Talbot, author of *The Holographic Universe*, reports that the experiment that conclusively proved this theory was conducted in 1982 at Paris University by physicist Alain Aspect and his team.[2] Aspect's experiment demonstrated that when subatomic particles affect each other across space, they do so without exchanging any apparent force, or energy. Rather than a transfer of energy, there is a direct transfer of information. In essence, information is passed without a carrier wave to transmit it and exists in both places simultaneously.

Access to specific information may be dependent on a second principle of quantum mechanics: entanglement. Basically, the exchange between subatomic particles is not random. It requires pre-existing connection; the particles must have already "met" each other. Once they have met, they become entangled and are able to transfer information from anywhere to anywhere. Once connected, always connected. There's no limit to the number of particles that can be connected, and an entire group can instantly receive information. In terms of psi phenomena, entanglement may determine what type of information you encounter as you engage your psychic abilities.

Developing Your Skills

Although intuition and psi ability are natural and innate, some people have greater access to using them than others. This may be due to having developed abilities in a past life, or from having fewer preconceptions about psi phenomenon and beliefs as to what is possible or impossible. In any case, the result of expanding awareness is the organic unfolding of your abilities. There's no benefit in forcing this; it happens as your development requires. The exercises in this chapter are only to provide support for what is occurring all on its own.

You can explore your abilities using subtle energy to transfer information, or you can use the principles of the hologram and align internally with the part of yourself that holds the knowledge you want to receive.

Either way, a sound meditation practice is the key to success. Practicing the energy exercises in this book will enhance your ability to move into deeper brain states, taking you to deeper domains of spiritual experience. The deeper you go within, the further your inner vision can travel. If you have trouble with the psi exercises, you may need to practice your meditation skills.

There are several internal qualities that, when present, assist the development of psi skills. A clear mental and emotional field, strong, protective boundaries, focused intent, and an open mind are elements of success.

Clear Emotional Field

Intuition develops out of your energy perceptions, which rely on your body as the antenna, receiver, and transformer. Any charged areas in your energy field will alter both the type of information you resonate with, and therefore receive, and how well you interpret it.

Information may be obtained as direct knowing (called gnosis), mental images, thoughts, or spoken words and body perceptions with emotional feelings. Usually, people receive in a combination of several modes. Natural intuitives are often empathic, called empaths or resonators, which means they feel and know what another person feels and knows. If you have this ability, you may have had a hard time as a child, possibly absorbing all the complex family interactions as your own feelings.

In order to get a clear read from your psychic insight, keep your energy field clear and grounded. Using the *Spiral Pillar of Light* and *Queen Nefertiti's Headdress* patterns will help you clear vibrations in your field. (Exercises in Chapter 13 offer more in-depth direction.)

Strong Boundaries and Protection

There are three key areas where strong boundaries are essential. Information exists on all levels. Low-level information is confusing, contradictory, and potentially harmful. Additionally, your own biases and projections can be reflected back to you, causing fear and/or delusions. When receiving psychic information, you can become inundated and overwhelmed with information, impressions, and emotions, especially if you're empathic. You can also become so enamored of and self-impressed with what you're receiving that you lose perspective and fall short in everyday responsibilities.

Strong, healthy boundaries help avoid inundation. Boundaries help you determine whether what you're sensing is true psychic information or your own projections. Adding elements of protection ensures that you avoid receiving thought forms, projections, or hooks from others as you open to receive information. The basis of protection is to stay in alignment with higher ideals, which means you have the added benefit of staying connected to high-level information. Higher ideals include aligning with unconditional love, compassion, and acceptance. Whether or not you become self-impressed is a choice. It helps when you honor the divine within all.

Once it is second nature to hold your boundaries and stay in alignment with higher ideals, additional protection won't be necessary. In the meantime, the *Celtic Cross* pattern provides excellent protection and is also a filter to allow higher information in, while shielding you from lower impulses. If you're concerned about protection, revisit the exercises in Chapter 12.

Intention and Mindset

Your intention is the road map for your experience. It guides the direction you take and determines what you resonate with. Your intention and the motivations behind it establish the level of connection and information you attract. Whatever your intention, always add the Reiki axiom "this for the highest and best good of all." Doing this will keep you aligned to higher levels of information.

Being open to other possibilities is essential to reduce resistance and to open to your inner knowing. Other qualities that reduce resistance are being unbiased, neutral, and non-judgmental toward the information you obtain. The moment you start judging what you're receiving, you inhibit the flow. This doesn't mean to accept everything you pick up as truth; it means to wait and examine it with discernment once you've finished.

Resonance to different information is achieved through your emotions. A strong connection to the person with whom you're attempting to connect or the information you want increases your success. Although you need to stay unbiased and neutral, emotions create energy links between people, as seen in Chapter 16. Use this to your advantage by building a strong feeling of love to fuel the strength of connection for a positive result. Resonate with the result you're seeking by matching your frequency to your target.

Psi Methods

Most people have three main reasons for wanting to develop their abilities: to connect more deeply with other people, to better understand events and the forces engaged in specific events, and to receive guidance for self, others, and/or the world. Although there are many types of psi practices, the following exercises explore visioning, telepathy, remote viewing/sensing, lucid dreaming, astral projection, and receiving a direct transmission.

Visioning and Journeying

Visioning is the practice of using deep meditative trance states for mental journeying into other realms. It's different from remote viewing, which seeks to mentally view an established target (location or object), and is different from astral projection, which seeks to project consciousness outside of the body. Visioning is an inner experience. It opens your inner eye to inner realms. You may be watching what is happening as an observer, or navigating the terrain as though you were present. Visioning is easy and very safe.

In this practice, energize your third eye and open a portal to other realms, observing what unfolds. You can activate the *Celtic Cross* pattern and use it as a vehicle and for protection. It's essential to set an intention for your journey before you start. It can be as simple as "What is the best way forward for me at this time?" or asking to meet your power animal or guide. You can also have a more complex intention, asking for insight into spiritual reality, asking to be shown information about the past or future, or asking for inspiration with a problem. The more you trust yourself and this process, the more complex your intention can become.

Visioning Exercise

1. Ground, center, and establish boundaries.

2. Active the *Spiral Pillar of Light* pattern to create a circle of safety and healing.

3. Activate the *Mystic Triangle* pattern and focus your attention on your Third Eye.

4. State your intention and invite your awareness to move further inward.

5. Imagine yourself moving into a dense mist. See and feel yourself surrounded by the white, swirling fog. If you feel moved to, activate the *Celtic Cross* pattern and intend it to be your vehicle for this journey. When you are inside, you are completely protected.

6. Move through the fog toward a source of light. As you move forward, feel yourself going deeper and deeper inside yourself.

7. Come out of the other side of the fog.

8. With no expectation, observe what you see, feel, hear, smell, and know.

9. Explore the terrain and interact with the beings, animals, and people you meet. Ask questions. Try not to analyze, direct, or dismiss the answers or any interaction you have.

10. Take any gifts you're given with thanks and gratitude. Sit in the light, and absorb healing and insight.

11. Stay for as long as there is energy, then give thanks and move back into the mist.

12. Emerge from the mist sitting in your meditation spot.

13. Close the activations.

14. Ground, center, and establish boundaries.

Telepathy: Person-to-Person Interaction

Dean Radin, author of *Entangled Minds: Extrasensory Experiences in a Quantum Reality*, defines telepathy as "feeling at a distance" the transfer of thoughts, feelings, or images directly from one person's mind to another's.[3] In general, it's easier to send and receive emotions than it is thoughts. Emotions are the most direct experience people have with non-local communication. When someone loves you, for example, you can feel the force of his or her emotion from across the room or across the country. Picking up the energy of emotions is familiar to everyone. We all have considerable practice feeling the emotional space in both personal and professional environments.

When practicing telepathy, two processes will make it more effective. First, link the thought you want to send with both an image and a strong emotion. Second, make an energy link with the person you're connecting with before you send the communication. As with any skill, practice makes perfect. Practicing with a friend or group of friends on a regular basis will dramatically improve your ability. When working with groups of people, remember to keep energy filters in place so that you don't inadvertently take on someone's thought forms or projections. The *Celtic Cross* pattern is an excellent filter for this type of work.

The more focused your mind is when you practice, the more your abilities will improve. However, try to avoid using willpower to send your message. The force of will can be perceived by the other person's body as aggression and cause him or her to subconsciously block your connection. It's best to connect with love and send your information along the energy between you.

You can perform this exercise with others in the same room or set it up so that everyone tunes in and meditates together at the same time from different locations. You can also try to simply send a message on and off throughout the day, then check in with each other in the evening to see if and when it was picked up. It's easiest to start by sending simple things like a basic shape in a primary color, or a basic playing card. Using energy activations to focus your intent creates a safe connection and augments your practice. Start any music or entrainment tools before you begin.

Developing Telepathy Exercise

1. Decide who is sending and who is receiving.

2. Ground, center, and establish your boundaries.

3. Establish any additional protection you may want, such as the *Celtic Cross* pattern.

4. Open the *Mystic Triangle* pattern and activate a triangle in your Third Eye.

5. Imagine a bridge of light flowing from your Third Eye to that of your partner's. Feel the emotion of your connection.

6. If you're sending, build the image/thought in your mind's eye and invest it with as much emotion as you can generate. If you're receiving, allow the bridge of light to join with your Third Eye and open to receive the image/message. Pay attention to what you see, feel and hear. Look for shapes, colors, and impressions.

7. When the communication feels ready, imagine it flying along the energy bridge you created. Say the message out loud, and imagine the sound traveling with the image along the bridge.

8. When the message reaches the triangle in the other person's Third Eye, imagine it waiting patiently outside to be received.

9. Try not to force any part of this. Simply focus your mind, feel the connection, and let the image be shared as part of the connection you feel.

10. When you feel the natural link begin to dissipate, let the bridge dissolve and write down what you experienced.

11. Close the activations.

12. Ground, center, and establish your boundaries.

Holographic Method

1. Decide who is sending and who is receiving.

2. Ground, center, and establish your boundaries.

3. Establish any additional protection you may want, such as the *Celtic Cross* pattern.

4. Open the *Mystic Triangle* pattern and activate a larger triangle inscribed around you. Sit inside the triangle and open a portal to the person with whom you wish to communicate.

5. Deepen your meditation and move into the nothing behind your eyes, allowing yourself to relax even more fully.

6. Be with your partner. Feel, smell, and hear him or her. Feel the frequency he or she emanates and match your frequency to his or hers.

7. Focus on the message you wish to send, or open to the message you're receiving.

8. Notice what you see, feel, hear, and sense.

9. Do not force any part of this. Simply allow the sending or receiving of a message.

10. When you feel the natural link begin to dissipate, bring your self back into daily awareness.

11. Close activations.

12. Ground, center, and establish your boundaries as you disconnect

This exercise can be done with three people as well. Follow the steps and, when you activate the *Mystic Triangle*, allow one person to sit in each corner. Come into resonance with each other. You might be surprised to find that you can have an entire conversation with the other two people that you will be able to verify.

Remote Viewing/Sensing

In its original form, remote viewing (RV) was developed at Stanford Research Institute and used in Central Intelligence Agency (CIA) programs. According to a recent article on the Military Remote Viewing Website titled "CIA-Initiated Remote Viewing at Stanford Research Institute" by H. E. Puthoff, the CIA was involved for 20 years in researching and developing RV techniques. What they developed was employed in intelligence gathering. The documents on how and why they used psi techniques were declassified and approved for release in 1995.[4]

The RV technique extends your awareness to touch other places and times on a screen in your mind's eye. You can watch events unfold, ask questions, and receive insight into intentions and motivations. It's often considered a form of clairvoyance; however, there are differences. Clairvoyants receive vivid and clear pictures that are married to sensations that provide additional information. Remote Viewing techniques consider vivid pictures to be the product of the imagination, representing an alpha brainwave level of awareness.

An RV experimenter seeks to use a delta or theta brainwave and looks for impressions, shapes, textures, smells, and other non-distinct pieces of information that together reveal a target. The point isn't to interpret information; it's to gather it. This technique is used with a blind control. The person looking at the target doesn't know ahead of time what he or she is viewing. He or she is simply given the target coordinates and asked to connect.

This technique is useful for developing confidence because you have direct and immediate feedback that allows you to hone your skills. If you're having difficulty with visioning or telepathy, employing RV will help you develop skill and confidence. (To try an easy blind RV training exercise, go to the Greater Reality Website at *www.greaterreality.com/rv/instruct.htm*.)

The following Remote Viewing/Sensing exercise is not a traditional RV format. It incorporates emotional and sensory information with mental images. It's also not a blind experiment. Pick a place and time you would like to see, or a piece of information you would like to understand better. The information you receive usually arrives very quickly and you won't need to spend more than a few minutes observing. Take the first images you receive, no matter how nonsensical they seem.

Remote Viewing/Sensing Exercise

1. Ground, center, and establish boundaries.
2. Activate the *Spiral Pillar of Light* pattern and incorporate additional protection as desired.
3. Sit in a relaxed, comfortable, warm place where you won't be disturbed.
4. Activate the *Mystic Triangle* pattern and open a triangle in your third eye.
5. Visualize another triangle around the place and time you want to see. Imagine that you sit in one corner of the triangle and that the other two corners are held by time and location. If you're working in a group, other people can sit in the other two corners.

6. Send your energy from your mind's eye through the portal to the target, building an energy bridge.

7. Keeping your mind relaxed and alert, pay attention to the images you receive. Notice shapes, colors, relationships. Pay attention to any sensations, emotions, or feelings you encounter. If you see people or scenery, look at the details: What types of buttons are on the coat? What are the shoes like? Look at the trees, the grass, the furniture. Try to obtain as much small detail as possible.

8. Ask questions and observe how the scene changes to reflect the new input.

9. As soon as the information starts to fade or feel stale, stop and write down everything. You may be able to move in and out of receiving and writing to refresh details.

10. When you are finished, close the activations, ground, center, and establish boundaries.

Direct Guidance

Some people are developing psi abilities in order to engage, receive, and hold higher frequency for the world. (It's such an important subject that receiving higher frequency is the focus of Chapter 20.) Many people want to channel higher beings, archangels, or aliens. Naturally you want to avoid dialing in a lower-level entity that doesn't have anything useful to offer. The Akashic Record is the name given to the hologram of Universal Consciousness from which you can channel direct guidance. The method is the same as for Remote Viewing/Sensing, only instead of connecting with a time and place, connect with your highest level of guidance or the Akashic Record hologram.

Direct Guidance Exercise

1. Ground, center, and establish boundaries.

2. Open the *Spiral Pillar of Light* pattern and invite the guides and guardians of the highest order to be present.

3. Activate the *Mystic Triangle* pattern and open a triangle in your third eye.

4. Imagine you're sitting in a triangle that is a portal to higher consciousness.

5. Vibrate with the frequency of the highest love and resonate with higher consciousness. Allow a flow of energy; imagine yourself growing in light as you connect with the highest love.

6. Ask for the guidance you seek for yourself, another person, or humanity at large.

7. As information flows, ask questions. Stay engaged as long as there is an energy flow of light.

8. When you're finished, close the activations, ground, center, and establish your boundaries.

Lucid Dreaming

Lucid dreams are dreams in which you are aware that you're dreaming. These are very powerful states of mind and used by Shamans to travel into other realms. Anything is possible in a dream; you can go anywhere, do anything, and have access to any truth. Dreams happen in delta brain states. (A delta brain state is a deep and highly connected state.)

Tibetan monks consciously dream, calling it Dream Yoga, which is a specific path of enlightenment. Awake or asleep, you can create your reality. Learning how to shape the elements of a dream can help you learn how to shape the elements in your life. Theosophists believe we travel in our dreams to meet with guides, to help souls cross over, and to attend etheric universities. Using lucid dreaming, you can meet with higher-dimensional beings, receive healing, and learn new skills and techniques.

Lucid dreams often happen spontaneously. You can be in the middle of a dream and suddenly become aware that you're dreaming. Typically when this happens, it's so surprising that people immediately wake up. The trick is to both induce the experience and then maintain it.

The first step to maintaining awareness in dreams is to improve your dream recall. Keep a journal near your bed and note your dreams. Write down whatever details you can remember right away; more details will often emerge as you write. A secondary benefit of doing this is that it increases your awareness of the average dream state, which will help alert you to a lucid dream.

Your subconscious mind also alerts you in a lucid dream that you are dreaming, giving you a chance to take control of the experience. It does this by having something odd occur so that you suddenly realize that you're dreaming. Flying is the most common cue. The next time you fly in a dream, wake up and continue your dream with awareness. To program yourself to lucid dream, simply place the intention as you go to sleep. Intend to immediately take control of the dream as soon as you are alerted to it being a dream. Using this practice every night can help you induce the experience.

Lucid Dream Programming Exercise

1. Every night, go to bed and activate the *Spiral Pillar of Light* pattern. Intend that it stay active and protective through the night.

2. Go to sleep with a threefold intention:

   a. Program yourself to wake up in your dream. As you create the intention, imagine it happening. See a cue and imagine yourself waking up.

   b. Program yourself to perform an action that will alert you to the fact that you have control. In his book *Don Juan: A Yaqui Way of Knowledge*, Carlos Castaneda suggests programming yourself to immediately look at your hands as soon as you realize that you're dreaming.[5] You will be surprised how hard this is to accomplish, but when you can do it, you can become conscious in your dreams.

   c. Program yourself to wake up when the dream is over. If you wake up in the night, immediately write down what you remember even if you don't think you had a lucid dream. Theosophists say we have regular lucid dreams but simply don't remember. Writing may jog your memory.

3. Use the time between waking and sleeping to support your program. This state is called the hypnogogic state and is in the realm of theta and delta brainwaves. This is a powerful time for visioning and will support maintaining your intention.

   a. As you are falling asleep, imagine yourself having a lucid dream. See yourself in a dream; feel the wind, sun, or other elements. Smell where you are. Engage all of your senses. This trains you to pay attention to when you wake up dreaming.

   b. Use recurring dreams as a focus for creating a lucid dream. As you go to sleep, re-write your recurring dream. Remember the dream in detail, and then at key points change the outcome in your imagination. This will not only help you take control of a frightening situation, it also programs your to wake up and become conscious when you have this dream.

4. Write down your dreams first thing in the morning before you engage in any activity, even using the bathroom. If you have to get up, jot down keywords to help you remember when you sit back down.

5. Once you begin to lucid dream, add to your program the intention you want in your dream. Do you want to meet with masters or learn about a past life? Your dreams can take you anywhere you intend to go.

6. Start your day by grounding, centering, and establishing boundaries.

Practicing Discernment

Whatever method you use, it takes time and practice to get consistent, clear, and useful results. Trust your first hit; it's usually less contaminated by your inner critic and judge. Once you start doubting yourself, your mind in-fills with what it thinks should be happening, and your results will more likely reflect your own bias. Always test your results and fine-tune your approach.

As you start receiving intuitive information, never assume you know what's right for another person. Your hit might not be what he or she needs in the moment. The other person is working on his or her own growth, and your insight may or may not be helpful. As no one else knows what is right for you, the only person who knows what's right for another person is himself or herself.

Chapter 19

HEALING: RECONNECT AND REPAIR

Your body is a self-healing organism, programmed with all the physiological and energetic mechanisms needed to maintain and restore health. Healing work is supporting what your body does naturally. When healing is obstructed, there are three primary causes: There may be a path and purpose beyond what you can readily see, you don't have the necessary ingredients (nutrients, sunlight, and so on), and/or something is getting in the way of your natural processes. Obstructions can be toxins interrupting cell function, DNA mutation, stored emotional trauma, or any number of physical or energetic causes.

Oftentimes, as discussed in Chapter 9, physical signs and symptoms are a communication from the bodymind that some aspect of your life is out of balance. This discussion can be a minefield, as it's easy to oversimplify a complex matter or to blame a person for being ill. Your illness might have a simple message, such as you need better food and more exercise, yet underneath have a more complex message, such as needing to value yourself, develop confidence, or believe in your path. Sometimes an illness can be as simple as needing to take a rest. Rather than approaching health challenges as a battle, try to be open to what you can learn. Your illness or injury may not have happened "in order to teach you something"; however, everything is an opportunity to grow.

Your body, from an energy perspective, is organized and maintained by a template that is part of your aura. When the connection between your template and your body is disrupted, the conditions for illness have been created. Your body no longer has appropriate instruction, similar to a cell receiving unhealthy information from mutated DNA. Ultimately, healing requires both a physical and energetic response. Be sure to receive the medical help you need, and at the same time you can use the practices here to connect and energize your energy template, optimizing conditions for healing.

Any time you use healing techniques on other people, be sure you have permission. As much as you may want to help someone else, it's arrogant to think you know what someone else needs.

Is There Science in Energy Healing?

Although having an energy template is a standard and ancient metaphysical concept, you may wonder if there is any scientific interest or support for this idea. Certainly, there has been scientific study into the power of prayer in assisting healing, and the use of visualization is now standard in the care of cancer patients. The idea of an energy field as the organizing principle for life was hypothesized in the 1950s by Dr. Harold Saxton Burr, a Yale University professor of anatomy.

Burr was studying cell differentiation in the developing embryo and looking at the long-standing question: If all cells have the same DNA blueprint, what activates the DNA in one cell to become a toe and another to become an eye? Through his research with the electric potential of salamander embryos, Burr determined that cellular development was activated and organized in accordance with a biological electromagnetic field, which he called the L-field, or life-field.[1]

Burr's theory was put to the test by Dr. Robert Becker, who was able to initiate limb regeneration in frogs and other animals. In his book *The Body Electric*, Dr. Becker describes the conditions created in the body for the healing of wounds. Basically, many physical functions are built on the use of electrical action potentials. Action potentials are generated across cell membranes via positively and negatively charged ions, and initiate muscle contraction, nerve conduction, and many other body functions. Becker found that injury disrupts ionic flow, creating a positively charged field around the wound. The first response of the body to initiate healing is to flood the area with a negative charge. Only in a negatively charged field does healing begin, and if a positive charge is artificially created during the healing process, healing stops.[2]

The need for a negative field in healing is one of the bases for magnetic products used in orthopedics to help relieve pain and heal bones and joints. It also may explain the healing properties of power spots on the planet, as natural areas have more negatively charged ions, especially where there is moving water. Becker also measured the magnetic field at different body sites and found that the hands carry a greater charge of negative ions than other parts of the body. The natural instinct to hold an area that has been hurt seems to be a healing response.

Technology to see energy fields was possible to a limited extent with the advent of a Russian technique called Kirlian photography. In 1939, Semyon Kirlian discovered that objects on a photographic plate created a coronal discharge, or aura, when subjected to an electric current. The discharge was seen as radiance around the object. The differences between an object and a living form were clearly detectible by the degree and complexity of light emission. The technology has been refined and advanced, and is now used to visualize the human aura on both photographic film and live video.

Kirlian photography reveals an important feature of the aura. In a study called "The Phantom Leaf Experiment," Kirlian photographs taken of a leaf showed a radiant light around and suffusing it. The leaf was then torn in half and re-photographed. If, as conventional science claimed, the corona was a discharge from the physical leaf, the aura of the re-photographed leaf should follow the physical contour of the torn leaf. It did. But it also continued to radiate, with lesser brilliance, revealing the shape of the entire leaf before being torn. This unexpected result revealed that damage to the physical body, through injury or illness, does not change the structure of the aura, only its radiance. The aura itself and the information it contains remains intact.[3]

In the past two decades, studies have blossomed, and many doctors and scientists have risked their reputations promoting energy medicine, such as former NASA astrophysicist Barbara Brennan, author of *Hands of Light: Guide to Healing Through the Human Energy Field* and *Light Emerging: The Journey of Personal Healing*, and medical doctor Donna Eden, author of *Energy Medicine: Balancing Your Body's Energies for Optimal Health, Joy, and Vitality*.[4] If you're interested in the science behind energy healing, more recent studies can be found in James Oschman's book, *Energy Medicine: The Scientific Basis*.[5]

Conditions for Healing

The construct presented thus far is that the templates for health that are in the aura transmit information into the body through the chakras then distribute it along the meridians to each cell. Obstruction in this system inhibits the body's healing processes.

The Institute of Resonance Therapy (IRT), in Cappenberg, Germany, identified three essential components for healing. Using energy to restore damaged ecosystems in the 1990s, they established guiding principles when they discovered that the healing of an ecosystem (or body) has three requirements: information on what to do, enough energy to be able to enact the information (vitality), and flow.[6] Establishing these three conditions creates an optimal healing environment.

Information

Energetically, the information needed to heal is stored in two specific layers of the aura. The first layer holds the template for organizing your physical body and is directly related to your genetic and karmic programs. Just as your genes represent your ancestral past and affect the conditions of your physical body, your karmic past is reflected in your physical body as well. You can see this in the way your past actions are stored in your energy field as charged areas that attract your conditions.

Past-life karma is programmed into your template as well. Research into children's memories of past lives conducted by Dr. Ian Stevenson, who was the head of the department of psychiatry at the University of Virginia, demonstrates this connection. The children Dr. Stevenson researched had memories of their death in previous lives, and birth marks, deformities, and health issues in this life seemed to correlate to the wounds they claimed killed them in the past.[7]

The fifth layer of the aura maintains the template for the ideal, or perfected human body. It can be used to adjust the first layer to a higher level of function. Connecting the information between the first and fifth layers of the aura optimizes the conditions for your body to heal. However, it doesn't replace medical care.

The most miraculous healing effects are the result of an influx of divine energy, often described as light. Quantum physicist David Bohm stated in an interview with Renee Weber that light "is energy and it's also information-content, form and structure. It's the potential of everything."[8] Another way of saying this is that light is the building block of matter. Encoded on light is information that interacts with the wisdom contained in the body to promote healing.

Vitality

Vitality is the amount of energy available for living and is determined by physical, energetic, and spiritual conditions. Your level of vitality determines how fully your body can respond to the need to heal. Without vitality there is no force to initiate healing processes.

Physically, vitality depends on having the necessary nutrients to build a healthy body, as well as clean air, sunlight, water, and exercise. Vitality in a healthy person can be drained by mental and emotional worry, physical exhaustion, and energy attachments. (See Chapter 12.) Spiritually, vitality is renewed through your connection to Source, and the amount of spiritual energy you channel through your body is the most important condition for health.

Flow

Physical, mental, emotional, and spiritual health is a result of flow—the flow of energy and blood to each cell, the flow of nerve supply to tissue, the flow of emotion and energy between people, the flow to and from one's spiritual source. Isolation causes disease: Cells isolated from blood flow die; tissues isolated from nerve supply atrophy; isolation from the flow of information and chi causes a loss of connection and function: isolation within one's family or community, or from one's spiritual Source causes mental suffering, emotional anguish, and physical decline. Babies deprived of touch, die.

Physical, emotional, and energetic aspects of life are entwined, and supporting the flow of energy supports the health of all. As energy changes, everything else has the potential to change as well. Flow is the quality that connects vitality to information. Flow between the layers of the aura and the body connect the body to higher levels of healing. Flow between the chakras allows for communication and growth. Flow along the meridians keeps every cell connected to the whole. The most common impairment to healing is an interruption in flow, which is felt as an imbalance.

Energy Healing Methods

The most important thing to remember in doing healing work is that when you're working with another person, you are not his or her healer. The person who is healing is the healer. You are the witness to their process, holding space for light and energy to flow. The work presented here is about the process, not the end result. No one knows the path and purpose of another, and to assume you know what is best for another is ego-based. Always seek permission before you work with someone's energy.

Interrupted flow and loss of vitality can be felt as an imbalance in the distribution of energy. In meridians, a block will cause an excess of energy to accumulate, as it continues to flow into the obstructed area. The area beyond the block will show a deficiency of energy. In chakras, a block appears as an over-function in one area and an under-function in another.

One chakra will do all the processing and thus perception and awareness are limited. In the aura, charged areas will influence mental, emotional, and physical function.

Using your hands to help balance energy is a natural instinct, and the negative charge your hands carry helps establish a healing environment. Using your hands has the added benefit of focusing your mind. Where your hands are placed attracts the attention of the mind, and where the attention goes, energy follows. Of course you can bypass the use of hands and direct your energy with your mind. With any exercise that uses the hands, simply substitute your attention for your hands and, with your breath, visualize moving energy through your body. In the following exercises, you can use your hands or your mind to scan and balance energy.

The first skill to practice is feeling imbalances in energy structures. The practices in Chapter 11 sensitized your hands to feeling subtle energy. Now that skill can be put to use for balancing energy.

Excess energy can be felt as a strong magnetic repulsion, intense vibration, roiling sensation, heat, stickiness, and so forth. Most commonly deficiency is felt as emptiness, magnetic attraction to the area, coldness, and lack of movement or "deathly" stillness. Here is a simple exercise to help.

Energy Scan Exercise Using Your Hands

1. If you're scanning yourself, sit in a comfortable chair. If you're scanning another person, have him or her lie down on a massage table or couch. You should be comfortable while sensing, or you will be distracted and have difficulty focusing.

2. Ground, center, and establish boundaries.

3. Activate the *Five-Hearts Open* pattern.

4. Connect the energy beam from the soles of your feet into the Earth and draw energy into your body, strengthening the energy in the palms of your hands.

5. Meridians:

   a. Start scanning at the feet. Holding your hands 2 to 3 inches above the body, slowly glide your hands from the feet up the legs all the way to the top of the body.

   b. Notice any areas where you feel the signs of excess or deficiency.

   c. Notice any areas where your attention is drawn for any reason.

6. Chakras:

   a. If you're working on yourself, sit or lie down. If you're working on another person, stand on the right side of the table.

   b. Place your right hand at the level of the person's knees around 10 inches above the body. Face your palm toward the person's Base chakra. If you're working on yourself, just position your right hand as low as possible and face your palm toward the Base chakra around 10 inches above your body.

   c. Keeping your right hand focused on the Base chakra, place your left hand 10 inches above the person's second chakra, between the pubic bone and the belly button. Notice what you feel between your two hands.

   d. Move your left hand to the third chakra between the breast bone and the belly button, and your right hand to the second chakra. Notice what you feel in your hands between these two chakras.

   e. Continue to move up the body one chakra at a time, noting where you feel excess, deficiency, and anything else to which your attention is drawn.

   f. Practice taking your hand further away and closer to the chakras to feel differences.

7. Aura:

   a. If you're exploring your own aura, extend your arms in front of you with palms facing inward. If you're exploring someone else, rest both hands in the air about 2 feet above your friend's body.

   b. Slowly bring your hands toward the body, then away, moving toward and away several times, as if compressing the energy between your hands and the body.

   c. Keep bouncing your hands and patting the air until you start to feel resistance against your hands.

   d. The resistance is a plane of energy forming a layer; explore the contours of this layer all around the body.

   e. Try to find additional layers that lie out further and closer in; explore what you find.

   f. Take note of what you feel.

8. When you're finished, close the activations, and ground, center, and establish boundaries.

Using your hands is only one way to assess someone else's field. Feeling the condition of another person often happens spontaneously as the result of empathy. When you're empathic, you may feel a reflection in your body of the other person's condition. If you are scanning someone and suddenly begin to feel aches and pains you haven't noticed before, stop, re-ground, and allow the feelings to melt away.

Empathic awareness is a natural phenomenon and some people use it quite well to assess another person's condition. If you decide to work this way, think of it as if you were putting on someone else's coat: You can wear it to see what it feels like, but it does not belong to you, so take it off when you have the information you need. You don't need to carry around someone else's imbalance. If you have difficulty knowing which symptoms are your own and which belong to someone else, place your hand on your body where you're feeling the symptom and direct your body to release anything that isn't yours. If it is someone else's, it will go away when you do this.

Balancing Chi

The body is constantly employing homeostatic mechanisms to maintain balance. However, different conditions can obstruct the process, and when there are many demands, maintaining balance may lose priority to something more urgent. In this way accommodations are made around imbalances. Once the body accommodates an imbalance, a new set point, or normal, is established. The new set point becomes familiar, and awareness of real normal can be forgotten.

Restoring balance requires re-awakening awareness. The process is actually very easy and relies on light as the building blocks of matter. You can use this exercise while you're feeling imbalances in the Energy Scan Exercise Using Your Hands (page 230).

Balancing Chi Exercise

1. Ground, center, and establish boundaries.
2. Activate the *Winged Disk* pattern and allow your hands to fill with light.
3. After performing the body scan, simply connect an area of excess with an area of deficiency, and allow the body to reestablish balance. You can do this by placing one hand on the area of deficiency and

one on the area of excess, or if you can't reach, simply hold both areas in your mind's eye, imagining that your hands are holding them.

4. You don't have to do anything to create balance. Once you have brought attention and energy to the imbalance, the body knows what it needs to do.

5. While the areas are in exchange, you may feel a flow of energy. When it stops, or when the two areas feel equal, you are finished in that area.

6. Once balanced, allow light to vitalize both areas, filling each with information.

7. Repeat on as many areas as you feel called to. Include chakras and areas of the aura. Don't limit your self to balancing chakra to chakra or aura to aura. You can balance a chakra to any area of the body, such as the Base chakra to the feet, or you can balance an area in the aura to a part of the body. Let yourself feel drawn to different areas and explore.

8. When you're finished, close the activation, ground, center, and establish boundaries.

Healing With the Energy Templates

The first layer of the aura maintains the template of the physical body, and the fifth layer of the aura maintains the template for the ideal physical form. (You may want to review Chapter 7 to refresh how this works.) In this exercise, the idea is to bring the information from the fifth layer down into the first layer, connecting ideal health to your physical form.

Healing Through the Energy Template Exercise

1. Ground, center, and establish boundaries.

2. Lie down and relax your mind and body.

3. Activate the *Living Matrix* pattern and feel suspended in the flow of the universe.

4. Imagine the light of pure love streaming into your aura from your spiritual Source and illuminating your fifth layer template. Visualize the grid work of the template glowing with energy.

5. Allow the light to stream from the fifth layer through the lower layers until it reaches the first. You can imagine this looking like rain fall through a canopy.

6. Visualize the first layer awakening as it is informed with light, reflecting the template of ideal health.

7. Notice where you have a harder time seeing your physical template enlivened with light. Focus your attention here and even put your hands over this area.

8. When light has transfused your entire field, relax and absorb the experience.

9. When you're ready to get up, close the activation, ground, center, and establish boundaries.

Repairing Energy Structures

In the challenges of daily living, energy structures can be damaged. Fibers can become psychically torn and tattered, as we saw in Chapter 16, and the aura can acquire holes or be compressed and unable to relay information. The meridians become blocked and the flow to each cell interrupted. Here are some easy approaches.

Balancing Chakras and Repairing Energy Fibers Exercise

1. Ground, center, and establish boundaries.

2. If you already know where your fibers have been damaged, move to Step 5.

3. Activate the *Chakra Fibers* pattern. Use this meditation to scan your chakras and sense the fibers leaving each one.

4. Assess the strength and health of each fiber, and see where your attention is drawn.

5. Activate the *Weaving the Nadis* pattern and weave Earth energy up and sky energy down along the nadis.

6. As energy weaves back and forth along the nadis, increase the vitality and spin in each chakra as each one comes into healing balance.

7. Allow light to stream from the chakras through the associated fibers. Focus on the area where you have sustained damage.

8. Continue until the energy is full and calm and radiating light.

9. Ground, center, and establish boundaries.

Restoring the Aura Exercise

1. Ground, center, and establish boundaries.

2. Activate the *Spiral Pillar of Light* pattern by inhaling and imagining a pillar of light coming down into, through, and around you to the Earth, creating a circle of safety and peace. Merge the *Spiral Pillar of Light* with your aura.

3. Activate the *Earth and Sky* pattern and fill your core with light.

4. Send the light that shines from your core into your aura.

5. Close your eyes and sense your boundary. If you could see it, what would it look like? How far out is it from your body? Is it the same all the way around? Is it weaker in some areas, or empty? Get a good, strong image of all aspects of it.

6. Observe your energy emanation. What is it like? Does it fill all the space within your boundary? Does it radiate beyond the perimeter? What does your emanation convey? How does it interact with your boundary? Do you see any thought forms, projections, or hooks? These might look like dark areas. You might want to visit Chapter 12 if there are more than a few of these areas.

7. Now bring your attention to your center, the core that is home to your spiritual essence. Allow your essence to shine.

8. Use your imagination to energetically examine your aura with the light fibers from your solar plexus. As you engage the edge of your field, you might feel resistance when your fibers push against the boundary. They may tingle, vibrate, and/or relate a sense of integrity. You may have a vision in your mind's eye of the energetic grid that surrounds you. The overall feeling will be one of connectedness.

9. Ask to see/feel any holes and notice those places where your attention is drawn. Things you might feel when you engage a hole in aura are emptiness, hollowness, extreme stillness, or an out-flowing of energy. You may have visions of darkness and feel drained.

10. If you find a hole, envision it filling with light as your light fibers weave the boundary back together.

11. Send light to each area of aura that drew your attention and visualize the light re-weaving the strands of your aura.

12. When you feel complete, inhale through the *Earth and Sky* pattern into your core; exhale your radiance into your aura, and shine your light.

13. Close activations, ground, center, and establish boundaries.

Rejuvenating the Meridians Exercise

1. Ground, center, and establish boundaries.
2. Activate the *Circle of Life* pattern and use the external energy pathway of the Central Channel meridian; inhale energy up your spine and over the top of your head, and exhale energy down the front of your body and around under your torso.
3. As the energy circulates along this pathway, activate the *Earth and Sky* pattern, and circulate power and light through your Central Channel.
4. Visualize light flowing along all the meridians in the body, as the Central Channel is the source that feeds them.
5. Allow any block or stagnant energy to melt away and join the flow of life force.
6. When you feel complete, collect the energy in your Dan Tein, or Hara, by placing your hands over your lower abdomen and breathing your energy into this area, known also as the Sea of Nourishment.
7. Know that energy is available from your Hara and will automatically fill your meridians as needed.
8. Ground, center, and establish boundaries.

Revitalizing All the Energy Structures Exercise

1. Ground, center, and establish boundaries.
2. Activate the *Queen Nefertiti's Headdress* pattern and allow light to clear your aura.
3. When the aura is clear, activate the *Weaving the Nadis* pattern and run energy until your chakras are balanced, clear, and full of light.
4. Activate the *Circle of Life* pattern and let energy circulate along the Central Channel until all your meridians are energized and flowing.
5. Ground, center, and establish your boundaries.

Healing Old Trauma: Mental and Emotional Pain

The after-effects of trauma can live as unresolved emotions in your aura and body, causing blocks to the energy flow. Healing old traumas can often be done by using awareness techniques that allow you to give back another person's projections (see Chapter 12), or you can simply own and accept your emotions, allowing them to clear. Receiving help from a qualified therapist, energy worker, or counselor can support your progress. The *Chakra Clarity* activation can help you retrieve the deeper information that was caught in your body and release it.

Trauma-Clearing Exercise

1. Ground, center, and establish boundaries.
2. Sit in a quiet, relaxed place, and activate the *Spiral Pillar of Light* and *Earth and Sky* patterns. Imagine yourself in a circle of safety and healing, surrounded by loving guidance. Actively invite any guides and angels you work with to join you.
3. When you feel grounded and centered, bring your attention to an old, emotional pattern that is limiting you. It can be anything: fear of mice, fear of intimacy, anger at injustice, grief over abandonment— anything that has become a limiting pattern for you.
4. In the circle of safety, allow yourself to fully feel the depth of emotion you carry. If you need to, imagine a time you felt this emotion very strongly. Recall every detail and grievance until you are completely in the throes of it. Accept it.
5. Notice where in your body you feel your emotion the most strongly. Is it in your heart? Your solar plexus? Your belly? You may feel the emotion as physical pain, heat, vibration, weakness, and so on.
6. Focus your attention on the chakra in the area where your physical sensation resides. If you feel an ache in your chest, take your attention to your Heart chakra; if you feel butterflies in your stomach, take your attention to your Solar Plexus chakra; and so on.
7. Observe the quality of energy in this chakra. Look at the color, texture, brightness, vibration, and so forth. If it were a room, what type or room would it be? If it were an animal, what animal would it be?
8. Ask the energy/room/animal/color if it has any information for you. Be still and open to whatever comes to mind. Don't rush the process; just hold the question. It may be a good idea to keep a journal handy to write things down.
9. When you feel you have an answer, or if you decide you aren't going to get one, ask what gift this energy/room/animal/color has for you.
10. When you're ready to shift the past, ask what, if anything, would like to be different. What would this chakra like to look like? Would it like to be a different color? A different shape, density, flavor? Does

the animal need something from you? Would the room like to be redecorated? Allow the chakra to morph into what it would most like to be. Notice how you feel as this occurs.

11. Now it's time to release the past. Put everything involved with the old situation into a sacred container: the people, the injury, trauma, hurt, and anger. Make the container as beautiful as you can. As you're creating the container and putting things in, forgive yourself and everyone involved. Understand that everyone had something to learn here, including you. The only time you are truly a victim is when you choose not to learn from the events that occur. Accept the higher learning. (You may also want to retrieve your projections and give back the projections you hold of others; see Chapter 12.)

12. Release the container and everything inside. You can bury it and give it to the Earth to keep. You can burn it and send the smoke to the heavens; you can pass it to your guides.

13. Now open your chakra to light and breathe in golden, dancing, living star light. Let yourself expand.

14. Send the golden dancing stars to every cell in your body, and feel your aura expand. You can activate the *Circle of Life* pattern to facilitate this if you would like more pizzazz.

15. When you feel complete, close the activations, ground, center, and establish boundaries.

Recovering From Karmic Backlash

When you use your energy skills and personal power to manipulate and influence a person or set of circumstances to your favor at the expense of another, you are incurring karma of a deep and profound nature. This type of behavior shows a lack of integrity or knowledge of your own wholeness. Feeling yourself as incomplete allows your actions to be driven by fear. This is not a judgment on you; everyone has periods in their life where their actions are fueled by fear. It is a natural part of developing true personal power and awareness. You will, however, have to transmute the karma you incurred in order to grow.

Karmic backlash describes a chain of events where life challenges beset you in order that you learn to function from a place of love. The challenges force you into growth and awareness of the harm you've caused others. This is not something to be afraid of; as soon as you recognize the nature of your karma, simply forgive and move on. It can be difficult to tell the difference between karmic backlash and attracting growth challenges in order to expand. In reality it doesn't matter which it is, because what you need to do is the same.

Overcoming Karmic Backlash Exercise

1. Ground, center, and establish boundaries.
2. Activate the *Mystic Triangle* pattern.
3. Imagine the triangle inscribed on the ground with you sitting in one corner, a guide sitting in another corner, and the third corner open.
4. Invoking the highest and best good of all, call in someone you have harmed and invite him or her to sit in the third corner.
5. Honor the divine within the other person.
6. Give an accurate detail of all the ways you have harmed this person and offer a sincere apology.
7. Ask the person to give you your projections back.
8. When he or she has, give thanks and blessings.
9. Forgive yourself, the other person, and anyone else in the situation.
10. Release each other from any need to continue a karmic pattern.
11. Send love and light to the other person and, when it feels complete, disconnect.
12. If the other person did not return your projections or did not receive your apology, forgiveness, and love, then respect his or her choice. State that you release him or her from any karmic pattern with you.
13. Ground, center, and establish boundaries.

Death and Dying

In this culture, people seem to perceive death as failure: People succumb to death, give in to their disease, weren't strong enough to heal, or didn't have a good enough doctor. However, death is the natural result of birth, and there is no way around it. Death is not the end of consciousness. You are conscious before you're born, and your consciousness continues after you leave your body. Whatever your belief about what occurs after death, it is not the end of consciousness. People who have died and been brought back to life—an experience called a near-death experience, or NDE—all report a continuation of awareness during the time their physical body was declared dead. They all share a surprisingly similar chain of events. For the vast majority, the death experience is very positive; for a small minority it is distressing.

Positive experiences usually begin with the person leaving his or her body and seeing a tunnel of light that draws him or her inside. In the tunnel, the person is guided by friends and family who have already died. When the tunnel ends, the person is in a light-filled place, in a body made of light, with others they recognize and know. NDEs change a person. He or she no longer has a fear of death and sees the priorities of life differently. For more information, read the account of Danion Brinkley, who has had two NDEs, one during which he was declared dead for a full hour and a half.[9]

People who have a negative experience often don't actually leave the body. While the body is dying they feel sucked out, often toward a dark tunnel, and struggle to stay in the physical body. It is a natural, pro-grammed instinct to fight for life. When a person's awareness sees death approaching before he or she has left the body, and the body is struggling to stay alive, it's understandable that he or she would cling to the body and resist. Clearly it wasn't time for this person to die, and he or she was still strongly linked to the physical body.

Everybody deserves to be with someone when he or she dies. It is a unique opportunity to act in concert with those on the other side to care for someone as he or she is passing over. The following exercise can offer support if you are with another person during their death process or are dying yourself. It can also be helpful if you are healthy and have a strong fear of dying. This exercise is not meant to take you to the other side; that will happen naturally in the right time, and you will have all the support you need in the process. This exercise is to help you feel your connection to the continuity of consciousness that exists through death.

Easing Death Exercise

1. Ground, center, and establish boundaries.
2. Open the *Spiral Pillar of Light* pattern.
3. Connect with your Star. Feel the love and energy from your spiritual Source surround you.
4. Imagine the faces of people you love who have already passed. Ask them for company and support in your passage. Feel their presence and know they will be with you when you are ready to go over.

5. Imagine the faces of people who are living to whom you have a strong attachment. Let them know how much you love them and ask that they send you energy on your journey to the other side. Assure them that you will be there to assist their passage when it is time for their own journey.

6. If you need to make peace with anyone you are leaving behind or anyone you will be seeing on the other side, call his or her image to your mind's eye. Say what you need to say to this person, and ask to be forgiven for any transgressions. Give forgiveness where needed.

7. If you have projections with anyone, use the exercise in Chapter 12 to retrieve them.

8. Activate the *Living Matrix* pattern and feel yourself suspended in the matrix of a living universe. Feel your connection to Source and to the power of love.

9. Let the peace and love of your source fill you.

10. When you feel complete, close the activations, ground, center, and establish boundaries.

Healing Events and Situations

Any situation can benefit from healing energy. Use the *Mystic Triangle* pattern and create a portal to whatever situation or event you would like healed—past, present, and future. Simply sit yourself in one corner, your guide in another, and whatever people are involved in the third corner. In the center, place the situation or event. Activate the *Spiral Pillar of Light* pattern all around the triangle and visualize healing rainbows of color flooding the situation with love. Affirm that the healing is for the highest and best good of all.

Chapter 20

EMBODYING CHANGING CONSCIOUSNESS

Right now, at this moment, you have the option to awaken. Inside is everything you need to experience expanded consciousness. When you do, you will open to higher frequencies of energy whose vibration will enliven your energy body and alter your physical structure. You will be an active part in anchoring higher frequency and spiritualizing matter. You will be helping others access a paradigm shift.

The frequencies you will be receiving are not new. They have always been right here, however never as accessible as they are today. The ability and opportunity to receive them has been the goal of a multitude of spiritual practices whose dedicated adepts spend lifetimes seeking connection. Today something unique is happening. Mystics have foretold this period as one where the separation between dimensions is sheered and access to higher frequencies is available to everyone as part of the paradigm shift underway. What each person does with it is his or her personal choice.

You may have heard it said that "time is speeding up." This is another way of saying that the vibration of the universe is quickening. The result is change—change in our society, our psyches, and our bodies. One result of the quickening is that the amount of time between what we think and what our thoughts create is becoming very short, teaching us to discipline our minds and consciously create the world. The paradigm shift is the acknowledgment that there is no separation between the seen and the unseen domains—between the material and the hidden forces that guide it. As ancient cultures have taught, the world is alive—all parts of it, animate and inanimate.

Receiving higher frequencies and expanding your consciousness instigates change in your physical and energetic bodies. Ever-increasing numbers of people are exhibiting signs and symptoms of this transformation.

This chapter discusses the mechanisms involved, how receiving higher frequency might affect you, including the areas of your body being engaged, and how to make the transition easier.

Due to the importance of the information in this chapter, current research is reviewed in detail. If you are more interested in the experience, simply turn to the end of the chapter and read the suggestions for embodying changing consciousness.

Perspective From the Maya

A compelling source of insight about the current changes comes from the prophecy related to the ancient Maya Long count calendar, said to be ending in 2012. The exact date is under debate; however, all agree that the calendar's end falls within the present time period.

The Maya astronomers of the past were true mathematical scholars. Through continuous study and observation of the night sky, they developed knowledge of the mechanisms of the universe as they explored the depths of consciousness. Using mind-expanding techniques, they delved into the mysteries of time, energy, the interconnections of time and space, and synchronicity. Through their eyes we learn that we are part of natural cycles and connections previously beyond our scope of understanding.

The ancient Maya lived in what is now southern Mexico, the Yucatan Peninsula, Guatemala, and parts of Honduras and El Salvador. They left behind a legacy of flat-topped pyramids, exotic cities, and astronomical observatories located throughout the jungle. The Maya were architectural, mathematical, and astronomical geniuses; their calendar system has proven to be as accurate as current time-keeping methods. They used more than 17 different calendars that tracked short cycles, like the moon orbiting the Earth (a month) and the Earth orbiting the Sun (a year), as well as long cycles such as the approximate 26,000-year progression of constellations across the night sky called the Precession of the Equinox.

One reason the Maya were interested in astronomical and terrestrial cycles was because of the energetic impulse released through different cycles. Spiritual energy, called k'ul, was the foundation of Maya cosmology. K'ul energy flowed in pathways through the Earth, accumulating in specific places, and the Maya structured life to coincide with this flow, harnessing the energy to power ceremonies and structures. They observed that celestial happenings interacted with Earth energy and influenced the movement of k'ul from one accumulation spot to another.

Consequently, they tracked the stars, the progression of alignments, eclipses, and so on, using the information to plan their daily activities including planting crops, performing ceremonies, building cities, and even charting the course of war. Old buildings, temples, and pyramids were destroyed and new ones created to coincide with the ending of old cycles and the beginning of new ones.[1] This allowed the Maya to take advantage of the energy being brought on to the planet with each cosmic alignment the calendars marked. The present shift is no different.

Major John Jenkins, a renowned researcher and author of *Maya Cosmogenesis 2012: The True Meaning of the Maya Calendar End-Date*,[2] has determined that the end of the Maya Long count calendar in 2012 coincides with an alignment of our solar system with the center of the galaxy. Present-day Maya elders Don Alejandro, Hunbatz Men, and Carlos Barrios say that in their cosmology the center of the galaxy is the home of Hunab k'u, the spiritual source of the universe. They claim the alignment will provide an influx of new energy from this spiritual center onto the planet heralding the Golden Age of the Maya Prophecy.[3]

According to Jenkins, the end of the Long count calendar also coincides with the completion of a cycle of the Precession of the Equinox. This 26,000-year cycle was known to the Maya as an "Age" or "World," which was a very significant turning point in their creation myths. The end of an Age meant the destruction of the current way of doing things. This is not the first Age to end for the Maya, but the fourth. Because the end of the Long count calendar represents the end of a time period called a World, the mass media began heralding 2012 as the end of the world. This was never the case.

The *Popul Vuh*, written by the Quiche Maya, is one of five ancient Mayan books, or codices, that survived the Jesuit purging of documents in the 1500s. In it are details of the Maya creation myths, stories that tell how previous Ages began and ended. It also tells the story of how this present Age began and predicts how it will end. It describes the changing of the Ages as being marked by economic, social, and environmental collapse when "people distrust their government and religious leaders."[4] The old must crumble as new frequencies from the spiritual center of the universe provide the impetus for the new world we are creating.

Looking around today, no one can dispute that the social structures of religion, government, and finance are all struggling with challenges to the old and the need to create something new. We are in an evolutionary bottleneck. Change is happening because it must; the way things have been cannot be sustained into the future.

This time period of change is an experiment. There are no guaranties. What happens as a result of this shift is determined by what each of us chooses to hold precious. As always, the choices we make will determine the world we will inhabit. The difference is that the choices we are making now will impact life on this planet for an entire Age to come.

Dimensionally Wired

Another way to look at expanding consciousness is becoming aware as a multidimensional being. As you remember from Chapter 7, each layer of your aura corresponds to a different level, or dimension, of reality. To experience different dimensions all you have to do is use your energy senses.

Descriptions of subtle energy are simply constructs—ways of organizing information to be able to observe patterns. Constructs change as information and awareness change. The popular construct used to describe the human energy system comes from India, brought into Western thought through the Theosophists at the turn of the 20th century. Let's review this information, keeping in mind that it is changing:

- There are seven dimensional planes, or levels of reality.

- Each plane vibrates at a specific rate.

- Humans are connected to these dimensional levels through our own energy field, the aura.

- The aura is our personal energy field and also contains seven distinct layers.

- Each dimensional plane corresponds to a layer of the aura through which we receive information from these planes of reality.

- Each layer of the aura has a corresponding chakra, or energy center, that takes the information from the aura and steps it down to a level where it can be accessed by the body. The chakras are the aura's connection to the physical body.

- As we grow in awareness we move from lower chakra information to higher chakra information.

In the past, expanding consciousness was viewed as rising through the chakras from the lower, more physical levels into the higher, more spiritual levels. Growth was a step-by-step progression with the assumption of a basic duality where spirit is good and material is not. Spiritual growth required transcending the lower physical planes. However, being truly multidimensional is having the ability to encompass and inhabit all levels of reality simultaneously. This is the intention of the shift underway.

Rather than being a trap, the body is the anchor for us as spiritual, multidimensional beings to interact with the physical plane. We often overlook the gift of a physical body and identify this plane with pain, suffering, and ego. Some seek to escape through ascension into higher consciousness. In truth, we would not be in physical form if it didn't have meaning and purpose. Rather than escaping matter, we are here to spiritualize matter—to open the doors between the realms bringing the gifts of each to bear on the other.

Spiritualizing matter is often mischaracterized as bringing spirit into matter. Of course, matter is already imbued with spirit; all life has spirit: human spirit, Nature Spirits, and so on. Matter is nothing more than the infusion of spirit into form. What is meant by spiritualizing matter is the raising of frequency such that matter loses its hold on our consciousness and we are free to come and go at will.

Receiving New Frequencies

New frequencies are bringing change, and change is often uncomfortable. To understand how we are being impacted by changes in frequency, let's review some key thoughts from Chapter 6. First, the difference between what we call energy and matter is only the rate of its vibration, as described by Einstein in $E=MC^2$. Beyond the parameters of force, frequency, and wavelength, there is no difference between what we call matter and what we call energy.[5] As we access higher frequencies, matter is raised in vibration and becomes more energetic.

Subtle energy is similar to physical energy in that is it a force that organizes matter. The information that organizes matter into form is coded in the frequency or vibration of the energy carrier wave. Hans Jenny's study of frequency and its effect on the organization of matter and Masaru Emoto's study of the impact of thoughts and emotion on crystalline structure demonstrate that physical form is held in place by a subtle energy template.[6,7] Changing frequency changes the geometrical structure of matter. Because our thoughts and emotions are expressions of frequency, they have tremendous power.

To put it more personally, as frequency increases in both rate and amplitude of vibration, it's received in your energy field, and impacts your thinking and worldview as well as your physical body.

Mechanisms of Change: Resonance and Kundalini

Higher frequencies reaching the Earth influence the human aura through resonance. When the aura changes vibration, the step-down process increases the vibration through the body down to a cellular level. Cells, tissues, and organs vibrate with their own signature frequency, the basis of diagnostic procedures such as electroencephalograms (EEGs), which measure brainwaves, or electrocardiograms (ECG/EKGs), which measure the electrical activity of the heart. Organs and body systems stay in sync with each other through vibration.[8] As higher frequency changes the vibration of the physical body, a series of physical and psycho-spiritual changes occur.

The increase in vibration is activating dormant Kundalini in the Base chakra at the root of the spine. Kundalini is the germ of consciousness that is each person's spiritual essence. When it awakens, it lifts out of the Base chakra in the sacrum and travels on three central channels that run along the spine and through the chakras. As it rises, it activates and awakens each chakra. When it reaches the Crown chakra, Kundalini streams from the top of the head like a fountain and opens the person for mystical, divine union.

Advancing up the spine to the Crown chakra doesn't usually happen in one sitting. The progression can take years or even lifetimes to complete, depending on the preparedness of the person. However, in the current quickening Kundalini is being activated and is rising whether people are fully prepared or not. The awakening magnifies unresolved emotional issues in the chakras that may manifest as external events in order to be resolved. Consequently, people are coming face to face with multiple life lessons. This can be uncomfortable and disruptive. Ultimately, it is forcing each of us to find new solutions to lifelong problems.

Physical Interface

The energy being transmitted through resonance and rising with Kundalini is fed by the chakra system into the body through the meridians and the neuroendocrine system. The nervous and endocrine systems are the master regulators of the body, overseeing all body activities. They are also the first two physical systems to receive subtle energy input. The extremely high-powered energy of Kundalini can challenge the circuits of the nervous system, causing many uncomfortable symptoms. The pineal gland and amygdala area in the brain are also at the forefront of this shift. The more conditioned your neuroendocrine system is to higher frequency, the easier the transition will be.

Pineal Activation

The pineal gland is about the size of a grain of rice, looks something like a pinecone, and sits in the back of the brain at the level of the root of the nose. Medicine once considered it the nonfunctioning vestigial remnant of a third eye that used to be in the center of the forehead. The pineal gland receives and responds to light and electromagnetic energy. It produces the hormone melatonin and maintains our circadian rhythm, the biological rhythms that govern body functions in response to day/night, seasonal cycles, and the daily cycles in the Earth's magnetic fields. It can be disrupted by artificial light and magnetic fields.

Still one of the body's mysteries, the pineal gland is a neuroendocrine transducer, meaning that it converts incoming nerve impulses into outgoing hormones, releasing hormones in response to bioelectrical messages received through the eyes. Through the act of receiving light, this gland energizes the entire body.

Spiritually, the pineal gland has long been considered a portal to self-awareness, higher consciousness, and states of bliss by yogi masters including Paramahansa Yogananda, author of *Autobiography of a Yogi*.[9] In esoteric literature it corresponds to the Third Eye chakra and when activated increases psychic ability, intuition, wisdom, and insight. It's considered a doorway for inter-dimensional experiences, and its activation is essential for experiencing multidimensionality.

Given both its physical and spiritual functions, it's no surprise that the pineal gland is central to receiving higher frequencies. The energy activating this expansion is coded on light that may be triggering the gland to produce yet another substance. In addition to melatonin, the pineal gland seems to produce a molecule associated with altered states of consciousness, dimethytyptamine (DMT.) DMT is a neuropeptide that acts as a natural hallucinogen. It was first discovered in the human body in the 1950s but its function and role are still not completely understood. Dr. Rick Strassman, author of *DMT: The Spirit Molecule*, speculates that DMT is involved with dreaming and is found in high concentrations in the pineal gland during near-death and out-of-body experiences.[10] As discussed in Chapter 18, more and more people are experiencing altered states and enhanced intuitive capability that may be directly related to stimulation of the pineal gland.

Pineal Crystals

A strange anomaly has been discovered in the pineal gland within the past 30 years. A new type of crystal has been found forming in the tissue.

What it means is far from clear. However, the large amount of conjecture about it warrants a lengthy discussion.

Whereas the presence of crystals in the body is not new, this type of crystal is. Hydroxyapatite is a form of calcium phosphate that is found throughout the body in functional and non-functional placement. It forms the crystal component in the mineral matrix of bones and in the otoconia crystals in the inner ear. Hydroxyapatite crystals have also been observed in the pineal gland; they are called pineal sand and are considered to the product of poor nutrition. They can appear in all age groups and have piezoelectric properties, meaning they can release electricity when placed under mechanical pressure.[11]

The new crystals found growing within the pineal gland are different. They're not hydroxyapatite; they're calcite crystals and have become the focus of interest in relation to the spiritual unfolding underway. Colleen Behan of the Spirit of Light Wellness Studio (*www.spiritoflight.org*) in Wallingford, Connecticut, teaches a Pineal Activation and Cranial Temple Activation to assist people in accommodating new frequencies. She intuitively believes the crystals are receiving higher frequencies and helping to uplift and spiritualize the human body. On the other hand, medical researchers wonder if the presence of the crystals is a pathological condition.

The calcite crystals are small, usually under 20 microns, which is truly microscopic, as there are 25,400 microns in 1 inch! The crystals are formed with sharp edges with a rough surface. They were first reported in the late 1970s and early 1980s. The initial scientific studies concluded that they were aging artifacts, even though they had previously not been seen in older people. A study done in 1986 and reported in *The Journal of Neural Transmission* hypothesized that their presence was the result of the inability of aging cells to break down calcium.[12] A study done in Italy found the crystals occur more in women than men.[13]

In support of this assessment, during the 30 years since these crystals have been discovered, people have been ingesting massive amounts of calcium supplementation to prevent osteoporosis, especially older women. At the same time there is an epidemic of Vitamin D deficiency. Vitamin D is a nutrient needed to metabolize calcium and incorporate it into bone tissue. It is obtained from the sun, and its deficiency is related to the fear of skin cancer which has caused people to avoid sun exposure and use sunscreen. It's tempting to assume the presence of these crystals is related to over-calcification and Vitamin D deficiency. However, this might not be the full picture.

An Israeli study conducted in 2002 looked at the impact of this new form of crystallization with regard to the human bio-magnetic field. The study states that the crystals are "the only known non-pathological occurrence of calcite in the human body" and theorizes that they are "biologically significant having a possible non-thermal interaction with external electromagnetic fields."[14] The study theorizes a functional interaction between the piezoelectric hydroxyapatite and the calcite.

Crystals act as transmitters, receivers, and amplifiers of frequency, making them useful in watches and computer technology. Many people, including Colleen Behan, believe the new pineal crystals have developed to assist transformation. She intuits they are meant to help us receive and interact with the new frequencies.

Another interesting study from the Ukraine looks at the new phenomenon of calcite crystals showing up in the intercellular spaces in plants. The study, conducted in 2004, was able to initiate the production of calcium crystals in plants by placing them in a weak magnetic field. The study postulates that increased magnetic field exposure is responsible for the calcification.[15]

If the pineal crystals are not due to improper calcium metabolism, are they the result of electromagnetic pollution from cell phones, WiFi overhead power cables, and so forth? Or are they caused by changes in the Earth's electromagnetic field from the new frequencies being received? Research may never be conclusive, and you will need to use your own intuitive capability to determine the importance, if any, of these crystals, to the process underway.

Regardless of the presence of crystals, the pineal gland is certainly an important player in spiritual expansion. This gland can be said to be guiding the enfoldment of light into the body, helping to activate your energy systems and expand your consciousness. Consider this comment made by physicist David Bohm in an interview with Renee Weber: "Light in its generalized sense (not just ordinary light) is the means by which the entire universe unfolds into itself."[16]

Brain Awakening

The amygdala is the part of the brain that deals with emotion and emotionally stored memory. The almond-shaped groups of nuclei are located deep within the temporal lobes of the brain as part of the limbic system. They are specifically involved in how we process and remember emotional reactions.[17] Their location is also home to the instinctual sensory system that allows prey to know when a predator is approaching, even without seeing, hearing, or smelling it.

Given the amygdala's function, many believe it's the part of the brain where we perceive paranormal experiences. A Canadian study published in *Brain Cognition* journal in 1992 concluded that periods of intense meaningfulness, including sensing a spiritual presence and experiencing enhanced creativity, correlated with increased burst-firing in the hippo-campus-amygdala complex.[18] Studies conducted by Russek and Schwartz demonstrated an ability of a subject to feel the presence of a hand or to feel when someone is looking at the back of his or her head for an extended period. The study showed subjects had a 57.6 percent positive performance in knowing when they were being looked at from behind. The ability to perceive someone's eye contact increased with the belief in some type of spiritual reality.[19]

Given that the amygdala senses prey without any physical signals, can we suggest that the ability of subjects in the Russek and Schwartz experiments to sense subtle energy happens in the amygdala as well?

Signs and Symptoms of Change

The new influx of frequencies is creating change at physical, emotional, psychological, and spiritual levels. It's being felt in lifestyle, interpersonal dynamics, and health.

Some of the effects are uplifting and gratifying; others are causing discomfort. Essentially, signs and symptoms represent the decision to grow and to do it quickly; however, that doesn't mean it isn't difficult. Additionally, each sign and symptom could be the result of a mild or seri-ous medical condition. One of the questions many people have is how to discern whether a physical symptom is caused by an underlying physical problem or by an energy effect of expansion. The truth is that every physi-cal symptom has both an energetic and physical component, and needs be addressed on both levels.

As you read through the lists of symptoms and identify those you have, remember that using the energy exercises throughout this book will reduce their effect. There are additional exercises at the end of this chapter; however, you already have all the techniques you need.

Here are some of the indicators you may be experiencing as the transition is underway.

Psycho-Spiritual Indicators

As the amygdala and pineal gland are being stimulated you may join others in the following experiences:

- Being more open to sensing guides, angels, and feeling a beneficial presence.
- Feeling subtle energy.
- Noticing increased amounts of synchronicity and deja-vu.
- Having an increasing ability to focus healing energy.
- Hearing voices and auditory spiritual guidance.
- Having higher levels of intuition and psychic ability, especially telepathy.
- Feeling more aware and in control of your own fate.

All these experiences are positive and beneficial; however, try not to get lost in them. The job at hand is to inhabit both realms while maintaining discernment and balance between this level of reality and the dimensions to which you are gaining access. Without discernment, you can lose the ability to function on this plane.

As you embrace higher frequencies, more information is being downloaded. This can either catapult you into a whole new awareness, or provide your ego with a lot of self-importance. It's easy to lose your moorings and get caught up in the trappings of ego.

Some of the more challenging psycho-spiritual aspects are:

- Feeling overloaded.
- Having overwhelming emotional responses.
- The reemergence of old emotional patterns.
- Being presented with life challenges at an accelerated rate.
- Depression, anxiety, psychosis.

Use *Queen Nefertiti's Headdress*, the *Circle of Life*, and the *Chakra Clarity* patterns to ease the psycho-spiritual effects.

Interpersonal Dynamics

The first place you may feel the effects of change is in your personal relationships. The incoming frequencies are affecting everyone, bringing each person's issues to the surface. Relationships are the arena in which we work out our issues, and thus there is large potential for interpersonal stress. In addition, as you grow the people around you may not understand what's happening. (Use the practices in Chapter 10 to keep your bearings.)

As with everything, the effects can happen at either end of the extremes. Here are some of the relationship impacts, both good and bad:

- New awareness of energy linkages between you and your partner.
- Stronger bonds based on deeper intimacy.
- Finding new ways to solve long-standing problems.
- Polarization with family members and friends as deep-seated beliefs surface, creating friction.
- Intolerance of differences.
- Distrust and fear-based thinking.

Try some of the practices in Chapter 16 to ease the challenges and expand the enjoyment in interpersonal expansion.

Physical Indicators

Physical signs and symptoms happen though an excess amount of energy that either overwhelms the body or causes it to burn out.

Nervous and endocrine system indicators include:

- Restless legs.
- Tingling.
- Trembling, shaking, vibrating sensations.
- Body jolts.
- Roving twitches.
- Memory and cognitive changes/ brain fog, memory loss.
- Headaches.
- Waking between 3 a.m. and 5 a.m. (receiving downloads of information).
- Weight gain and weight loss.
- Extreme fatigue or heightened levels of energy.
- Hot and cold flashes.

Sensory indicators include:

- Hearing voices.
- Sounds in the ear (clicking and high-pitched frequencies).
- Proprioceptive confusion (not knowing where you are in space).
- Sensations of pressure and heat racing through your body.
- Seeing light flashes.
- Seeing shadowy shapes out of the corner of your eyes.
- Seeing auras and color around people.

Miscellaneous indicators include:

➤ Multiple chemical sensitivities.

➤ Vivid dreaming.

➤ Temporal-spatial disorientation.

Easing the Transition

It's difficult to tell from reading a list how disconcerting some of these signs can be. For example, people report driving down the road and suddenly not knowing where they are or where they're going, even though they've driven that road hundreds of times before (temporal-spatial disorientation). Hearing voices or seeing shadows moving in corners can be scary for some, and many people report feeling as though they are going crazy or losing control. It's a good idea to find other people who are aware of the changes underway and form a support group for each other.

The best way to ease the transition is to learn how to use the changes that are happening to you in positive ways. For example, instead of worrying about how much sleep you're losing when you consistently wake at 3 a.m., use the time to actively interact with the information coming in. Sit with a journal and write. Meditate and connect with other realms. If you have hot flashes, see lights, and hear tapping noises, try to identify what is happening at that moment that is triggering it. What else do you notice? What patterns can you discern? Use the signs as a wake-up bell and pay attention.

Added inputs of energy cause the body to function at a higher metabolic rate and burn more nutrients. A sound nutritional program with added supplementation is essential. If you feel overwhelmed or confused, you can obtain a focused naturopathic consult through the Website *www.thepathofenergy.com*. A consult will not include medical diagnosis and advice, but it can give you directions to investigate and suggestions to ask your medical provider.

Using some of the basic meditations in Chapter 3 can significantly help. *Weaving the Nadis* assists in smoothing Kundalini and easing some of the nervous system discomfort, and *The Living Matrix* will help you adjust to living in higher frequency. Here are a few focused exercises.

Smoothing the Flow of Kundalini

Many of the signs and symptoms of expansion are caused by the rising of Kundalini and the overwhelming of the system with large influxes of energy. Preparing the pathways for Kundalini rising and grounding the excess energy will help ease any stress. This is especially helpful in reducing the effects of restless legs.

Easing Energy Overload and Smoothing Kundalini Exercise

1. If possible, go to your power spot. Sit in a chair or on a rock with your feet on the ground, or sit on the ground in cross-legged position.
2. Ground, center, and establish boundaries.
3. Smoothe Kundalini flow:
   a. Activate the *Weaving the Nadis* and the *Earth and Sky* patterns.
   b. As you inhale, imagine Earth energy flowing into your sacrum and up the two parallel pathways of the Nadis, weaving in one side of a chakra, out the other, and then up to the next.
   c. At the Crown chakra, exhale and send the energy into the sky.
   d. Inhale and bring energy down from the sky thorough your crown and let it flow down the Nadis, through each chakra, to your sacrum. Exhale and send it down into the Earth.
   e. Continue breathing the *Earth and Sky* pattern through the Nadis.
4. Ground excess energy:
   a. Open the *Circle of Life* pattern.
   b. With your breath, circulate energy along the outer pathway.
   c. Inhale energy up the spine and then exhale energy down the front of your body for three complete rounds.
   d. Open your Base chakra and, as energy circulates down your front, instead of sending it up your spine, imagine it flowing into the Earth; imagine it being received by a ley line and streamed away.
   e. Continue until the excess energy subsides.
5. Close the patterns, and ground, center, and establish boundaries.

Activating the Etheric Pineal Gland and Amygdala

Activating your pineal gland and amygdala will help you open to new frequencies, receive heightened information, and adjust more easily to transformation. The basis of this self-aligning process was part of a Lightworkers' activation course taught by Colleen Behan. The shift to a self-activation process was inspired on a trip to Malta during a group energy exercise and offers an effective way of helping you align to the changes underway. (To take part in Colleen's activation course, visit *www.thespiritoflight.org*. For illustration of activation see *www.thepathofenergy.com*.)

Activating the Etheric Pineal Gland and Amygdala Exercise

1. Ground, center, and establish boundaries.

2. Activate the *Pyramid Purification* pattern and imagine two identically sized pyramids superimposed over each other. Rotate one pyramid so that the two bases overlap. This forms a sacred geometry that receives the new frequency.

3. Visualize your head inside this structure.

4. Imagine a beam of light coming from your personal Star, your Source, entering the top of the pyramids through your Crown chakra to focus on your pineal gland, located in the center of your head at the level of the bridge of the nose.

5. Visualize an infinity sign forming in your head with the pineal gland in the center. The figure-eight pattern is horizontal. One edge hits the Third Eye and the back edge hits the back of the head.

6. As light continues to enter the top of the pyramid, imagine the infinity sign rotating counter-clockwise. As it rotates it creates a torus spinning around the pineal gland.

7. Rotate the two pyramids in a clockwise direction. The pyramid and torus create two fields of energy, rotating in opposite directions. The torus is inside your head and the pyramid is outside your head.

8. Continue to focus on the rotating fields and see if they want to change direction. Notice what you feel throughout your body as they do. Let the fields rotate back and forth in different directions until your brain and body feel awakened, energized, and balanced.

9. Acknowledge that your third eye is now activated and visualize your connection to spiritual impulses.

10. When you feel complete, close the activations, ground, center, and establish boundaries.

COMPLETING THE CIRCLE

"The significant problems we face today cannot be solved at the same level of thinking we were at when we created them."

—Albert Einstein

Accepting your place as a spiritual being who is co-creating this reality is the essence of the transformation underway—the paradigm shift we are undergoing. The focus of this book has been to expand your energy awareness so you are able to navigate in this realm with ease. Ultimately, energy awareness is a spiritual practice. Activating new energy patterns and shifting your awareness will allow you to fully participate in the path and purpose of your life. As you remember your essence, you will awaken to the realization that humans are magnificent beings with unlimited potential.

Many different prophecies have foretold the times we are now in. The Mayan prophecies say this is the ending of an Age, or World. In the creation stories as told in the Mayan *Popol Vuh*, previous Ages ended as humans either could not or would not worship the gods. What does it mean to worship the gods? Perhaps it is a metaphor for acknowledging the god force within. Worshiping the gods may be as simple as honoring the divine within all, putting spiritual reality first in our choices and actions. What would it mean in your life and choices if you did?

In this moment we are creating the direction of the future. What that direction will be depends on the awareness with which we make our choices. How each of us behaves in the trials of this transition will determine the future we are creating; what we do depends on what we hold precious and what we believe about reality. It's time to define what you believe and what your treasure is, and then align your actions accordingly.

When conflict and fear seem to prevail, react with thoughtfulness, calmness, and love. Practice living without conflict. Choose to transform

< 257 >

your anxious, fear-filled, and angry thoughts. Most importantly, we are being asked to re-identify ourselves, to shift out of the old and be our new selves, and to align with the frequency of the new paradigm.

When embracing the new, there is always a moment of fear where we wonder how. How do I become the new me? Energetically, it is the moment when you disengage your energy fibers from their attachments and float free. Then you create a vision, send your fibers to attach to it, and let yourself be pulled forward. The secret is to vision a compelling future.

Shifting Identity

Shifting your identity is a function of your attention. Throughout this book you've been asked to pay attention—to expand your awareness through the use of intentional attention. Directing your attention is the single most important factor in developing energy skills. Learning to pay attention is only half the picture; learning how to pay attention is the other.

Your attention and what you see, feel, and experience through your attention is linked to your imagination. You cannot see what you cannot imagine; you have no frame of reference. You may have heard the story about the native people on the shore when Columbus landed who were not able to see his ships in the harbor. They had no frame of reference to recognize ships. The Spaniards, it is said, seemed to appear out of thin air. Whether or not this story is true, it illustrates something called in-attentional blindness, also known as perceptual blindness.

In-attentional blindness, is a term coined by Arian Mack and Irvin Rock in 1998 and is the phenomenon of not being able to perceive things that are in plain sight. Two examples of this are being unable to find keys that are sitting on the table and hitting another car that you never saw, although it was in plain view and you looked before turning. Christopher Chabris and Daniel Simons, two Harvard psychologists, investigated this subject with an experiment called the Selective Attention Test, which you can take online (*www.youtube.com/watch?v=vJG698U2Mvo.*)

The test asks people to view a short video of six basketball players passing two balls. In the video, three of the players are wearing white t-shirts and three are wearing black t-shirts. The viewer is asked to count the number of times the white-shirted players pass a ball. By paying close attention as the players weave quickly around each other passing the balls, viewers will get the right answer (the ball is passed 15 times). However, at the same time that the ball is being passed, a man in a gorilla suit walks onto the court into the middle of the players, faces the camera, and thumps his chest before walking off. Half the viewers who watch this video see the gorilla; the other half do not.

The fact of paying singular attention closed down the viewers' perceptions. They became so focused that they closed down parts of their awareness and missed the bigger picture. More importantly, they simply couldn't see what they weren't expecting and never imagined. Your ability to perceive subtle energy and create a compelling future depends on your ability to expand your imagination. How can you create what you cannot imagine? The type of attention required to perceive subtle energy is wide and soft and accepting. It uses your whole self, allowing information in, rather than requiring it to conform to what you already know. Imagine walking through a forest. How much of the life around you are you aware of? Lose your expectations and expand.

To imagine something more requires an expansion of consciousness. The best part is that you are wired for expansion. You are linked to other levels and dimensions of reality through your energy structures. Expanding consciousness is simply opening your awareness; it is the driving force in life. The spiritual evolution at hand does not mean ascending out of matter into higher dimensions. Spiritualizing matter does not mean making the creation something different. The universe is imbued with spirit. The evolution at hand is waking up and being aware of what is here!

The frequency influx onto the planet is vibrating us into new awareness. Being multidimensional is free movement in and out of all levels of reality. Open your imagination, and perceive with your whole mind and heart. The practices in this book will help you transition; five minutes a day to connect inwardly are all you need. Their effect will be gentle and the change in your life subtle, until all at once you realize everything is different. You don't have to do all the exercises. In fact, it isn't about doing at all: It's about being.

Singularity Consciousness

As seen in Chapter 20, people are undergoing rapid change at both cellular and energetic levels. There are many social signs of transition, and the list of physical signs and symptoms is long. However, the largest impact of the change underway is being felt on the level of personality.

Our personalities want things to stay the same, even as our spirits want change. Some people are responding to change with fear and clinging to

< The Path of Energy >

old behaviors of flight or fight reactions. Others are embracing change and letting go of old limitations. Everyone must face the consequences of his or her own karma—of past choices and beliefs—to move away from identification with polarization (physical vs. spiritual, good vs. evil, light vs. dark) to that of unity. Some people call this the singularity consciousness.

Singularity consciousness is not new. It's a return to an ancient way of seeing life. It is the step *beyond* the realization that all life is interconnected. It's the step *beyond* realizing that we are all part of the whole. It's the moment we shift from knowing we are connected to knowing we are one. It's the moment we shift our perception from being part of the whole to being the whole—and not just the whole of humanity, or the whole of the Earth; it's the whole of all creation.

In a small way we incorporate this awareness every time we hold each other in a vision of wholeness. In the book, *The Game of Life and How to Play It*, author Florence Scovel Shinn proposes that if even one person holds you in a vision of wholeness, you cannot fail.[1] This concept is life-changing. How do you see the people around you: your parents, children, partners, friends? Is the first thought of them of their failures, or how they've let you down? Or, can you be the one person who sees them in the wholeness of their path—as people with divine essence, working to grow?

In a large way everything we are and every choice we make changes with this realization. The Tibetan Lamas and tribes of the Sierra Nevada care for the planet and provide us room to grow because they know this. We are not all connected; we are one. How many times has this been said and by how many spiritual traditions? And if each of us really believed it, what would change? Would we be better stewards of the Earth? Would we be able to follow the prime directive of all religions to love one another like we love ourselves? Would we feel safe and less defensive?

In the words of Maxwell Igan, "How would the world be different if you really did treat everyone else as if they were you?"[2]

To paraphrase Machaelle Small Wright, how would the world change if we really behaved as if the God in all life mattered?

Here is the bottom line:

We are all in this together, and in the transition underway,
none of us makes it unless all of us do.
Enjoy life, enjoy this process of expansion, and choose love.
Move beyond the polarity of good and bad,
and of us and them, into singularity.
Follow your heart and engage the path of energy.

< 260 >

Appendicies

Five-hearts Opened

Origin of the Meditations

I became fascinated with subtle energy early in life, convinced there was a deeper reality than what I could see and feel. My parents were intelligent, professional people with open minds who studied the Edgar Cayce material, and there were many books around the house for me to browse. When I was 13, I read Edgar Cayce's book *Auras: An Essay on the Meaning of Colors* and found validation for my inner conviction. For the next several years, I spent many cross-eyed hours trying to see auras. I never did, at least not that way. However, one day while petting my cat, Lamar, I started to notice something I never expected.

I was 20 when it happened, and by that time I had read Carlos Castaneda's book *The Teachings of Don Juan: A Yaqui Way of Knowledge*, which had changed my life. The practices in that and subsequent Castaneda books altered my perceptions, opening me for what was about to happen. I had also already succeeded in actually seeing an aura: a brief glimpse of a blue field surrounding my yoga teacher. In the relaxed, altered state induced by the two hours of practice, I opened my eyes to clearly see the field of light around him and to observe that it was comprised of tiny filaments of light emanating from his body and looking something like a sea anemone. It was brilliant, awe-inspiring, and so shocking that I was immediately jolted out of my ability to see it.

Thus prepared, I was sitting on my bed reading and petting Lamar, when I felt a strong resistance against my hand each time I approached her body to stroke her. The resistance felt like two north poles of a magnet being pushed toward each other. It had not occurred to me that auras could be felt; the vehicle of touch seemed far too gross for the subtlety of energy! I explored the resistance and was able to define a border around her entire body. I was further startled to notice that Lamar responded to my feeling her aura exactly as if I were petting her fur. She rotated her head to expose her ears and rolled to expose her belly as my hand passed over. I had the distinct awareness that she could feel my ministrations clearly and that we were interacting on a level highly satisfactory to us both.

This event expanded my awareness, opening me to the kinesthetic experience of energy. It also launched my career into massage therapy and energy bodywork. As I became more proficient at feeling and moving energy, I began to see in my mind's eye what I was unable to will my physical eyes to see. In this way, my inner vision was developed.

The patterns in this book were discerned over a period of 30 years. I have not received this information passively; I went searching for it. I am not special because of what I've experienced, as my relatives and friends will attest! I did not find this information because I'm a good human being; however, in exploring these patterns and the practices in this book, I am becoming a better human being. Each person is capable of discovering truth. Each person has everything he or she needs inside, and truly, no one is more special than any one else. I offer these activations and practices with respect, from one person walking her path to another. I fully expect that each person who works with these will modify each one for him or herself.

The decision to write a book featuring the energy activations came about during a 40-day mantra meditation exercise in August 2005. On a day about halfway through, I finished the daily repetition of the Mantra and sat in the vibrant silence that comes in the after time. My body pulsated and my energy field was brilliantly clear. In the empty space behind my eyes, I saw the book take form and present itself in a complete version, chapters laid out with topics and content. I flipped through the pages and realized I was being inspired to put everything I had ever learned about energy into a book. It seemed impossible, yet still I said yes.

The Spiral Pillar of Light

I was introduced to the basics of this pattern in a channeling session with Barbara Marciniak and the group she channels called the Pleiadians, also known as the P's. Barbara opened the session by calling on the Pillar of Light to access the P's and to provide protection. I began to work with this meditation on a regular basis, observing how it impacted the aura, and activated higher connection and developed a slightly different variation that created a more expanded experience for me.

Professionally, I use the *Spiral Pillar of Light* in all of my bodywork sessions, and also use it to clear and cleanse my treatment room and energy tools. Personally, I use this to deepen my meditation practice, to clear my personal space, and for grounding during stressful encounters.

One of the aspects of this pattern that I love is its ability to contain my own harmful projections when I am out of balance, ensuring I don't harm or drain another person. Like you, I work each day to clear my field and take responsibility for what I transmit and project. Sometimes I fail, and when I do, I have the *Spiral Pillar of Light*.

Earth and Sky

The first time I felt this flow I was doing a simple conscious breathing exercise. Sitting cross-legged, I followed my breath and moved into a deepened meditative state. I became aware of the movement of energy above my head and below my feet, corresponding to my breathing pattern as described in the activation. I could easily see the image of a tree with my body as the trunk, and the energy entering and leaving my Crown and Base chakras, forming branches above my head and roots below my feet. The more grounded I became in the Earth, the more expanded I became in the sky. I had the profound experience of being the place humans hold as bridge between Earth and Sky and felt the responsibility we have in that position.

Being centered, grounded, and energetically aware, changed from being a simple matter of personal growth to something much larger. I saw each person in the context of a system. What each of us does impacts the quality of all life. I have since seen this mediation in various forms in different practices, proof we all have access to universal energy information.

Circle of Life

Circle of Life is one of the meditations that originates in a traditional practice. This is based on the Great Central Channel meridian of Chinese medicine. The Central Channel is composed of two paired channels or meridians. The front or yin meridian, named the Conception Vessel, flows down the center front of the body and under the torso. It changes into the Governing Vessel and rises up the spine and over the top of the head. Together, the two make a continuous circuit. The Great Central Channel is the first set of meridians to develop in the embryo. It interacts with the chakras and feeds all other meridians.

I first learned to meditate with this channel during the study of Jin Shin Do Bodymind Acupressure and later saw it as a Taoist meditation called the microcosmic orbit. The traditional meditation focuses on accumulating chi in the Hara that is then sent along the pathway of the Governing and Conception Vessels.

The variations in this book focus on the coccyx as the collecting place of chi rather than the Hara, an adaptation based on the need to alleviate the effects of Kundalini energy that has been activated before the person is fully ready. People were presenting in treatment with energy accumulating in the sacrum and causing vibration, heat, and agitation. Asking for insight into how to relieve the symptoms without prematurely inciting Kundalini, I saw this coccyx variation. The alteration changed the focus from accumulating energy to distributing it, easing the physical discomfort of awakening Kundalini while using the excess energy to help in the clearing process.

The second variation is based on the inner channel of the traditional flow. In this flow, both Governing and Central channels flow up the center of the body through the Hara line and create a fountain of energy at the crown. I use this pattern more regularly than the other two, primarily because this variation lends itself to the more advanced practices in Part III of this book.

Chakra Clarity

This is the second traditional meditation. Meditating with the chakras is often used to access blocks and limitations, as well as clarify developmental issues. This practice supports spiritual evolution. It is used here as a tool for self-exploration and the development of visioning skills to access imagery and metaphor to communicate with the subconscious mind. The information stored in the deeper layers of the subconscious mind directs our responses to daily stimuli and perceived limitations in life. When we learn the language of imagery, we can begin to discover the unconscious script we live by. Once we learn the process of accessing imagery, we can apply it to all meditative practice.

Chakra Fibers

The first time I saw my yoga teacher's aura was while attending college at Michigan State University in the late 1970s. Every Saturday at 7 a.m., a wonderful man provided two hours of free yoga in the Student Union. One day, toward the end of the session, I was in a deeply relaxed state in sitting meditation with my eyes semi-open and with a soft gaze. I was quietly looking at the instructor with a clear mind, devoid of random thoughts, and gently taking in the environment. I became aware, in a detached sort of way, that I was gazing at the instructor's aura. Although there was a field of silver blue around him, what was more striking was the energy streaming off him in fibers or filaments of light. It actually looked and acted like flames, and was unlike any light I had ever seen. It clearly contained consciousness, was alive, and was interactive with the surroundings.

Immediately, I connected what I was seeing to the fibers described by Carlos Castaneda, who teaches that the chakra fibers are anchors to reality and sensors to explore. Since that experience, I have seen the living light filaments in several different circumstances. Kinesthetically, it is the most prominent aspect of the energy fields I feel around people. This activation challenges us to pay attention to how attached we are to dogmatic or habitual ways of being and thinking, and how free and available we are for inspiration.

My first direct experience of how the fibers connect in love relationships happened when I first met my husband. Our chakras linked together with a distinct popping sound as each one connected. Since then, I have worked extensively with love connections between people and can attest to the fact that the fibers become damaged with violent treatment.

Weaving the Nadis

The primary nadis are pathways between the chakras that regulate the flow of energy and assist communication. They are involved in the development of psychic perception. I had never thought too much about the nadis, although my eldest daughter described them to me when she was a young child. She saw auras and energy fields until around 10 years of age.

The *Weaving the Nadis* activation revealed itself in 2002 when a client came for treatment after a severe car accident. The impacted car had spun in many circles before stopping, and the woman was knocked unconscious during part of it. As I worked on her field, I felt with my hands and saw in my mind's eye the pathway of the nadis. They appeared as shoelaces, tying her energy structures in alignment. In her case, the laces on the right side were too loose with too much of the lace pooled on that side. The left side was too tight, restricting all energy flow. The spin of the car pulled her right side to the outside with centrifugal force pulling her even further to the right. I ran my hands along the pathway as described in the activation pattern until the right and left sides were even.

After this session, I began to meditate with the pattern, gaining insight into its function and found evenness along this pathway allowed a gentle rise of Kundalini. As energy flows more smoothly between the chakras, issues are resolved, creating a vacuum that invites Kundalini to rise. When Kundalini rises organically as the result of clear pathways, it is a gentle and powerful expansion. *Serenity* is the keyword for this activation. It is calm, gently flowing water, soothing the bodymind and healing the spirit.

Queen Nefertiti's Headdress

I saw this activation pattern in 2003 during a session with a client coming for depression. Although this client is a very beautiful and extremely talented woman who is liked and respected by everyone who knows her, she was caught in old patterns of low self-esteem and an inability to manifest joy in her life. She had a history of severe childhood illness that formed her belief system and sense of identity.

We had worked together on and off for many years; in this session we were both opened for something new. I sat next to her and when I asked for inspiration, the headdress appeared in her energy field. I saw immediately how the striations of the headdress interacted with the aura and described what I was seeing. We proceeded to breathe together through the cone. I watched my client's aura while experiencing in myself the different layers beginning to vibrate. Negative thoughts and beliefs stood out in relief against the vibrating field. As the frequency increased, the belief-thoughts burst like bubbles, followed by a feeling of lightness.

We both left that day feeling light, free, and very happy. This activation has to be used on a regular basis to be permanently effective. I compare it to taking a shower: something we do daily when possible, but needed more some days than others. In time, as the chakra work is also being done and core issues are being resolved, the remnants to be cleared in the field become less and less. Still, I do enjoy a daily shower.

Five-Hearts Open

This activation opened during a session in 1999. I was providing a simple relaxation, rejuvenation massage and was flowing along in a free form state of mind when I noticed my Hara line light up as rays of energy descended into my crown, flowing down the Hara line into my heart. The energy built up in my heart until it became almost uncomfortable, then streamed down into my hands and feet. I was overwhelmed by the sense of my "self" extending outward and meeting the world at a different level of matter. As I massaged this person's body, the energy from my hands extended into her body and met an inner plane of her energy. I was simultaneously massaging her skin with my hands as well as a deeper plane of energy with my energy extension. My feet were experiencing the same expansion: physically on the ground and energetically connected to a deeper, inner plane of Earth energy.

This experience stayed with me the rest of the day. As I walked, it was from the energy plane of the Earth, lifting my knees high, stepping deeply, and building charge. My hands and heart touched into the essence of what was around me. I kept seeing the image of an Egyptian relief with the people walking with knees high and hands raised with palms outward. Suddenly, I had a new understanding of the phrase *walk like an Egyptian*. I find this activation initiates itself when needed with clients. I activate it myself when I want to charge my system from the heart of the Earth.

Winged Disk

I've been drawn to the symbol of the winged disk my entire life. I find the symbol hidden in objects all around me. It has appeared at milestone moments, a synchronistic reminder to stay true to myself. This activation came in meditation. The symbol simply descended from the sky until the disk was located over my heart and my arms became the wings. While profoundly energizing, it is essentially a very gentle, nurturing flow, ministering to the aches, pains, and exhaustion of the heart and soul.

Celtic Cross

This was the first activation I received. It was the summer of 1980 or 1981, and I was living in Canada, at the end of a period working with Greenpeace. I was visiting a friend in Montréal, a woman who had just ended a dramatic relationship with a deeply disturbed man. She lived in an apartment over a shop, and when I arrived I was surprised to see debris strewn along the stairway to her rooms. She explained that the man she had broken up with was engaged in an ongoing battle of revenge, littering her space, painting obscenities on the stairway walls in red paint, and psychically attacking her in her sleep.

Although intrigued by the details, I wasn't overly concerned. We had a wonderful day exploring Montreal and by bedtime I was exhausted and fell deeply asleep. I was awakened suddenly in the early hours of the morning with a deep sense of dread. Opening my eyes, I was assailed by the image of a man's face, enlarged and enraged, filling the entire ceiling. His eyes bore into me, emanating anger and hatred. I felt he was jealous that I was near his love object. The room seemed to spin, and I was concerned for my safety as well as my friend's. Completely unprepared to deal with the situation, I simply asked what to do and saw the Celtic Cross, as described in the meditation, form around both myself and my friend. We were completely protected from the attack, which quickly ended. There was no further assault during the rest of the visit.

When I met my husband, Colin Andrews, more than 10 years later, I was surprised to learn that this pattern had played a significant role in his life. Colin is a crop circle researcher who co-authored the first book on the subject published in 1989 and has been in the forefront of investigation since 1983. This pattern of five circles, with one in the middle surrounded by four satellites, appeared as a crop circle in the late 1980s. Colin named the formation the Celtic Cross, and I have kept the name for my meditation. The Celtic Cross played a critical role in Colin's research into the mysterious phenomenon and is one of the many links that tie us together.

Mystic Triangle

My first contact with this activation was in the mid-1980s. I tried to spend time each day at sunrise and sunset, facing the sun, and expressing appreciation and gratitude for all that each day brought. During the practice, I would bring my hands together over my third eye and make a triangle using the two index fingers and thumbs. It felt like drawing in sunlight and filling my Third Eye; it was very grounding, energizing, and somehow deeply familiar.

The advancement of this activation happened in the fall of 1993, a month or more after Colin and I were married. We were sound asleep when we were both awakened shortly after 3 a.m. Colin suddenly sat up and appeared to be filled with light, which expanded him like a balloon. Lying there, I felt unable to move. It was as though I were turned off, simply there to observe and unable to formulate the thought to move.

While filled with light, Colin began talking about triangles in the landscape between sacred sites and crop circles. Part of his research focused on the placement of the crop formations in relation to sacred sites, to ley lines, and to each other. He seemed to be channeling important information about using the Earth energy created when the crop circles formed in patterns that made triangulations with each other in the natural landscape. After a few minutes, the light left him and he simple deflated. He attempted to move to the side table and write the experience down, but was interrupted. As the light left him, it moved over to me and poured into me, expanding and bringing me to life. I began talking as I saw triangles in the human body focused on the palms of the hands and the third eye. After about five minutes, the light simply went out and I deflated as well. We wrote down the information with no idea what to do with it.

We understood how to use this information after an event in March 2006 when we used triangulations to create a communication portal as described in the meditation. What kind of portal is created depends on your intention and on the level of awareness you bring to the practice.

Pyramid Purification

This activation came in summer 2006. My husband and I were working with the dynamics of forgiveness, especially self-forgiveness. The political climate seemed to match our personal turmoil, and the anger and sadness we felt over the path the world was taking was at times overwhelming. Although we wanted to simply rail against the politicians, we were trying for something higher.

Throughout the past 25 years we have both been deeply touched by the commitment of some cultures to stabilize the spirit of the planet in times of crises. The Tibetan Lamas and the Tribes in the Sierra Nevada in Columbia are two examples that have inspired us. We decided to take the hurt and anger, as well as our inspiration, into our nightly meditation in an attitude of service. We wanted to be positive, yet felt powerless to make a difference.

One night as we settled into meditation, we were joined by two energy beings. Neither of us could tell if we were meeting with the light body of living people, with people who had passed over, or with spiritual guides. My feeling was that they were living people. The four of us were positioned in a square that became a four-sided pyramid. Each sat in a corner of the pyramid in cross-legged position as described in the meditation. Our job was to hold the construct while spirit worked.

As we sat in this configuration, shadows and vapors began to be drawn into the base of the pyramid and were fed to the violet flame. The energy became brilliant, living light that was beamed out through the apex. We were witnessing the calling home of negative thought forms and the returning to the light of pain, humiliation, sadness, and all the emotions that led us to destructive actions. It was humbling and a little frightening.

The Living Matrix

This is the newest of the meditations. It arrived in 2010 while I was working with an exceptional client. This client is working to manifest her spiritual matrix in all aspects of her life. As she lay on the table, I saw the 20 light filaments entering her fingers and toes. I started to tell her what I saw, but before I could say more than three words, she told me the same information from the perspective of how it felt in her body. We went back and forth, sharing in the description of the Living Matrix as it came into being in her body. Afterward, we both felt connected, uplifted, and in harmony with a higher order of affairs.

The next time I saw this was in my regular long-distance meditation with Johanna Sayre. As we met in the etheric and settled into our meditation, the pattern that had emerged in my client the day before activated in my body. I saw Johanna and myself floating in white clouds within a matrix of criss-crossed lines of force. It was like being the crossing point in dimensional fishnet stockings! We were side by side, linked together along with others, lines of force going to the level above and connecting all of us to our guides, lines of force going below to the people we guided. It was a profound awareness of the manner in which we interconnect!

Dancing with the Elements

This moving meditation is dedicated to my first energy mentor, Louisa Poole. She taught me how to be free and to move forward fearlessly, even when terrified. She taught me how to extend my energy senses to meet the world. This meditation is modified from a weekend spent with her at Killam's Point in Branford, Connecticut, where we danced with the Devas and fairies of the Earth.

Pineal Self-Activation

Colleen Behan originally taught me how to activate the pineal gland as a Lightworkers technique. While in Malta at a conference where I was lecturing, I told a room full of people during my workshop that I was available to perform the activation on anyone who wanted to try it. Of course, everyone did. Knowing that I could not offer everyone individual time, I opened to a solution and saw that self-activation was necessary. The process in this book is the result.

The Adventure Continues

Writing *The Path of Energy* has been an incredible journey through many realms. Every suggestion made has been proven through life experience. The question I am frequently asked is: How will it impact my life to use these practices? I am answering this question with a series of novels that demonstrate the adventure of energy awareness. The first is completed; keep your eyes open for its publication!

RESOURCES

Books

Andrews, Colin, with Stephen J. Spignesi. *Signs of Contact* (New Page Books, 2003).

Andrews, Synthia, with Colin Andrews. *The Complete Idiots Guide to the Akashic Record* (Alpha Books, Penguin, 2010).

Andrews, Synthia, with Colin Andrews. *The Complete Idiots Guide to 2012* (Alpha Books, Penguin, 2008).

Andrews, Synthia, with Bobbi Dempsey. *Acupressure and Reflexology for Dummies* (Wiley, 2007).

Becker, Dr. Robert, and Gary Seldon. *The Body Electric* (Quill Press, 1985).

Bodanis, David. *E=mc²: A Biography of The World's Most Famous Equation* (The Berkley Publishing Group, 2000).

Braden, Gregg. *The Language of the Divine Matrix.* (Hay House, 2008).

Brinkley, Dannion, with Kathryn Brinkley. *Secrets of the Light: Lessons from Heaven* (HarperOne, 2009).

Brinkley, Dannion, with Paul Perry. *Saved by the Light: The True Story of a Man who Died Twice and the Profound Revelations He Received* (HarperOne, reprinted 2008).

Castaneda, Carlos. *The Teachings of Don Juan: A Yaqui Way of Knowledge, 3rd Edition* (University of California Press, 2008).

Chopra, Deepak. *The Seven Spiritual Laws of Success: A Practical Guide to the Fulfillment of Your Dreams* (Amber-Allen Publishing, 1994).

Dychwald, Ken. *Bodymind* (Tarcher Putman, 1986).

Ereira, Alan. *The Elder Brothers' Warning* (Taironal Heritage Trust, 2009).

Ereira, Alan. *The Elder Brothers* (Knopf, 1992).

Emoto, Masaru. *Messages from Water, Vol. 1* (Hado Publishing, 1999).

Hay, Louise. *You Can Heal Your Life, 2nd Edition* (Hay House, 1984).

Hurtack, J.J. *An Introduction to The Keys of Enoch* (Academy for Future Science, 4th edition, 1997).

Jennings, Hans. *Cymatics: A Study of Wave Phenomena & Vibration, 3rd Edition* (Macromedia Press, 2001).

Kenyon, Tom. *Brain States* (World Tree Press, 2001).

Kafatos, Menas, and Robert Nadeau. *The Conscious Universe: Parts and Wholes in Physical Reality* (Springer, 1999).

Keyes, Ken. *Handbook to Higher Consciousness* (Eden Grove Editions, 1997).

Lovelock, James. *Gaia: A New Look at Life on Earth* (Oxford University Press, 2000).

Marcinak, Barbara. *Path of Empowerment: New Pleiadian Wisdom for a World in Change* (New World Library, 2004).

Marcinak, Barbara. *Family of Light: Pleiadian Tales and Lessons in Living* (Bear and Company, 1998).

Marcinak, Barbara. *Earth: Pleiadian Keys to the Living Library* (Bear and Company, 1994).

Marcinak, Barbara, with Tera Thomas. *Bringers of the Dawn: Teachings from the Pleiadians* (Bear and Company, 1992).

McTaggart, Lynn. *The Field, A Quest for the Secret Force of the Universe* (HarperPerennial, 2002).

McTaggart, Lynn. *The Intention Experiment: Using Your Thoughts to Change Your Life and the World* (Free Press, 2008).

Melchizedek, Drunvalo. [*The Ancient Secret of the Flower of Life: Vol. I and Vol. II* (Light Technology Pub., 2000).

Mitchell, Dr. Edgar. *The Way of the Explorer, Revised Edition* (New Page Books, 2008).

Oschman, Dr. James L. *Energy Medicine: The Scientific Basis* (Churchill Livingston Publishing, 2000).

Pert, Dr. Candace. *Molecules of Emotion: The Science Behind Mind-Body Medicine* (Simon & Schuster, 1999).

Radin, Dean. *Entangled Minds: Extrasensory Experiences in a Quantum Reality* (Paraview Pocket Books, 2006).

Radin, Dean. *The Conscious Universe* (Harper Edge, 1997).

Sheldrake, Rupert. *A New Science of Life* (Park Street Press, 1995).

Sheldrake, Rupert. *The Presence of the Past: Morphic Resonance and the Habits of Nature* (Park Street Press, 1995).

Shinn, Florence Scovel. *The Game of Life and How to Play It* (DeVorss & Company, 1978).
Small Wright, Machaelle. *Behaving as if the God in All Life Matter, 3rd Edition* (Perelandra, Ltd., 1997).
Small Wright, Machaelle. *Perelandra Garden Workbook: A Complete Guide to Gardening with Nature Intelligence* (Perelandra, 1993).
Talbot, Michael. *The Holographic Universe* (HarperCollins, 1992).
Targ, Russell, and Jane Katara. *Miracles of Mind, Exploring Non-local Consciousness and Spiritual Healing* (New World Library, 1998).
Targ, Russell. *Mind-Reach: Scientists look at Psychic Abilities* (Hampton Roads Publishing, 2005).
Tipping, C. Colin. *Radical Forgiveness, Making Room for the Miracle* (Quest Publishing & Distribution, 2002).
Tolle, Eckhart. *A New Earth: Awakening to Your Life's Purpose* (Plume Books, 2005).
Wilbur, Ken. *The Theory of Everything* (Shambhala, 2001).
Williams, Paul. *Das Energie* (Entwhistle Books, 1982).
Willimas, Paul. *Remember Your Essence* (Entwhistle Books, 1999).
Young-Sowers, Meredith. *Agartha: Journey to the Stars (reprint)* (New World Library, 2006).
Young-Sowers, Meredith. *Spirit Heals: Awakening a Woman's Inner Knowing for Self-Healing, 1st Edition* (New World Library, 2007).
Young-Sowers, Meredith. *Wisdom Bowls: Overcoming Fear and Coming Home to your Authentic Self* (New World Library, 2006).

Mayan
Calleman, Carl Johan. *The Mayan Calendar and the Transformation of Consciousness* (Inner Tradition, 2004).
Freidel, David, Linda Schele, and Joy Parker. *Maya Cosmos: Three Thousand Years of the Shaman's Path* (Perennial, 2001).
Jenkins, John Major. *Maya Cosmogenesis 2012* (Bear and Company, 1998).
Stray, Geoff. *Catastrophe or Ecstasy: Beyond 2012* (Vital Signs Publishing, 2005).

Remote Viewing
Buchanan, Lyn. *The Seventh Sense: The Secrets of Remote Viewing as Told by a "Psychic Spy" for the U.S. Military* (Pocket, 2003).
McMoneagle, Joseph. *Remote Viewing Secrets* (Hampton Roads Publishing, 2000).

Morehouse, David. *Remote Viewing: The Complete User's Manual for Coordinate Remote Viewing* (Sounds True, Incorporated, 2007).

Targ, Russell. *Limitless Mind: A Guide to Remote Viewing and Transformation of Consciousness* (New World Library, 2004).

Sacred Geometry

Melchizedek, Drunvalo. *The Ancient Secret of the Power of Life, Vol.1* (Knight Technology Publications, 1999).

Michell, John. *The New View Over Atlantis* (Thames and Hudson, 2001).

Pogacnik, Marko. *Sacred Geography: Geomancy: Co-creating the Earth Cosmos* (Lindisfarne Books, 2008).

Schneider, Michael. *A Beginner's Guide to Constructing the Universe: Mathematical Archetypes of Nature, Art and Science* (HarperPerennial, 1995).

Stewart, Malcolm. *Patterns of Eternity: Sacred Geometry and the Starcut Diagram* (Floris Books, 2010).

Subtle Energy and Energy Structures

Brennan, Barbara. *Light Emerging: The Journey of Personal Healing* (Bantam Books, 1993).

Brennan, Barbara. *Hands of Light* (Bantom Books, 1988).

Gerber, Richard, *Vibrational Medicine: The #1 Handbook of Subtle-Energy Therapies* (Bear & Company, 2001).

Judith, Anodea, and Selene Vega. *The Sevenfold Journey: Reclaiming Mind, Body and Spirit Through the Chakras* (Crossing Press, 1993).

Myss, Caroline. *Anatomy of the Spirit: The Seven Stages of Power and Healing* (Three Rivers Press, 1997).

Pond, David, *Chakras for Beginners: A Guide to Balancing Your Chakra Energies* (Llewellyn, 1999).

Shumsky, Susan G. and Dannion Brinkley, *Exploring Auras: Cleansing and Strengthening Your Energy Field* (New Page Books, 2005).

Teeguarden, Iona Marsaa. *The Joy of Feeling: Body Mind Acupressure, 2st Edition* (Japan Publications (USA), 1987).

Websites
Training Centers
Astral projection: *www.monroeinstitute.org*
Energy awareness training: *www.thepathofenergy.com*

Jin Shin Do Bodymind Acupressure: *www.jinshindo.org*
Pineal gland and cranial temple activation: *www.thespiritoflight.org*
Remote viewing: *www.virtualviewing.org*

Nature Co-Creation and Flower Essence
Findhorn: *www.findhorn.org*
Flower Essences: *www.earthlightessence.com*
Perelandra: *www.perelandra-ltd.com*
A Place Called Hope, Inc.: *www.aplacecalledhoperaptors.com*

Consciousness Research, Teaching and Products
The Academy for Future Science: *www.affs.org*
Brainwave activating audio programs: *www.daael.com/precognition.htm*
Dannion Brinkley: *www.dannion.com*
Circles Phenomenon Research: *www.colinandrews.net*
Consciousness Research Laboratory: *www.deanradin.com/default original.html*
Edgar Cayce's Association for Research and Enlightenment:
    www.edgarcayce.org
Greater Reality: *www.greaterreality.com/rv/instruct.htm*
Healing Rhythms—Wild Divine: *www.wilddivine.com*
Inspiration: *www.creativethinkingwith.com*
The Institute of Consciousness Research: *www.icrcanada.org*
The Institute of Noetic Sciences: *www.noetic.org*
Intentional Peace Experiment:
    www.theintentionexperiment.com/the-peace-intention-experiment
The Life of Gandhi: *www.mkgandhi.org*
Lucid Dreaming: *www.lucidity.com* and *www.world-of-lucid-dreaming.com*
Meaningful Coincidences, Synchronicity & Synchrodestiny:
    www.meaningoflife.i12.com/coincidence.htm
Drunvalo Melchizedek: *www.drunvalo.net*
Monroe Institute: *www.monroeinstitute.org*
The Paradigm Research Group: *www.paradigmresearchgroup.org*
The Pleiadians, channeled by Barbara Marciniak: *www.pleiadians.com*
Prosperity: *www.abundance-and-happiness.com/inspiration.html*
Society of the Inner Light: *www.innerlight.org.uk*

Mayan Elders

Don Alejandro: *www.spiritofmaat.com/may09/don_alejandro_message.html*

Hunbatz men: *www.experiencefestival.com/a/Mayan_Elder_Hunbatz_Men/ id/2371*

Carlos Barrios: *tribes.tribe.net/mayawisdom/thread*

Psychic Readers

Deb Hastings: *debrahastings@sbcglobal.net*

Pam Hogan: *pamhogan@mac.com*

NOTES

Chapter 5

1. Michael Talbot, "The Universe as a Hologram," *The Universe News*, April 20, 2010, 19:21.

Chapter 6

1. David Bodanis, $E = MC^2$: *A Biography of the World's Most Famous Equation* (Berkley Books, 2000).
2. Hans Jennings, *Cymatics: A Study of Wave Phenomena & Vibration, 3rd Edition* (Macromedia Press, 2001).
3. Masaru Emoto, *Messages from Water, Vol. 1* (Hado Publishing, 1999).

Chapter 7

1. Caroline Myss, *Anatomy of the Spirit: The Seven Stages of Power and Healing, 1st Edition* (Three Rivers Press, 1997).
2. Carlos Castaneda, *The Teachings of Don Juan: A Yaqui Way of Knowledge, 3rd Edition* (University of California Press, 2008).
3. Barbra Brennan, *Light Emerging: The Journey of Personal Healing* (Bantam Books, 1993).
4. Barbara Marciniak, *Earth: Pleiadian Keys to the Living Library* (Bear and Company, 1995).

Chapter 8

1. Marie Jones and Larry Flaxman, *The Resonance Key* (The Career Press, 2009).
2. James Lovelock, *Gaia: A New Look at Life on Earth* (Oxford University Press, 2000).
3. Bruce Cathie, *The Energy Grid: Harmonic 695: The Pulse of the Universe, The Investigation into the World Energy Grid* (Adventures Unlimited Press, 1997).
4. Ibid.
5. Rupert Sheldrake, *A New Science of Life: The Hypothesis of Morphic Resonance* (Park Street Press, 1995).
6. Tim Wallace-Murphy. *Hidden Wisdom: The Secrets of the Western Esoteric Tradition* (The Disinformation Company, 2010).

7. Robert Coon, *World Alchemy Earth Chakras: The Definitive Guide* (self-published, 2009).
8. Maud Worcester, *The Book of the Jaguar Priest: A translation of the Book of the Chilam Balam of Tizi* (1951).
9. Alfred Watkins, *Old Straight Track-Its Mounds, Beacons, Moats, Sites and Mark Stones* (1972).
10. Drunvalo Melchizedek, *The Ancient Secret of the Flower of Life: Vol. I and Vol. II* (Light Technology Pub., 2000).
11. *www.Bristichdowsers.org*
12. *www.Findhorn.org*
13. *www.perelandra-ltd.com*

Chapter 9
1. Ken Dychwald, *Bodymind* (Tarcher Putman, 1986).
2. Candace Pert, *Molecules of Emotions: The Science behind Mind-body Medicine, 1st Edition* (Simon & Schuster, 1999).

Chapter 11
1. N.E. Thing Enterprises, *Magic Eye, 1st Edition* (Andrews and McMeel Publishing, 1993).

Chapter 16
1. Barbra Brennan, *Light Emerging: The Journey of Personal Healing* (Bantam Books, 1993).

Chapter 17
1. Machaelle Small Wright, *Behaving as if the God in All Life Matters, Revised Edition*, (Perelandra, Limited, 1997).
2. Lynn McTaggart, *The Field: The Quest for the Secret Force of the Universe, updated edition* (Harper Paperbacks, 2008) and Lynn McTaggart, *The Intention Experiment: Using Your Thoughts to Change Your Life and the World* (Free Press, 2008).

Chapter 18
1. Michael Talbot, "The Universe as a Hologram," *The Universe News,* April 20, 2010, 19:21.
2. Michael Talbot, *The Holographic Universe, First Edition* (Harper Perennial, 1992).
3. Dean Radin, *Entangled Minds: Extrasensory Experiences in a Quantum Reality* (Paraview Pocket Books, 2006).
4. H.E. Puthoff, PhD, "CIA-Initiated Remote Viewing At Stanford Research Institute," *militaryremoteviewers.com.* Original source: H.E. Puthoff, "CIA-Initiated Remote Viewing Program at Stanford Research Institute," *Journal of Scientific Exploration, volume 10, number 1*: 63–76, *www. scientificexploration.org/journal/jse_10_1_puthoff.pdf.*

5. Carlos Castaneda, *The Teachings of Don Juan: A Yaqui Way of Knowledge,* *3rd Edition* (University of California Press, 2008).

Chapter 19

1. Ronald E. Matthews, MS, "Harold Burr's Biofields: Measuring the Electromagnetics of Life," *Subtle Energies & Energy Medicine, 2007, volume 18, number 2:* 55–61.
2. Dr. Robert Becker and Gary Seldon, *The Body Electric* (Quill Press, 1985).
3. Dr. Richard Gerber, *Vibrational Medicine, 3rd Edition* (Bear & Company, 2001).
4. Barbara Brennan, *Hands of Light: Guide to Healing Through the Human Energy Field* (Bantom Books, 1988); Barbara Brennan, *Light Emerging: The Journey of Personal Healing* (Bantam Books, 1993); and Dr. Donna Eden, *Energy Medicine: Balancing Your Body's Energies for Optimal Health, Joy, and Vitality, Revised Edition* (Tarcher, 2008).
5. Dr. James L. Oschman, *Energy Medicine: The Scientific Basis* (Churchill Livingston Publishing, 2000).
6. Dr. Franz Lutz and Hans Andeweg, *Resonance Therapy in Eight Steps* (Institute for Resonance Therapy, Cappenberg Germany, 1995).
7. Dr. Ian Stevenson, *Children Who Remember Previous Lives: A Question of Reincarnation* (McFarland & Company, 2000).
8. Renee Weber, *Dialogues with Scientists and Sages: The Search for Unity* (Penguin (Non-Classics), 1990).
9. Dannion Brinkley, and Paul Perry, *Saved by the Light: The True Story of a Man Who Died Twice and the Profound Revelations He Received, Reprint Edition* (HarperOne, 2008).

Chapter 20

1. David Freidel and Linda Schele, *A Forest of Kings: The Untold Story of the Ancient Maya* (HarperPerennial, 1992).
2. John Major Jenkins. *Maya Cosmogenesis 2012: The True Meaning of the Maya Calendar End-Date* (Bear & Company, 1998).
3. Don Alejandro: *www.spiritofmaat.com/may09/don_alejandro_message.html*; Hunbatz men: *www.experiencefestival.com/a/Mayan_Elder_Hunbatz_Men/ id/2371*; Carlos Barrios: *tribes.tribe.net/mayawisdom/thread.*
4. Maud Worcester, *The Book of the Jaguar Priest: A translation of the Book of the Chilam Balam of Tizi* (1951).
5. David Bodanis, $E = MC^2$: *A Biography of the World's Most Famous Equation* (Berkley Books, 2000).
6. Hans Jennings, *Cymatics: A study of Wave Phenomena & Vibration, 3rd Edition* (Macromedia Press, 2001).
7. Masaru Emoto, *Messages from Water, Vol. 1* (Hado Publishing, 1999).

8. Dr. Robert Becker, *The Body Electric: Electromagnetism and the Foundation of Life, 1st Edition* (Harper Paperbacks, 1998).
9. Paramahansa Yogananda, *Autobiography of a Yogi* (Self-Realization Fellowship, 2006).
10. Dr. Rick Strassman, *DMT: The Spirit Molecule* (Park Street Press, 2000).
11. Sidney B. Lang et al. *Piezoelectricity in the Human Pineal Gland, 1996. Departments that participated in the study:* Department of Chemical Engineering (Ben-Gurion University, Israel), Department of Orthopaedic Surgery and Department of Cellular Biology and Anatomy (LSU, Shreveport, LA), Department of Materials and Interfaces (Weizmann Institute of Science, Israel), Department of Pathology (LSU, Shreveport, LA), Department of Medicine, Nephrology Section (LSU, Shreveport, LA).
12. R. Kristic, "Pineal Calcification: Its Mechanism and Significance," *Journal of Neural Transmission Supp. 1986, 21*: 415–32.
13. I. Galliani, E. Falcieri, F. Giangaspero, G. Valdre, R. Mongiorgi. "A preliminary study of human pineal gland concretions: structural and chemical analysis," *Bollettino Della Societa Italiana di Biologia Sperimentale, July 1990, 66(7)*: 615–22.
14. S. Baconnier, SB Lang, M. Polomska, B. Hilczer, G. Berkovic, G. Meshulam, "Calcite Micro Crystals in the Pineal Gland of the Human Brain: First Physical and Chemical Studies," *Bioelectromagnetics 2002, October 23 (7)*: 488–95.
15. NA Belyavskaya. "Biological Effects Due to Weak Magnetic Field on Plants," *Advances in Space Research, 2004, 34*(7): 1566–74.
16. Renee Weber, *Dialogues with Scientists and Sages: The Search for Unity* (Penguin (Non-Classics), 1990).
17. Ben Best, *The Amygdala and the Emotions, www.benbest.com/science/anatmind/anatmd9.html.*
18. MA Persinger, K. Makarec, "The Feeling of a Presence and Verbal Meaningfulness in Context of Temporal Lobe Function: Factor Analytic Verification of the Muses?" *Brain Cognition, November 1992, 20(2)*: 217–26.
19. Gary E.R. Schwartz and Linda G.S. Russek, "Registration of Actual and Intended Eye Gaze: Correlation with Spiritual Beliefs and Experiences," *Journal of Scientific Exploration, 1999, Vol. 13, No. 2*: 213–29.

Conclusion

1. Florence Scovel Shinn, *The Game of Life and How to Play It* DeVorss & Company, 1978).
2. "In Lak'etch–I am another yourself" by Maxwell Igan. Youtube video, *www.youtube.com/watch?v=HNdlf5TavAU.*

INDEX

About the Author

Synthia Andrews is a naturopathic doctor with a foundation in massage therapy, specializing in the underlying emotional and spiritual components of health and healing. She was on faculty for 15 years at the Connecticut Center for Massage Therapy, taught in the Kripalu School of Massage, and is an authorized teacher of the Jin Shin Do Foundation. For the past 20 years she has joined her husband, research-author Colin Andrews, in the study of consciousness and spirituality. She is co-author of three previous books *Acupressure and Reflexology for Dummies* (Wiley, 2007), *The Complete Idiots Guide to 2012* (Penguin, 2008), and *The Complete Idiots Guide to the Akashic Record* (Penguin, 2010)] and currently maintains a private clinic in Guilford, Connecticut. She can be reached at *www.andrewshealingarts.com* or *www.thepathofenergy.com*.

Continue your exploration at...

You are a vessel of infinite potential becoming a spiritual realization.